THE AUSTRALIAN
Women's Weekly

Retro

THE COMPLETE COLLECTION

Contents

Pamela Clark *then*

Pamela Clark *now*

Reviving
RETRO

Take a walk down memory lane as you flick through this delightful collection of our favourite retro recipes, some dating back to the 1950s – they're as good today as they were yesterday.

Retro recipes just refuse to go away, more than likely because the food is so yummy, cosily familiar and connected to fond memories of favourite times with family and friends.

My time at The Weekly's famous Test Kitchen started in 1969, and even back then we talked about food from the 1950s as being retro. Now, nearly 50 years on, we're still talking about the same recipes but with some new additions. So how far back is retro?

Back then...

Baking at home was done routinely by stay-at-home mums, usually once a week, so there was always something sweet and delicious to have for children's lunch boxes or after school snacks, or for when friends dropped in for a 'cuppa'. Today, people are more likely to buy something to fill these same needs from the supermarket or local bakery.

BAKING WITHOUT COOKBOOKS

My mother was famous for her boiled fruit cake and apple pie slice, both treats were legendary in the family. No one ever knew my Mum's recipe for the apple slice, which is still known as 'Jeannie's apple pie slice', she just 'threw it together'; I well remember the sweet perfume of stewing apples filling the kitchen. Not so many years ago I decided to try to copy Mum's recipe – you can see my version on page 214, it's pretty close, but could never be quite the same.

Mothers and grandmothers around the world are famously remembered for handing down family recipes using the 'at your mother's knee' technique; that is, teaching you the recipe verbally as you grew up helping them. These days we know better, and write every recipe down before it is lost in the mists of time.

Fond memories

Memories of favourite food seem to grow out of all proportion to reality – no one made better scones than my great grandmother! Apart from the baking and dessert recipes in this book, there are many much-loved savoury recipes that you will recall with fondness.

This is a retro cookbook – with feeling!

Pamela Clark

TEA TIME

Crab, avocado &
CUCUMBER SANDWICHES

- 2 GREEN ONIONS (SCALLIONS), SLICED THINLY
- 1 FRESH LONG RED CHILLI, SEEDED, CHOPPED FINELY
- 227G (7 OUNCES) CRAB CLAW MEAT
- 2 TABLESPOONS COLESLAW DRESSING
- 1 LEBANESE CUCUMBER (130G)
- 8 SLICES WHITE BREAD (360G)
- 1 SMALL AVOCADO (200G), SLICED THINLY

1 Combine onion, chilli, crab and dressing in a small bowl. Season.
2 Using a vegetable peeler, slice cucumber into thin ribbons.
3 Top half the bread slices with cucumber, crab mixture and avocado then remaining bread. Cut off crusts; discard. Cut each sandwich into three fingers.

tip Sandwiches can be made several hours ahead; refrigerate, covered tightly. If making ahead, drizzle a little lemon juice over the avocado before using.

Salmon & herb
CREAM CHEESE SANDWICHES

- 330G (2 OUNCES) CREAM CHEESE, SOFTENED
- 1 TEASPOON FINELY CHOPPED FRESH DILL
- 1 TEASPOON FINELY CHOPPED FRESH CHIVES
- 1 TEASPOON LEMON JUICE
- 1 TEASPOON RINSED, DRAINED BABY CAPERS, CHOPPED FINELY
- 4 SLICES WHITE BREAD (180G), CRUSTS REMOVED
- 125G (4 OUNCES) SMOKED SALMON SLICES
- 4 LARGE ROCKET LEAVES (ARUGULA), TRIMMED

1 Combine cream cheese, dill, chives, juice and capers in a small bowl. Season to taste.

2 Using a rolling pin, roll over one slice of bread to flatten slightly. Spread with a quarter of the cream cheese mixture; top with a quarter of the smoked salmon and one rocket leaf, then roll tightly to enclose filling.

3 Repeat with remaining bread, cream cheese mixture, smoked salmon and rocket. Trim ends then slice each roll into four circles.

Smoked trout
RIBBON SANDWICHES

- ⅓ CUP (100G) MAYONNAISE
- 1 TEASPOON FINELY GRATED LEMON RIND
- 2 TEASPOONS LEMON JUICE
- 1 TABLESPOON FINELY CHOPPED FRESH CHIVES
- 8 SLICES MULTIGRAIN BREAD (360G)
- 140G (5 OUNCES) SKINLESS SMOKED TROUT, FLAKED FINELY

1 Combine mayonnaise, rind, juice and chives in a small bowl.

2 Spread bread with mayonnaise mixture. Sandwich trout between bread slices. Discard crusts; cut each sandwich into three fingers.

Plum & almond TURNOVERS

- 825G (1¾ POUNDS) CANNED WHOLE PLUMS IN NATURAL JUICE
- ¼ CUP (55G) CASTER SUGAR (SUPERFINE SUGAR)
- 3 CARDAMOM PODS, BRUISED
- 2 TABLESPOONS CORNFLOUR (CORNSTARCH)
- 1 TABLESPOON WATER
- 250G (8 OUNCES) MARZIPAN, CHOPPED COARSELY
- ⅓ CUP (80ML) THICKENED (HEAVY) CREAM
- 6 SHEETS PUFF PASTRY
- 1 EGG, BEATEN LIGHTLY
- ¼ CUP (20G) FLAKED ALMONDS
- 1 TABLESPOON DEMERARA SUGAR
- 2 TEASPOONS ICING SUGAR (CONFECTIONERS' SUGAR)

1 Drain plums over a small bowl; reserve ½ cup of juice, discard remainder. Cut plums into quarters; discard stones.

2 Place plums, reserved juice, caster sugar and cardamom in a medium saucepan; stir over high heat, without boiling, until sugar dissolves. Bring to the boil; boil, uncovered, for 5 minutes or until mixture is thickened slightly. Blend cornflour with the water in a small jug, add to pan; cook, stirring, until mixture boils and thickens. Cool for 2 hours. Discard cardamom.

3 Meanwhile, blend or process marzipan and cream until smooth.

4 Preheat oven to 200°C/400°F. Grease oven trays; line trays with baking paper.

5 Cut 30 x 9cm (3¾-inch) rounds from pastry sheets. Spread rounded teaspoons of marzipan mixture over each pastry round, leaving a 1cm (½-inch) border. Divide plum mixture into centres of pastry rounds. Brush edges with egg; fold rounds in half to enclose filling, pinch edges to seal.

6 Place turnovers on trays about 5cm (2 inches) apart. Brush tops with egg; sprinkle with nuts, then demerara sugar.

7 Bake turnovers for 25 minutes or until golden. Cool on trays. Serve warm, dusted with icing sugar.

serving suggestion Ice-cream, custard or cream.

CARROT CAKE
with cream cheese frosting

- 3 EGGS
- 1⅓ CUPS (250G) FIRMLY PACKED BROWN SUGAR
- 1 CUP (250ML) VEGETABLE OIL
- 3 CUPS COARSELY GRATED CARROT
- 1 CUP (120G) COARSELY CHOPPED WALNUTS
- 2½ CUPS (375G) SELF-RAISING FLOUR
- ½ TEASPOON BICARBONATE OF SODA (BAKING SODA)
- 2 TEASPOONS MIXED SPICE
- 15G (½ OUNCE) BUTTER
- 2 TEASPOONS BROWN SUGAR, EXTRA
- 2 TEASPOONS GROUND CINNAMON
- 1 CUP (100G) ROASTED WALNUTS, EXTRA

CREAM CHEESE FROSTING

- 65G (2 OUNCES) BUTTER, SOFTENED
- 165G (4 OUNCES) CREAM CHEESE, SOFTENED
- 2¼ TEASPOONS FINELY GRATED LEMON RIND
- 3½ CUPS (540G) ICING SUGAR (CONFECTIONERS' SUGAR)

1 Preheat oven to 180°C/350°F. Grease a deep 22cm (9-inch) round cake pan; line base with baking paper.

2 Beat eggs, sugar and oil in a small bowl with an electric mixer until thick and creamy. Transfer mixture to a large bowl; stir in carrot and walnuts, then sifted dry ingredients. Pour mixture into pan.

3 Bake cake about 1¼ hours. Leave cake in pan for 5 minutes before turning, top-side up, onto a wire rack to cool.

4 Meanwhile, melt butter in a small saucepan over medium heat; stir in extra brown sugar, cinnamon and extra walnuts. Cool.

5 Make cream cheese frosting.

6 Split cold cake in half, place bottom layer onto a serving plate, cut-side up; spread with half the frosting. Top with remaining cake layer; spread top with remaining frosting. Decorate with caramel walnuts.

CREAM CHEESE FROSTING Beat butter, cream cheese and rind in a small bowl with an electric mixer until light and fluffy. Gradually beat in sifted icing sugar.

tips You will need 3 large carrots (540g) for the amount of grated carrot in this recipe. This cake will keep in an airtight container in the fridge for up to 3 days, or freeze, without the frosting and walnuts, for up to 3 months.

Mini cherry
BAKEWELL TARTS

- 90G (3 OUNCES) UNSALTED BUTTER, SOFTENED
- 2 TABLESPOONS CASTER SUGAR (SUPERFINE SUGAR)
- 1 EGG YOLK
- 1 CUP (150G) PLAIN FLOUR (ALL-PURPOSE FLOUR)
- ½ CUP (60G) GROUND ALMONDS
- 2 TABLESPOONS STRAWBERRY JAM
- 12 RED GLACÉ CHERRIES, HALVED

ALMOND FILLING

- 125G (4 OUNCES) UNSALTED BUTTER, SOFTENED
- ½ TEASPOON FINELY GRATED LEMON RIND
- ½ CUP (110G) CASTER SUGAR (SUPERFINE SUGAR)
- 2 EGGS
- ¾ CUP (90G) GROUND ALMONDS
- 2 TABLESPOONS PLAIN FLOUR (ALL-PURPOSE FLOUR)

LEMON GLAZE

- 1 CUP (160G) ICING SUGAR (CONFECTIONERS' SUGAR)
- 2 TABLESPOONS LEMON JUICE, APPROXIMATELY

1 Beat butter, sugar and egg yolk in a small bowl with an electric mixer until combined. Stir in sifted flour and ground almonds, in two batches. Knead dough on a floured surface until smooth. Wrap pastry in plastic wrap; refrigerate for 30 minutes.

2 Preheat oven to 200°C/400°F. Grease two 12-hole (2 tablespoons/40ml) flat-based patty pans.

3 Make almond filling.

4 Roll pastry between sheets of baking paper until 3mm (⅛-inch) thick. Cut 24 x 6cm (2¼-inch) rounds from pastry; gently press rounds into pan holes. Divide jam then filling into cases.

5 Bake tarts for 20 minutes. Cool in pans for 10 minutes before turning, top-side up, onto a wire rack.

6 Meanwhile, make lemon glaze.

7 Spoon glaze over warm tarts; top with cherries. Cool.

ALMOND FILLING Beat butter, rind and sugar in a small bowl with an electric mixer until light and fluffy. Beat in eggs, one at a time. Stir in sifted ground almonds and the flour.

LEMON GLAZE Sift icing sugar into a small bowl; stir in enough juice to make glaze pourable.

NOW.

ONE POUND

Arnott's

FAMOUS

ASSORTED CREAM

BISCUITS

★ *There is no Substitute for Quality* ★

in the NEW TRANSPARENT *MOISTURE PROOF* WRAPPING...

Arnott's *famous* **ASSORTED CREAM** **Biscuits**

There is no Substitute for Quality.

Best-ever LAMINGTONS

- 6 EGGS
- ⅔ CUP (150G) CASTER SUGAR (SUPERFINE SUGAR)
- ⅓ CUP (50G) CORNFLOUR (CORNSTARCH)
- ½ CUP (75G) PLAIN FLOUR (ALL-PURPOSE FLOUR)
- ⅓ CUP (50G) SELF-RAISING FLOUR
- 2 CUPS (160G) DESICCATED COCONUT, APPROXIMATELY

CHOCOLATE ICING

- 3 CUPS (500G) ICING SUGAR (CONFECTIONERS' SUGAR)
- ½ CUP (50G) COCOA POWDER
- 15G (½ OUNCE) BUTTER, MELTED
- ⅔ CUP (160ML) MILK

1 Preheat oven to 180°C/350°F. Grease and line a deep 23cm (9-inch) square cake pan.

2 Beat eggs in a medium bowl with an electric mixer for 10 minutes or until thick and creamy. Gradually add sugar, beating until sugar dissolves after each addition. Fold in triple-sifted flours. Spread mixture into pan.

3 Bake cake about 30 minutes. Leave cake in pan for 5 minutes before turning, top-side up, onto a wire rack to cool.

4 Make chocolate icing.

5 Cut cooled cake into 16 squares. Dip squares in icing, drain off excess; toss squares in coconut. Place lamingtons on a wire rack to set.

CHOCOLATE ICING Sift icing sugar and cocoa into a large heatproof bowl; stir in butter and milk. Place bowl over a large saucepan of simmering water; stir until icing is of a coating consistency.

tips The cake is easier to handle if it has been made the day before. Sponge or butter cake can be used.

You can fill the lamingtons with jam and cream, if you like.

Lamingtons can be stored in an airtight container for up to 2 days.

Prize
WINNING

EDITOR'S
Favourite

NEENISH TARTS

- 1¾ CUPS (260G) PLAIN FLOUR (ALL-PURPOSE FLOUR)
- ¼ CUP (40G) ICING SUGAR (CONFECTIONERS' SUGAR)
- 185G (6 OUNCES) COLD BUTTER, CHOPPED COARSELY
- 1 EGG YOLK
- 2 TEASPOONS ICED WATER, APPROXIMATELY
- ⅓ CUP (110G) STRAWBERRY JAM

MOCK CREAM

- ¾ CUP (165G) CASTER SUGAR (SUPERFINE SUGAR)
- 1½ TABLESPOONS MILK
- ⅓ CUP (80ML) WATER
- ½ TEASPOON POWDERED GELATINE
- 185G (6 OUNCES) UNSALTED BUTTER, SOFTENED
- 1 TEASPOON VANILLA EXTRACT

GLACÉ ICING

- 1½ CUPS (240G) ICING SUGAR (CONFECTIONERS' SUGAR)
- 15G (½ OUNCE) UNSALTED BUTTER, MELTED
- 2 TABLESPOONS HOT MILK, APPROXIMATELY
- PINK FOOD COLOURING
- 1 TEASPOON COCOA POWDER

1 Process flour, sugar and butter until crumbly. With motor operating, add egg yolk and enough of the water to make ingredients come together. Turn dough onto a floured surface, knead gently until smooth. Wrap pastry in plastic wrap then refrigerate for 30 minutes.

2 Grease two 12-hole (2-tablespoon/ 40ml) deep flat-based patty pans. Roll out half the pastry between sheets of baking paper until 3mm (⅛-inch) thick. Cut out 12 x 7.5cm (3-inch) rounds; press rounds into holes of one pan. Prick bases of cases well with a fork. Repeat with remaining pastry. Refrigerate for 30 minutes.

3 Preheat oven to 220°C/425°F.

4 Bake pastry cases for 12 minutes or until golden. Stand cases in pans for 5 minutes before turning, top-side up, onto wire racks to cool.

5 Meanwhile, make mock cream and glacé icing.

6 Divide jam between pastry cases; fill cases with mock cream, level tops with a spatula. Spread pink icing over half of each tart; cover remaining half with chocolate icing.

MOCK CREAM Stir sugar, milk and ¼ cup of the water in a small saucepan over low heat, without boiling, until sugar dissolves. Sprinkle gelatine over remaining water in a small jug; stir into milk mixture until gelatine dissolves. Cool to room temperature. Beat butter and extract in a small bowl with an electric mixer until as white as possible. With motor operating, gradually beat in cooled milk mixture; beat until light and fluffy.

GLACÉ ICING Sift icing sugar into a medium bowl; stir in butter and enough of the milk to make a thick paste. Divide icing between two small heatproof bowls; tint icing in one bowl with pink colouring and the other with sifted cocoa. Stir each bowl over a small saucepan of simmering water until icing is of a spreadable consistency.

Apricot
CHOC-CHIP CAKE

- 1 CUP (150G) CHOPPED DRIED APRICOTS
- 1 CUP (250ML) APRICOT NECTAR
- 125G (4 OUNCES) BUTTER, SOFTENED
- ⅔ CUP (150G) RAW SUGAR
- 2 EGGS, SEPARATED
- 1½ CUPS (120G) DESICCATED COCONUT
- 1½ CUPS (225G) SELF-RAISING FLOUR
- ½ CUP (95G) CHOC BITS
- 1 TABLESPOON ICING SUGAR (CONFECTIONERS' SUGAR)

1 Combine apricots and nectar in a small bowl; stand for 1 hour.

2 Preheat oven to 180°C/350°F. Grease a deep 20cm (8-inch) round cake pan; line base of pan with baking paper.

3 Beat butter and sugar in a small bowl with an electric mixer until light and fluffy. Beat in egg yolks, one at a time, until combined. Transfer mixture to a large bowl; stir in coconut, then half the sifted flour and half the apricot mixture. Stir in remaining flour and apricots, then Choc Bits.

4 Beat egg whites in a small bowl until soft peaks form; fold into cake mixture. Spread mixture into pan.

5 Bake cake about 1¼ hours. Leave cake in pan for 5 minutes before turning, top-side up, onto a wire rack to cool. Dust with sifted icing sugar before serving.

tip This cake will keep in an airtight container for up to 3 days.

EDITOR'S
Favourite

Buttermilk SCONES

- 2½ CUPS (375G) SELF-RAISING FLOUR
- 1 TABLESPOON CASTER SUGAR (SUPERFINE SUGAR)
- ¼ TEASPOON SALT
- 30G (1 OUNCE) BUTTER, CHOPPED
- 1¼ CUPS (310ML) BUTTERMILK, APPROXIMATELY
- STRAWBERRY JAM AND WHIPPED CREAM, TO SERVE

1 Preheat oven to 240°C/475°F. Grease a deep 19cm (8-inch) square cake pan.

2 Place flour, sugar and salt in a large bowl; rub in butter with your fingertips. Make a well in the centre of the flour mixture; add buttermilk. Using a knife, cut the buttermilk through the flour mixture to make a soft, sticky dough. Gently knead dough quickly and lightly on a floured surface until smooth.

3 Press dough out evenly into a 2cm (¾-inch) thickness. Dip a 4.5cm (1¾-inch) round cutter into flour; cut as many rounds as you can from the dough. Place scones, just touching, in pan.

4 Gently knead scraps of dough together. Cut out more rounds; place, just touching, in pan. Brush scones with a little milk.

5 Bake scones for 15 minutes or until browned and scones sound hollow when tapped firmly on the top with your fingers. Serve scones warm or cooled with jam and cream.

tip The homemade berry jam on page 245 is just the thing to serve with these delicious scones.

Rosewater
MERINGUE KISSES

- 2 EGG WHITES
- ½ CUP (110G) CASTER SUGAR (SUPERFINE SUGAR)
- 1 TEASPOON ROSEWATER
- PINK FOOD COLOURING
- 2 TABLESPOONS POURING CREAM
- 90G (3 OUNCES) WHITE CHOCOLATE, CHOPPED FINELY
- 4 FRESH OR THAWED FROZEN RASPBERRIES

1 Preheat oven to 120°C/250°F. Grease oven trays; line trays with baking paper.

2 Beat egg whites, sugar, rosewater and a few drops of the colouring in a small bowl with an electric mixer for 10 minutes or until sugar is dissolved.

3 Fit a large piping bag with a 2cm (¾-inch) plain tube. Paint three stripes of pink food colouring on the inside of the piping bag. Spoon the meringue mixture into the bag. Pipe the mixture into 4cm (1½-inch) rounds, about 2cm (¾ inch) apart, onto oven trays.

4 Bake meringues for 50 minutes or until dry to touch. Cool on trays.

5 Meanwhile, bring cream to the boil in a small saucepan. Remove from heat; stir in chocolate until smooth. Push berries through a fine sieve over a small bowl to make a puree; you need 2 teaspoons puree. Stir puree into chocolate mixture with a few drops of pink colouring. Refrigerate for 20 minutes or until filling is spreadable.

6 Just before serving, sandwich meringues with filling.

tip You can use any colour of food colouring to paint inside the piping bag. For multi-coloured meringues simply paint a different colour for each stripe.

All about TEA

Tea has a rich and complex history that dates back hundreds of years and spans countries all over the world. The traditions and ceremonies that have developed around the drinking of tea are fascinating and exceptionally varied, often reflecting the culture of their origin. But regardless of its diverse history, where it is enjoyed, whether it is green, black, medicinal, a blend or a herbal infusion, tea brings us together, revitalises and warms us.

In London, as early as the 1700s, tea drinking was embraced as a social activity. It became popular to entertain guests in one's home and serve tea. Of course it didn't take long for the art of afternoon tea to be perfected. Scones, pastries, sandwiches and cakes accompanied black tea with milk, carefully brewed to create the finest possible cup.

Today, tea drinking is much more relaxed. We embrace many kinds of tea, and although tea bags are still the most commonly bought, loose-leaf teas are making a comeback. You really can taste the true flavour of a tea when you brew with loose leaves.

How to brew
THE PERFECT CUP

• Use loose leaves. They're almost always better quality.

• Fill the kettle with fresh, cold water and bring it to the boil (once only, to maintain the water's oxygen).

• Preheat your teapot by swilling hot water around in it. Pour it out, and then replace the lid.

• Know how many cups your pot makes so you can get the water-to-tea ratio right. Add one teaspoon of tea per person and one for the pot. As a guide, it's usually best to fill the pot to near the base of the spout.

• If making black or herbal tea, carry the teapot to the just-boiled kettle, and pour the water in immediately. Replace the lid straight away to retain the heat. Green tea is better brewed with water that is just off the boil, to avoid a bitter taste.

• Depending on the variety of tea, and whether the leaves are broken or whole, black tea is best brewed for 3 to 5 minutes; green and herbal should be brewed for 2 to 4 minutes.

• Milk or lemon can be added to black tea, along with sugar, if desired. Often honey or mint is added to green and herbal varieties.

• Milk first? Or tea first? Neither is incorrect, however the taste of your tea will differ. The fats in milk won't overheat if you slowly pour hot tea onto the cold milk. However, some do say that pouring a small amount of milk into a large cup of hot tea imparts a stale taste. Others simply prefer to add the milk afterwards as it's easier to gauge the desired amount. So, milk first or last? It's really up to you.

Chai

Gr

Tea
TYPES

Earl Grey

Chamomile

English Breakfast

Rosehip

arjeeling

TEA COSY

MATERIALS

- PURCHASED OR OLD JUMPER
- WOOLLEN QUILT BATTING
- WATER-SOLUBLE FABRIC MARKER
- SEWING THREAD AND NEEDLE
- 25MM-WIDE BIAS BINDING
- 2 WOOLLEN POMPOMS, MADE OR BOUGHT FROM CRAFT SHOPS (OPTIONAL)

1 Cut dome-shaped paper pattern from scrap paper to fit teapot. Pin pattern to jumper (front and back). Cut out shape from jumper (you will have two pieces). Cut two pieces of batting using the same pattern.

2 Lay batting pieces on top of each other; place jumper pieces, right-sides together, on top of batting. Trace a 1.5cm (¾-inch) border around the curved edge with a fabric marker – this is the sewing line. Pin all layers together. Sew around the sewing line through all layers. Don't sew across the bottom opening.

3 Trim the seam allowance to 5mm (¼-inch) and turn right-side out so the batting layers are on the inside. Fold the binding around the lower edge of the tea cosy; stitch in place with running stitch, catching both sides of the binding.

4 Cut the collar, or waistband, from jumper; sew running stitch along the bottom edge, using double thread for strength. Pull the thread tightly; curl the piece around itself into a rose. Stitch to the top of the cosy. Attach pompoms to each end of a piece of finger-knitted or crocheted cord; tie firmly around the rose.

STEP 1
Cut a dome-shaped pattern from scrap paper to fit teapot. Place pattern on jumper and cut out. Cut batting from pattern.

STEP 2
Pin batting and jumper pieces together. Trace around shape with a fabric marker. Cut around line, leaving a 1.5cm border.

STEP 3
Fold the binding around the lower edge of the cosy; stitch in place all around the bottom edge, using running stitch.

STEP 4
Stitch along the edge of the collar; pull thread tightly to curl collar into a rose. Attach rose and pompom to top of cosy.

Brandy SNAP BASKETS

- 2 TABLESPOONS GOLDEN SYRUP
- 60G (2 OUNCES) BUTTER
- ⅓ CUP (75G) LIGHTLY PACKED BROWN SUGAR
- ⅓ CUP (50G) PLAIN FLOUR (ALL-PURPOSE FLOUR)
- 2 TEASPOONS GROUND GINGER
- PINCH SALT
- 300ML THICKENED (HEAVY) CREAM
- 1 TABLESPOON CASTER SUGAR (SUPERFINE SUGAR)
- 1 TABLESPOON BRANDY
- 250G (8 OUNCES) STRAWBERRIES

1 Preheat oven to 180°C/350°F. Grease oven trays.

2 Stir syrup, butter and brown sugar in a small saucepan over low heat until butter has melted. Remove from heat; stir in sifted flour, ginger and salt until mixed well. Drop rounded teaspoonsful of mixture onto oven trays, allowing room for spreading (about two per tray).

3 For easy handling, bake one tray at a time. Bake snaps for 6 minutes or until they bubble and are golden brown. Stand 1 minute. Using a thin metal spatula or knife, carefully loosen snaps from tray; working quickly, shape snaps over an upturned small mould or glass into baskets. Transfer to a wire rack to cool. Repeat with remaining snaps.

4 Beat cream, sugar and brandy in a small bowl with an electric mixer until firm peaks form. Spoon cream mixture into a piping bag fitted with a 1cm (½-inch) fluted tube. Pipe brandy cream into baskets, top each with a strawberry.

Glazed lemon &
VANILLA MADELEINES

- 125G (4 OUNCES) BUTTER, MELTED
- 1 TABLESPOON PLAIN FLOUR (ALL-PURPOSE FLOUR)
- 2 EGGS
- ⅓ CUP (75G) CASTER SUGAR (SUPERFINE SUGAR)
- 1 TABLESPOON FINELY GRATED LEMON RIND
- 1 TEASPOON VANILLA BEAN PASTE
- ⅔ CUP (100G) PLAIN FLOUR (ALL-PURPOSE FLOUR), EXTRA
- ¼ TEASPOON BAKING POWDER

GLACÉ ICING

- 1 CUP (160G) ICING SUGAR (CONFECTIONERS' SUGAR)
- 2 TEASPOONS BUTTER
- ¼ CUP (60ML) LEMON JUICE, APPROXIMATELY

1 Preheat oven to 200°C/400°F. Grease 20 holes of two 12-hole (1½-tablespoon/30ml) madeleine pans with 1 tablespoon of the melted butter. Dust pan holes with flour.

2 Beat eggs, sugar, rind and paste in a small bowl with an electric mixer for 5 minutes or until thick and creamy.

3 Sift the extra flour and baking powder twice; fold into egg mixture with remaining butter. Spoon level tablespoons of mixture into the prepared pan holes.

4 Bake madeleines for 10 minutes or until golden and firm to touch. Stand in pans for 2 minutes before transferring to a wire rack set over an oven tray.

5 Meanwhile, make glacé icing.

6 Spoon icing over madeleines; stand for 5 minutes or until set.

GLACÉ ICING Sift icing sugar into a small heatproof bowl; stir in butter and enough juice to form a firm paste. Place bowl over a small saucepan of simmering water; stir until icing is of a pouring consistency. Do not overheat.

tip Madeleines are best made on the day of serving. They are suitable to freeze uniced.

Choc-strawberry
MERINGUE GATEAU

- 125G (4 OUNCES) BUTTER, SOFTENED
- 4 EGGS, SEPARATED
- ¾ CUP (165G) CASTER SUGAR (SUPERFINE SUGAR)
- 1 CUP (150G) SELF-RAISING FLOUR
- ⅓ CUP (35G) COCOA POWDER
- ½ TEASPOON BICARBONATE OF SODA (BAKING SODA)
- 1 CUP (250ML) BUTTERMILK
- ⅓ CUP (75G) CASTER SUGAR (SUPERFINE SUGAR), EXTRA
- ¼ CUP (30G) COARSELY CHOPPED ROASTED HAZELNUTS
- ⅔ CUP (160ML) THICKENED (HEAVY) CREAM
- 1 TABLESPOON ICING SUGAR (CONFECTIONERS' SUGAR)
- 250G (8 OUNCES) STRAWBERRIES, HALVED

1 Preheat oven to 160°C/325°F. Grease two 20cm (8-inch) round cake pans; line bases and sides with baking paper.

2 Beat butter, egg yolks and caster sugar in a medium bowl with an electric mixer until light and fluffy. Stir in combined sifted flour, cocoa and soda, then buttermilk. Divide mixture between pans.

3 Beat egg whites in a small bowl with an electric mixer until soft peaks form; gradually add extra caster sugar, a tablespoon at a time, beating until sugar dissolves between additions.

4 Divide meringue mixture over cake mixture in pans; using a spatula, spread meringue so cake mixture is completely covered. Sprinkle nuts over meringue mixture on one of the cakes.

5 Bake cakes for 25 minutes. Cover pans loosely with foil; bake for a further 20 minutes. Leave cakes in pans for 5 minutes before turning, top-side up, onto wire racks to cool.

6 Beat cream and icing sugar in a small bowl with an electric mixer until soft peaks form. Place cake without nuts on a serving plate; spread with cream mixture. Top with strawberries, then top with the remaining cake.

tip This recipe is best made on the day of serving.

Caramel ÉCLAIRS

- 395G (12½ OUNCES) CANNED SWEETENED CONDENSED MILK
- ½ CUP (125ML) WATER
- 60G (2 OUNCES) BUTTER, CHOPPED FINELY
- 1 TABLESPOON DARK BROWN SUGAR
- ½ CUP (75G) BAKER'S FLOUR
- 3 EGGS
- 2 CUPS (500ML) THICKENED (HEAVY) CREAM

CARAMEL ICING

- 30G (1 OUNCE) BUTTER, CHOPPED COARSELY
- ¼ CUP (55G) FIRMLY PACKED DARK BROWN SUGAR
- 1 TABLESPOON MILK
- ⅓ CUP (55G) ICING SUGAR (CONFECTIONERS' SUGAR)

1 Preheat oven to 220°C/425°F.

2 Pour condensed milk into a medium shallow baking dish; cover with foil. Place dish in a large baking dish; add enough boiling water to large dish to come halfway up sides of dish. Transfer to oven; bake, uncovered, for 1¼ hours or until condensed milk is golden brown and caramel. Cool to room temperature. Whisk caramel until smooth.

3 To make choux pastry, combine the water, butter and sugar in a medium saucepan; bring to the boil. Add flour; beat with a wooden spoon over medium heat until mixture comes away from the base of the pan. Transfer pastry to a medium bowl; beat in two of the eggs, one at a time. Whisk remaining egg with a fork, beat enough of the egg into the pastry until it becomes smooth and glossy but still holds its shape.

4 Spoon pastry into a piping bag fitted with a 1.5cm (¾-inch) plain tube. Pipe 8cm (3-inch) lengths, about 5cm (2 inches) apart, onto greased oven trays.

5 Bake éclairs for 10 minutes. Reduce oven temperature to 180°C/350°F; bake éclairs for a further 15 minutes.

6 Using a serrated knife, cut éclairs in half, remove any soft centres and return to the trays, bake for a further 5 minutes or until éclairs are dry. Cool on trays.

7 Meanwhile, make caramel icing.

8 Beat cream in a small bowl with an electric mixer until firm peaks form. Spread caramel into éclair bases; top with whipped cream. Position éclair tops on cream; spread with caramel icing.

CARAMEL ICING Melt butter in a small saucepan, add brown sugar and milk; cook, stirring over high heat, without boiling, until sugar dissolves. Bring to the boil. Reduce heat; simmer, uncovered, for 1 minute. Remove from heat; cool for 10 minutes. Whisk in sifted icing sugar. (If the icing becomes too thick, stir in 2 teaspoons boiling water for a better consistency.)

COFFEE & WALNUT CAKE
with toffee

- 30G (1 OUNCE) BUTTER
- 1 TABLESPOON BROWN SUGAR
- 2 TEASPOONS GROUND CINNAMON
- 2 CUPS (200G) ROASTED WALNUTS
- ½ CUP (125ML) MILK
- 1 TABLESPOON INSTANT COFFEE GRANULES
- 185G (6 OUNCES) BUTTER, SOFTENED, EXTRA
- 1⅓ CUPS (300G) CASTER SUGAR (SUPERFINE SUGAR)
- 3 EGGS
- 1 CUP (150G) SELF-RAISING FLOUR
- ¾ CUP (110G) PLAIN FLOUR (ALL-PURPOSE FLOUR)

TOFFEE

- ½ CUP (110G) CASTER SUGAR (SUPERFINE SUGAR)
- 2 TABLESPOONS WATER
- 3 TEASPOONS POURING CREAM

1 Preheat oven to 160°C/325°F. Grease a 22cm (9-inch) baba cake pan well; dust with flour, shake out excess flour.

2 Melt butter in a small saucepan over medium heat; stir in brown sugar, cinnamon and walnuts. Cool.

3 Combine milk and coffee in a small bowl; stir until coffee dissolves.

4 Beat extra butter and caster sugar in a small bowl with an electric mixer until light and fluffy. Beat in eggs, one at a time. Stir in sifted flours, then milk mixture.

5 Spread one-third of the cake mixture into the pan; sprinkle with half the nut mixture. Top with the remaining cake mixture.

6 Bake cake about 45 minutes. Leave cake in pan for 5 minutes before turning onto a wire rack set over an oven tray. Cool.

7 Make toffee. Working quickly, drizzle some of the toffee over top of the cooled cake, press on the remaining nut mixture, then drizzle with the remaining toffee.

TOFFEE Stir sugar and the water in a small saucepan over medium heat, without boiling, until sugar dissolves; bring to the boil. Reduce heat; simmer, uncovered, without stirring, until toffee becomes caramel in colour. Carefully add cream (take care as the toffee may splatter); stir for 1 minute or until thickened slightly.

tip This cake is best eaten the day it is made.

Chocolate ALMOND FINGERS

- 60G (2 OUNCES) BUTTER, SOFTENED
- 1 CUP (125G) GROUND ALMONDS
- ½ CUP (110G) CASTER SUGAR (SUPERFINE SUGAR)
- 2 EGGS, BEATEN LIGHTLY
- 2 TABLESPOONS PLAIN FLOUR (ALL-PURPOSE FLOUR)
- 100G (3 OUNCES) DARK (SEMI-SWEET) CHOCOLATE
- 1 TEASPOON VEGETABLE OIL

ALMOND TOPPING
- 60G (2 OUNCES) BUTTER, CHOPPED
- ⅓ CUP (75G) CASTER SUGAR (SUPERFINE SUGAR)
- ⅓ CUP (80ML) GLUCOSE SYRUP
- 1½ CUPS (120G) FLAKED ALMONDS
- 2 TABLESPOONS WATER

1 Preheat oven to 200°C/400°F. Grease a 23cm x 33cm (9-inch x 13-inch) swiss roll pan; line base and long sides with baking paper, extending the paper 5cm (2 inches) above the sides.

2 Beat butter, ground almonds and sugar in a small bowl with an electric mixer until smooth. Gradually beat in egg. Stir in sifted flour until combined. Spread mixture over base of pan.

3 Bake base about 10 minutes. Remove base from oven (leave oven on); cool base for 5 minutes.

4 Meanwhile, make almond topping.

5 Spread topping over base; bake for a further 10 minutes or until browned lightly. Cut while warm; lift onto wire racks to cool.

6 Place chocolate in a small heatproof bowl over a small saucepan of simmering water (make sure water doesn't touch the base of the bowl); stir until melted. Combine melted chocolate and oil. Dip biscuits diagonally into chocolate mixture; place on wire racks, stand until set.

ALMOND TOPPING Stir ingredients in a medium saucepan over medium heat, without boiling, until sugar is dissolved. Bring to the boil; simmer, uncovered, without stirring, for 4 minutes or until mixture thickens slightly.

Cinnamon TEACAKE

- 60G (2 OUNCES) BUTTER, SOFTENED
- ⅔ CUP (150G) CASTER SUGAR (SUPERFINE SUGAR)
- 1 TEASPOON VANILLA EXTRACT
- 1 EGG
- 1 CUP (150G) SELF-RAISING FLOUR
- ⅓ CUP (80ML) MILK
- 10G (½ OUNCE) BUTTER, EXTRA
- 1 TEASPOON GROUND CINNAMON
- 1 TABLESPOON CASTER SUGAR (SUPERFINE SUGAR), EXTRA

1 Preheat oven to 180°C/350°F. Grease a deep 20cm (8-inch) round cake pan; line base with baking paper.

2 Beat butter, sugar, extract and egg in a small bowl with an electric mixer until light and fluffy. Stir in sifted flour and milk until smooth. Spread mixture into pan.

3 Bake cake about 30 minutes. Turn cake, top-side up, onto a wire rack.

4 Meanwhile melt extra butter. Brush top of hot cake with melted butter; sprinkle with combined cinnamon and extra sugar while cake is still hot.

serving suggestion Serve warm with butter.

Chocolate
RASPBERRY KISSES

- 125G (4 OUNCES) UNSALTED BUTTER, SOFTENED
- ½ CUP (110G) FIRMLY PACKED BROWN SUGAR
- 1 EGG
- ¾ CUP (110G) PLAIN FLOUR (ALL-PURPOSE FLOUR)
- ⅓ CUP (35G) COCOA POWDER
- ¼ CUP (35G) SELF-RAISING FLOUR
- 1 TEASPOON BICARBONATE OF SODA (BAKING SODA)
- ⅔ CUP (160ML) BUTTERMILK
- 125G (4 OUNCES) FRESH RASPBERRIES, TORN

RASPBERRY BUTTER CREAM

- 125G (4 OUNCES) UNSALTED BUTTER, SOFTENED
- 1½ CUPS (240G) ICING SUGAR (CONFECTIONERS' SUGAR)
- 1 TABLESPOON MILK
- PINK FOOD COLOURING
- 2 TABLESPOONS RASPBERRY JAM

CHOCOLATE GANACHE

- 2 TABLESPOONS POURING CREAM
- 100G (3 OUNCES) DARK (SEMI-SWEET) CHOCOLATE, CHOPPED FINELY

1 Preheat oven to 200°C/400°F. Grease oven trays; line trays with baking paper.

2 Beat butter, sugar and egg in a small bowl with an electric mixer until light and fluffy. Beat in sifted dry ingredients and buttermilk, on low speed, until mixture is smooth.

3 Drop level tablespoons of mixture about 5cm (2 inches) apart onto trays. Bake cakes about 10 minutes. Cool on trays.

4 Meanwhile, make raspberry butter cream, then chocolate ganache.

5 Spoon butter cream into a piping bag fitted with a 2cm (¾-inch) fluted tube. Pipe butter cream on the flat side of half the cooled cakes.

6 Spread ganache over rounded side of remaining cooled cakes. Place on top of butter cream. Top kisses with raspberries.

RASPBERRY BUTTER CREAM
Beat butter in a small bowl with an electric mixer until light and fluffy. Beat in sifted icing sugar and milk. Tint pink with colouring; stir in jam.

CHOCOLATE GANACHE Bring the cream to the boil in a small saucepan. Remove from heat; stir in chocolate until smooth.

tip Unfilled cakes can be frozen for 2 months. Kisses, once filled, should be served within several hours.

Pink JELLY CAKES

- 125G (4 OUNCES) BUTTER, SOFTENED
- 1 TEASPOON VANILLA EXTRACT
- ½ CUP (110G) CASTER SUGAR (SUPERFINE SUGAR)
- 2 EGGS
- 1½ CUPS (225G) SELF-RAISING FLOUR
- ½ CUP (125ML) MILK
- 85G (3-OUNCE) PACKET RASPBERRY JELLY CRYSTALS
- 1 CUP (250ML) BOILING WATER
- 1 CUP (250ML) COLD WATER
- ½ CUP (125ML) THICKENED (HEAVY) CREAM
- 1 TABLESPOON ICING SUGAR (CONFECTIONERS' SUGAR)
- 2 CUPS (160G) DESICCATED COCONUT, APPROXIMATELY

1 Preheat oven to 200°C/400°F. Grease 18 holes of two 12-hole gem irons.

2 Beat butter, extract and sugar in a small bowl with an electric mixer until light and fluffy. Beat in eggs, one at a time, until combined. Stir in sifted flour and milk.

3 Drop tablespoons of mixture into gem irons. Bake cakes for about 15 minutes. Turn cakes, flat-side down, onto a wire rack to cool.

4 Meanwhile, dissolve jelly crystals in the boiling water; stir in the cold water until combined. Refrigerate for 45 minutes or until jelly is partly set.

5 Beat cream and icing sugar in a small bowl with an electric mixer until firm peaks form.

6 Level flat-sides of cakes; sandwich the flat-sides with cream. Dip cakes in jelly, then roll in coconut. Place on a tray; refrigerate for 30 minutes.

tip Old-fashioned gem irons, made from cast iron, are available from specialty cookware shops, or try second-hand shops.

Victoria SPONGE SANDWICH

- 250G (8 OUNCES) BUTTER
- 1 TEASPOON VANILLA EXTRACT
- 1 CUP (220G) CASTER SUGAR (SUPERFINE SUGAR)
- 4 EGGS
- ⅓ CUP (80ML) MILK
- 2 CUPS (300G) SELF-RAISING FLOUR
- ⅓ CUP (110G) RASPBERRY JAM, WARMED
- 2 TEASPOONS ICING SUGAR (CONFECTIONERS' SUGAR)

1 Preheat oven to 180°C/350°F. Grease two deep 20cm (8-inch) round cake pans; line bases with baking paper.

2 Beat butter, extract and sugar in a small bowl with an electric mixer until light and fluffy. Beat in eggs, one at a time; beat in milk. Transfer mixture to a large bowl. Stir in sifted flour, in two batches, until smooth. Divide mixture between pans.

3 Bake cakes about 30 minutes. Turn cakes, top-side up, onto baking paper-covered wire racks to cool.

4 Sandwich cakes with jam. Dust sponge with sifted icing sugar to serve.

tips For a light, buttery cake, make sure you beat the butter, sugar and egg mixture thoroughly. For other cake filling ideas, see pages 62-63. Fill the sponge with the homemade berry jam on page 245, if you like.

EDITOR'S
Favourite

Cake FILLINGS

Jazz up a victoria sponge (page 60) with these delicious fillings.

BLUEBERRY JAM

Sandwich the sponge cake layers with ⅓ cup blueberry jam and ¾ cup whipped thickened (heavy) cream. Serve sponge dusted with sifted icing sugar (confectioners' sugar).

LEMON BUTTER

Add a little delicious tartness with ⅓ cup lemon butter and ¾ cup whipped thickened (heavy) cream. Serve sponge dusted with sifted icing sugar (confectioners' sugar).

RASPBERRY CREAM

Use fresh fruit instead of jam and fold
125g (4 ounces) chopped fresh raspberries
through ¾ cup whipped thickened (heavy) cream.
Serve sponge dusted with sifted icing sugar
(confectioners' sugar).

PASSIONFRUIT CREAM

You can't go past passionfruit during summer; fill
your sponge with ¾ cup whipped thickened
(heavy) cream and the pulp from 2 passionfruit.
Serve sponge dusted with sifted icing sugar
(confectioners' sugar).

e best cup of
Coffee you've ever tasted

WITH DOUBLE-RICH

Carnation

JUST MAKE IT BLACK AND ADD CARNATION STRAIGHT FROM THE CAN.

What a delicious difference Carnation makes to coffee. Its double richness does so much to bring out the full fragrant coffee flavour. Make your coffee black the way you like it . . . ground, or with essence or powder, but, instead of using ordinary milk, 'cream' it with Carnation — straight from the can — and enjoy a richer, smoother creamier cup of coffee. It's much easier with Carnation, because there's no separate heating of milk and no messy saucepans to wash.

Your bedtime drink tastes nicer with Carnation . . . it's easier, too.

If you like hot chocolate, cocoa or any tonic beverage, use Carnation instead of ordinary milk. Make your favourite drink with boiling water, then simply stir in Carnation, and you'll find that Carnation's double-richness will give it a creamier, more delicious flavour.

CARNATION IS SO CONVENIENT
Carnation MILK
FROM CONTENTED COWS

FREE RECIPE BOOKLET: Send for the new Carnation Winter Recipe Booklet. For your copy write to Mary Blake, Carnation Home Economist, 252 Swanston Street, Melbourne, or ask your local grocer.

CHELSEA BUNS

- 4 TEASPOONS (14G) DRY YEAST
- 1 TEASPOON CASTER SUGAR (SUPERFINE SUGAR)
- 3 CUPS (560G) PLAIN FLOUR (ALL-PURPOSE FLOUR)
- 1½ CUPS (375ML) WARM MILK
- ½ TEASPOON GROUND CINNAMON
- ½ TEASPOON MIXED SPICE
- ¼ TEASPOON GROUND NUTMEG
- 2 TEASPOONS FINELY GRATED ORANGE RIND
- 1 TABLESPOON CASTER SUGAR (SUPERFINE SUGAR), EXTRA
- 1 EGG, BEATEN LIGHTLY
- 45G (1½ OUNCES) BUTTER, MELTED

- 15G (½ OUNCE) BUTTER, MELTED, EXTRA
- 2 TABLESPOONS RASPBERRY JAM
- ½ CUP (75G) DRIED CURRANTS
- ¼ CUP (55G) BROWN SUGAR
- ½ CUP (60G) COARSELY CHOPPED ROASTED PECANS
- 3 TEASPOONS WARMED HONEY

COFFEE ICING

- 1½ CUPS (240G) ICING SUGAR (CONFECTIONERS' SUGAR)
- 15G (½ OUNCE) BUTTER, MELTED
- 2 TABLESPOONS WARM MILK
- 3 TEASPOONS INSTANT COFFEE GRANULES

1 Combine yeast, caster sugar, 1 tablespoon of the flour, and the warm milk in a small bowl. Cover; stand in a warm place for 10 minutes or until frothy.

2 Combine remaining sifted flour, spices, rind and extra caster sugar in a large bowl, stir in egg, butter and yeast mixture; mix to a soft dough. Knead the dough on a floured surface for 10 minutes or until smooth and elastic. Place dough in a large greased bowl. Cover; stand in a warm place for 1 hour or until doubled in size.

3 Grease two deep 22cm (9-inch) round cake pans.

4 Turn dough onto a floured surface; knead for 1 minute. Roll dough into a 23cm x 36cm (9-inch x 14½-inch) rectangle. Brush dough with extra butter, spread with jam. Sprinkle with combined currants, brown sugar and nuts, leaving a 2cm (1-inch) border all around.

5 Roll dough up firmly from one long side like a swiss roll. Cut dough evenly into 12 pieces; place six pieces, cut-side up, in each pan. Cover; stand in a warm place for 30 minutes or until risen slightly.

6 Meanwhile, preheat oven to 200°C/ 400°F.

7 Bake buns for 30 minutes or until golden brown.

8 Make coffee icing. Turn buns, top-side up, onto a wire rack. Brush hot buns with honey, drizzle with coffee icing; cool.

COFFEE ICING Sift icing sugar into a small bowl; stir in butter, milk and coffee until smooth.

SPONGE ROLL
with jam & cream

- 3 EGGS
- ⅔ CUP (150G) CASTER SUGAR (SUPERFINE SUGAR)
- ½ CUP (75G) WHEATEN CORNFLOUR (CORNSTARCH)
- 2 TABLESPOONS CUSTARD POWDER
- ¾ TEASPOON CREAM OF TARTAR
- ½ TEASPOON BICARBONATE OF SODA (BAKING SODA)
- ¾ CUP (180ML) THICKENED (HEAVY) CREAM
- ⅓ CUP (110G) RASPBERRY JAM
- 1 TABLESPOON ICING SUGAR (CONFECTIONERS' SUGAR)

1 Preheat oven to 180°C/350°F. Grease a 25cm x 30cm (10-inch x 12-inch) swiss roll pan; line base and long sides with baking paper, extending the paper 5cm (2 inches) above the sides.

2 Beat eggs and ½ cup of the caster sugar in a small bowl with an electric mixer until thick and creamy and sugar is dissolved. Fold in the triple-sifted dry ingredients.

3 Spread mixture into pan; bake about 12 minutes.

4 Meanwhile, beat cream in a small bowl with an electric mixer until soft peaks form.

5 Place a piece of baking paper cut the same size as the pan on bench; sprinkle with remaining caster sugar. Turn sponge onto paper; peel lining paper away. Cool; trim all sides of sponge.

6 Spread sponge with jam, then cream. Using the paper as a guide, roll the sponge from one short side. Cover with plastic wrap; refrigerate for 30 minutes. Before serving, dust with sifted icing sugar.

tips You'll notice most sponge recipes call for triple-sifted flour. We sift the dry ingredients twice onto a piece of greaseproof paper (why create washing up by using a bowl) – this sifting not only mixes the ingredients thoroughly, but also incorporates some air into the flour. Hold the sifter up high as you sift. The third sifting is done over the egg mixture, seconds before you start folding the ingredients together.

Use the homemade berry jam on page 245 to fill the sponge roll, if you like.

Frou frou CUPCAKES

- 125G (4 OUNCES) BUTTER, SOFTENED
- 1 CUP (220G) CASTER SUGAR (SUPERFINE SUGAR)
- 3 EGGS
- ½ CUP (75G) PLAIN FLOUR (ALL-PURPOSE FLOUR)
- ¼ CUP (35G) SELF-RAISING FLOUR
- ½ CUP (40G) DESICCATED COCONUT
- ⅓ CUP (80G) SOUR CREAM
- 155G (5 OUNCES) FROZEN RASPBERRIES (SEE TIPS)
- 1 CUP (50G) FLAKED COCONUT, TOASTED
- 24 FRESH RASPBERRIES

CREAM CHEESE FROSTING

- 60G (2 OUNCES) BUTTER, SOFTENED
- 155G (5 OUNCES) CREAM CHEESE, SOFTENED
- 2 TEASPOONS COCONUT EXTRACT
- 3 CUPS (480G) ICING SUGAR (CONFECTIONERS' SUGAR)

1 Preheat oven to 180°C/350°F. Line a 12-hole (⅓-cup/80ml) muffin pan with paper cases.

2 Beat butter, sugar and eggs in a small bowl with an electric mixer until light and fluffy. Stir in sifted flours, desiccated coconut, sour cream and frozen raspberries. Spoon mixture into paper cases; smooth surface.

3 Bake cakes about 40 minutes. Leave cakes in pan for 5 minutes before turning, top-side up, onto a wire rack to cool. Remove paper cases from cold cakes.

4 Meanwhile, make cream cheese frosting.

5 Spread top and side of cakes with frosting; decorate with flaked coconut and fresh raspberries.

CREAM CHEESE FROSTING Beat butter, cream cheese and extract in a small bowl with an electric mixer until light and fluffy; gradually beat in sifted icing sugar.

tips Do not thaw the frozen raspberries as their colour will bleed into the batter. These cakes are best made on the day of serving. Unfrosted cakes can be frozen for up to 3 months.

Strawberry ALMOND FRIANDS

- 6 EGG WHITES
- 185G (6 OUNCES) BUTTER, MELTED
- 1 CUP (120G) GROUND ALMONDS
- 1½ CUPS (240G) ICING SUGAR (CONFECTIONERS' SUGAR)
- ½ CUP (75G) PLAIN FLOUR (ALL-PURPOSE FLOUR)
- 100G (3 OUNCES) STRAWBERRIES, SLICED THINLY
- 1 TEASPOON ICING SUGAR (CONFECTIONERS' SUGAR), EXTRA

1 Preheat oven to 200°C/400°F. Grease 12 x ½-cup (125ml) oval friand pans; stand on oven tray.

2 Place egg whites in a medium bowl; whisk lightly with a fork until combined. Add butter, ground almonds, sifted icing sugar and flour; using a wooden spoon, stir until just combined. Spoon mixture into pans; top with strawberry slices.

3 Bake friands about 25 minutes. Turn, top-side up, onto a wire rack to cool. Serve friands warm or at room temperature, dusted with extra sifted icing sugar.

VARIATIONS

PLAIN Omit strawberries; replace ground almonds with ground hazelnuts.

BLUEBERRY Omit strawberries and replace with 80g (2½ ounces) fresh or frozen blueberries.

BANANA Use either ground hazelnuts or ground almonds; top unbaked friands with a thin slice of banana.

CHOCOLATE Stir 100g (3 ounces) coarsely chopped dark chocolate into the egg white mixture; use either ground almonds or ground hazelnuts.

tip Friands are at their best made on the day of serving, but they can be stored in an airtight container for up to 2 days.

Prize
WINNING

PUMPKIN SCONES

- 40G (1½ OUNCES) BUTTER, SOFTENED
- ¼ CUP (55G) CASTER SUGAR (SUPERFINE SUGAR)
- 1 EGG, BEATEN LIGHTLY
- ¾ CUP COOKED MASHED PUMPKIN
- 2½ CUPS (375G) SELF-RAISING FLOUR
- ½ TEASPOON GROUND NUTMEG
- ⅓ CUP (80ML) MILK, APPROXIMATELY

1 Preheat oven to 220°C/425°F. Grease two 20cm (8-inch) round sandwich pans.

2 Beat butter and sugar in a small bowl with an electric mixer until light and fluffy; beat in egg. Transfer mixture to a large bowl; stir in pumpkin, sifted flour and spice, and enough milk to make a soft, sticky dough.

3 Knead dough on a floured surface until smooth. Press dough out evenly into a 2cm (¾-inch) thickness. Using a 5cm (2-inch) cutter, cut as many rounds as you can from dough. Place the rounds, just touching, in pans.

4 Gently knead scraps of dough together. Cut out more rounds; place in pans. Brush scones with a little extra milk.

5 Bake scones for 15 minutes or until browned and scones sound hollow when tapped firmly on the top with your fingers.

tip These scones can be stored in an airtight container for up to 2 days.

DATE & PECAN ROLL

- 30G (1 OUNCE) UNSALTED BUTTER
- ½ CUP (125ML) WATER
- ½ CUP (75G) FINELY CHOPPED SEEDED DRIED DATES
- ¼ TEASPOON BICARBONATE OF SODA (BAKING SODA)
- ½ CUP (110G) FIRMLY PACKED BROWN SUGAR
- 1 CUP (150G) SELF-RAISING FLOUR
- ¼ CUP (30G) COARSELY CHOPPED PECANS
- 1 EGG

1 Adjust oven shelves to fit an upright nut roll tin. Preheat oven to 180°C/350°F. Grease lids and the inside of an 8cm x 20cm (3-inch x 8-inch) nut roll tin evenly with melted butter; place base lid on tin, position tin upright on an oven tray.

2 Stir butter and the water in a medium saucepan over low heat until butter melts. Remove from heat; stir in dates and soda, then the remaining ingredients. Spoon mixture into tin; tap tin firmly on bench to remove any air pockets. Position top lid.

3 Bake roll about 1 hour. Stand roll for 5 minutes before removing lids. Shake gently to release roll onto a wire rack to cool slightly. Slice roll and serve, warm or cold, with butter.

tips Tall 8cm x 17cm, 850ml fruit juice cans (3-inch x 6¾-inch, 28 fl oz) make good nut roll tins. Use a can opener that cuts just below the rim to cut one end from the can. Carefully wash and dry the can thoroughly before greasing well. Use a double-thickness of foil to cover the top of the can and secure with string; slash a hole in the top of the foil to allow steam to escape during baking.

The nut roll tins (or fruit juice cans) need to be coated thickly with melted butter so the roll won't stick to the inside of the tin. Don't use cooking-oil spray as this doesn't give a good enough coating and the roll will stick and be hard to turn out.

The roll can be stored in an airtight container for up to 3 days.

Only **LAN·CHOO TEA** gives
DOUBLE ECONOMY

SAVE THIS LABEL

and share in the **LAN-CHOO BONUS PLAN.** There are over **400** useful presents to choose from.

YOU SAVE THAT EXTRA SPOONFUL

every time you make tea with **LAN-CHOO.** That's real economy!

Send now for your copy of the **LAN-CHOO** Catalogue of Bonus Presents

LAN-CHOO TEA COMPANY
364-372 Kent St., Sydney
452-460 Flinders St., Melbourne
Strike out address which does not apply.
Please send me a copy of the Lan-choo Tea Catalogue of Bonus Presents. I enclose 4d. in stamps for postage.

NAME

ADDRESS

W.W.25 9

LAN·CHOO
Ceylon's Choicest Tea

Tangy LEMON SQUARES

- 125G (4 OUNCES) BUTTER, SOFTENED
- ¼ CUP (40G) ICING SUGAR (CONFECTIONERS' SUGAR)
- 1¼ CUPS (185G) PLAIN FLOUR (ALL-PURPOSE FLOUR)
- 3 EGGS
- 1 CUP (220G) CASTER SUGAR (SUPERFINE SUGAR)
- 2 TEASPOONS FINELY GRATED LEMON RIND
- ½ CUP (125ML) LEMON JUICE
- 2 TEASPOONS ICING SUGAR (CONFECTIONERS' SUGAR), EXTRA

1 Preheat oven to 180°C/350°F. Grease a shallow 22cm (9-inch) square cake pan; line base and sides with baking paper, extending the paper 2.5cm (1 inch) above the sides.

2 Beat butter and sifted icing sugar in a small bowl with an electric mixer until smooth. Stir in 1 cup of the sifted flour. Press mixture evenly over base of pan.

3 Bake base for 15 minutes or until browned lightly.

4 Meanwhile, whisk eggs, caster sugar, rind, juice and remaining flour in a medium bowl until combined. Pour egg mixture over the hot base.

5 Return slice to oven; bake for a further 20 minutes or until firm. Cool slice in pan on a wire rack before cutting into squares. Just before serving, dust slice with extra sifted icing sugar.

tips When buying lemons, look for those that are bright and heavy; they have more juice and flavour. This slice can be stored, covered, in the refrigerator for up to 3 days.

PREP + COOK TIME 50 MINUTES (+ STANDING) MAKES 12

CREAM BUNS

- 4 CUPS (600G) PLAIN FLOUR (ALL-PURPOSE FLOUR)
- ¼ CUP (55G) CASTER SUGAR (SUPERFINE SUGAR)
- 4 TEASPOONS (14G) DRY YEAST (SEE TIP)
- 60G (2 OUNCES) BUTTER
- ½ CUP (125ML) LUKEWARM MILK
- 1 CUP (250ML) LUKEWARM WATER
- 1 EGG YOLK
- 1 TEASPOON WATER, EXTRA
- ¾ CUP (240G) RASPBERRY JAM
- 300ML THICKENED (HEAVY) CREAM, WHIPPED
- 1 TEASPOON ICING SUGAR (CONFECTIONERS' SUGAR)

1 Sift flour, sugar and yeast into a large bowl. Rub in butter until mixture resembles fine breadcrumbs. Make a well in the centre, add the combined milk and the water; mix to a soft dough.

2 Turn dough out onto a floured surface; knead for 5 minutes. Place dough in an oiled bowl; cover, stand in a warm place for 1 hour or until dough has doubled in size.

3 Preheat oven to 220°C/425°F. Grease two oven trays.

4 Punch dough down in bowl. Turn dough out onto a floured surface; knead for 5 minutes. Divide dough into 12 even portions. Knead each portion into a round. Place rounds on trays, allowing room for spreading. Stand in a warm place for 10 minutes or until half-doubled in size.

5 Brush buns with combined egg yolk and extra water. Bake for 10 minutes. Reduce oven temperature to 180°C/350°F; bake for a further 15 minutes or until golden brown. Place buns on a wire rack to cool.

6 Split buns, fill with jam and cream. Dust buns with sifted icing sugar.

tip If you are lucky enough to find a supply, you can substitute fresh (compressed) yeast for dry yeast; you will need to use 30g (1 ounce).

To use fresh yeast: Combine the yeast and 1 teaspoon of the sugar in a small jug; stir in milk. Stand for 10 minutes or until frothy. Rub the butter into the flour and remaining sugar in a large bowl; make a well in the centre, add yeast mixture and the water; mix to a soft dough. Continue recipe from step 2.

DATE SCONES
with whipped caramel butter

- 30G (1 OUNCE) BUTTER, SOFTENED
- ¼ CUP (55G) BROWN SUGAR
- 1 EGG YOLK
- 2½ CUPS (375G) SELF-RAISING FLOUR
- ⅓ CUP (50G) FINELY CHOPPED SEEDED DRIED DATES
- 1¼ CUPS (310ML) BUTTERMILK

WHIPPED CARAMEL BUTTER

- 150G (5 OUNCES) UNSALTED BUTTER, SOFTENED
- ¼ CUP (55G) BROWN SUGAR
- 2 TEASPOONS VANILLA EXTRACT

1 Preheat oven to 220°C/425°F. Grease a deep 22cm (9-inch) square cake pan.

2 Beat butter, sugar and egg yolk in a small bowl with an electric mixer until light and fluffy. Transfer mixture to a large bowl; add sifted flour, dates and buttermilk. Use a knife to cut the buttermilk through the flour mixture to make a soft, sticky dough. Turn dough onto a floured surface, knead gently until smooth.

3 Press dough into a 20cm (8-inch) square, cut into nine squares using a floured knife, then cut each square in half diagonally. Place scones side by side, just touching, in pan. Brush scones with a little extra buttermilk.

4 Bake scones about 20 minutes.

5 Meanwhile, make whipped caramel butter; accompany with warm scones to serve.

WHIPPED CARAMEL BUTTER

Beat ingredients in a small bowl with an electric mixer until light and fluffy.

tip Scones are best made on the day of serving. They can be frozen for up to 3 months. Thaw in oven, wrapped in foil.

ladies WHO LUNCH

Chicken, almond & tarragon
MINI ROLLS

- 1 CUP (160G) FINELY SHREDDED COOKED CHICKEN BREAST
- 2 TABLESPOONS FINELY CHOPPED FRESH TARRAGON
- 2 TABLESPOONS ROASTED SLIVERED ALMONDS
- ½ TRIMMED CELERY STALK (50G), CHOPPED FINELY
- 2 GREEN ONIONS (SCALLIONS), CHOPPED FINELY
- 2 TABLESPOONS MAYONNAISE
- 6 MINI BREAD ROLLS (180G)

1 Combine chicken, tarragon, almonds, celery, onion and mayonnaise in a medium bowl; season to taste.

2 Make a cut into the tops of the rolls; Spoon in chicken mixture.

tip You can use leftover barbecued chicken for this recipe; you will need about a quarter of a chicken.

Tuna & vegetable SALAD

- 2 MEDIUM ZUCCHINI (240G), SLICED THINLY
- 2 MEDIUM CARROTS (240G), CUT INTO MATCHSTICKS
- 425G (13½ OUNCES) CANNED TUNA IN SPRINGWATER, DRAINED
- 4 TRIMMED CELERY STALKS (400G), SLICED THINLY
- 1 SMALL WHITE ONION (80G), SLICED THINLY
- 1 TABLESPOON FINELY CHOPPED FRESH FLAT-LEAF PARSLEY
- 4 ICEBERG LETTUCE LEAVES

DRESSING

- ½ CUP (125ML) FAT-FREE FRENCH DRESSING
- 2 TABLESPOONS PLAIN YOGHURT
- 1 CLOVE GARLIC, CRUSHED
- 2 TEASPOONS CURRY POWDER

1 Blanch zucchini and carrots in a small saucepan of boiling water for 1 minute; drain. Refresh under cold water; drain.

2 Make dressing.

3 Place zucchini and carrots in a medium bowl with tuna, celery, onion, parsley and dressing; toss gently to combine.

4 Serve salad in lettuce leaves.

DRESSING Combine ingredients in a small bowl; season to taste.

tip We used iceberg lettuce in this recipe as it is important to use a crisp variety of lettuce; you could also use cos (romaine) lettuce.

Corned beef & pickle
SANDWICH

- 2 SLICES WHOLEMEAL BREAD (90G)
- 10G (½ OUNCE) BUTTER, SOFTENED
- 2 TABLESPOONS MUSTARD PICKLES
- 2 SLICES CORNED BEEF (60G)

1 Spread both slices of bread with butter; spread pickles on one slice, top with corned beef, season. Top with remaining bread. Cut diagonally into halves or quarters, to serve.

tips You can use slices of leftover corned beef (page 177) or buy sliced corned beef from your delicatessen. Use your favourite pickle or other condiment, if you prefer.
Double this recipe to make extra servings as part of a mixed sandwich platter.

CUTWORK PAPER DOILY

MATERIALS

- **SHEET OF TISSUE PAPER**
- **SOFT PENCIL**
- **RULER OR TAPE MEASURE**
- **SMALL SHARP SCISSORS**

1 Fold the tissue paper into quarters and mark a series of points, each 25cm (10 inches) from the inner folded corner. Use a soft pencil to join up the points into a curve. Cut along the curve to get a circle with a diameter of 50cm (20 inches). Do not unfold the tissue paper.

2 Fold paper in half again and cut a scalloped edge along the outer curve – do this by eye, there's no need to measure. Do not unfold. Fold the wedge in half again: it is now in sixteenths.

3 Starting on one folded edge, cut small diamond, circle, heart and square shapes through the layers. Repeat on the other side. Open out and re-fold the circle into eighths or sixteenths along another axis, so the folded edges are no longer cut.

4 Repeat the cutting process, noting that you might not be able to cut as close to the apex as before. Open out. You can press the doily very gently, using a cool iron and a clean tea towel as a pressing cloth.

STEP 1
Fold the paper into quarters, then mark a series of dots on the paper, 25cm from the inner folded corner.

STEP 2
Do not unfold. Join the dots to make a curve. Fold in half again and cut a scalloped or pointed edge along the outer curve.

STEP 3
Starting on a folded edge, cut small shapes (hearts, diamonds, circles, squares) through the layers.

STEP 4
Refold the paper so the fold is in a different place; repeat the cutting. Open out the doily very gently so as not to tear.

PRAWN COCKTAIL

- 1KG (2 POUNDS) COOKED MEDIUM KING PRAWNS (SHRIMP)
- ⅓ CUP (100G) MAYONNAISE
- 2 TABLESPOONS POURING CREAM
- 1 TABLESPOON TOMATO SAUCE (KETCHUP)
- 1 TEASPOON WORCESTERSHIRE SAUCE
- ½ TEASPOON TABASCO SAUCE
- ½ TEASPOON DIJON MUSTARD
- 2 TEASPOONS LEMON JUICE
- 8 BABY COS (ROMAINE) LETTUCE LEAVES
- LEMON WEDGES, TO SERVE

1 Shell and devein prawns.

2 Combine mayonnaise, cream, sauces, mustard and juice in a small bowl; season to taste.

3 Divide lettuce between four glasses; top with prawns, drizzle with sauce. Accompany prawn cocktail with lemon wedges.

tip Use a good quality whole-egg mayonnaise for this recipe.

Goat's cheese & zucchini
FLOWER QUICHES

- 12 BABY ZUCCHINI WITH FLOWERS ATTACHED (240G)
- 3 SHEETS SHORTCRUST PASTRY
- 100G (3 OUNCES) FIRM GOAT'S CHEESE, CHOPPED FINELY
- ⅓ CUP (25G) FINELY GRATED PARMESAN
- 2 TABLESPOONS FINELY CHOPPED GARLIC CHIVES

QUICHE FILLING

- 300ML POURING CREAM
- ¼ CUP (60ML) MILK
- 3 EGGS

1 Preheat oven to 200°C/400°F. Grease a 12-hole (⅓-cup/80ml) muffin pan.

2 Remove flowers from zucchini; discard stamens from flowers. Slice zucchini thinly.

3 Make quiche filling.

4 Cut 12 x 9cm (3¾-inch) rounds from pastry; press into pan holes. Divide combined sliced zucchini, cheeses and chives into pastry cases; pour filling into pastry cases. Top each quiche with a zucchini flower.

5 Bake quiches about 25 minutes. Stand in pan for 5 minutes before turning out. Serve quiches warm.

QUICHE FILLING Whisk ingredients in a large jug.

Prawn & caper SANDWICHES

- 300G (9½ OUNCES) COOKED MEDIUM PRAWNS (SHRIMP)
- 1 TABLESPOON RINSED, DRAINED CAPERS, CHOPPED FINELY
- ½ CUP (150G) MAYONNAISE
- ½ TEASPOON SWEET PAPRIKA
- 2 TABLESPOONS FINELY CHOPPED FRESH FLAT-LEAF PARSLEY
- 1 CLOVE GARLIC, CRUSHED
- 8 SLICES WHITE BREAD (360G)

1 Peel and devein prawns; chop prawns finely.

2 Combine prawns, capers, mayonnaise, paprika, parsley and garlic in a medium bowl; season to taste.

3 Sandwich prawn mixture between bread slices. Discard crusts; cut each sandwich into four triangles.

PREP + COOK TIME 30 MINUTES **MAKES** 16 TRIANGLES

Curried egg SANDWICHES

- 6 EGGS
- ⅓ CUP (100G) MAYONNAISE
- 2 TEASPOONS CURRY POWDER
- 2 CUPS SHREDDED ICEBERG LETTUCE
- 8 SLICES WHITE BREAD (360G)

1 Boil eggs in a large saucepan of water for 6 minutes or until hard-boiled. Cool, then shell eggs. Chop eggs coarsely.

2 Mash egg, mayonnaise and curry powder in a medium bowl; season to taste.

3 Sandwich egg mixture and lettuce between bread slices. Cut crusts from bread; cut each sandwich into four triangles.

DEVILLED EGGS

- 12 EGGS
- ⅔ CUP (200G) MAYONNAISE
- 1 TABLESPOON DIJON MUSTARD
- 2 TABLESPOONS FINELY CHOPPED FRESH CHIVES
- 2 TABLESPOONS FINELY CHOPPED FRESH FLAT-LEAF PARSLEY

1 Boil eggs in a large saucepan of water for 6 minutes or until hard-boiled. Cool, then shell and halve each egg.

2 Carefully scoop yolks from whites into a medium bowl. Place egg white halves on a serving platter.

3 Mash egg yolks with mayonnaise and mustard until smooth; stir in herbs, season to taste.

4 Spoon egg yolk mixture into a piping bag fitted with a 1.5cm (¾-inch) fluted tube; pipe mixture into egg white halves. Serve devilled eggs sprinkled with extra parsley or chives.

tip Use a good quality whole-egg mayonnaise for this recipe.

Cucumber SANDWICHES

- 1 TELEGRAPH (HOTHOUSE) CUCUMBER (400G)
- SEA SALT FLAKES
- 16 SLICES WHITE BREAD (720G)
- 50G (1½ OUNCES) BUTTER, SOFTENED

1 Peel and seed cucumber; slice as thinly as possible. Place cucumber in a strainer or colander, sprinkle with salt. Stand 20 minutes, then rinse cucumber with cold water; drain well. Pat dry with paper towel.

2 Butter bread slices. Sandwich cucumber between slices.

3 Cut crusts from bread; cut each sandwich into three fingers.

tip You can use a mandoline or V-slicer to cut the cucumber into paper-thin slices.

Slice your Kraft Cheddar
best cheese for sandwiches

This is the cheese that always slices smoothly, evenly. Depend on its mellow Cheddar flavour to make sandwiches all the family will like. It takes a gallon of milk to make every pound of this fine cheese . . . that's why Kraft Cheddar is so rich in strengthening protein, essential vitamins and minerals. Kraft Cheddar is truly a bargain in nutrition. Get Kraft Cheddar in the 8 oz., 1 lb. and family-size 2 lb. packets. Also in 1 oz. portions.

They'll love these

PROTEIN-RICH
LUNCH SANDWICHES

- Buttered wholemeal bread, with good thick slices of Kraft Cheddar.
- Sliced Kraft Cheddar with brains and Vegemite.
- Sliced Kraft Cheddar, with hard-boiled egg and Kraft Mayonnaise.
- Cooked sliced frankfurts and tomato sauce, with sliced Kraft Cheddar.
- Sliced cold lamb, sliced Kraft Cheddar and pickle.
- Sliced Kraft Cheddar, with chopped raisins and lemon juice.
- Vegemite, sliced Kraft Cheddar, and grated apple.
- Sliced Kraft Cheddar, mashed banana, and lemon juice.

Other ways to enjoy Kraft Cheddar in sandwiches.
- Shredded Kraft Cheddar, with grated carrot and Kraft Mayonnaise.
- Sweetcorn and shredded Kraft Cheddar.
- Mashed sardines and vinegar, and shredded Kraft Cheddar.

FROM THE 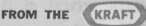 **KRAFT KITCHEN**

KR219

Illustration featured in *The Australian Women's Weekly* magazine, circa 1960

Champagne
MINI CUPCAKES

- 125G (4 OUNCES) BUTTER, SOFTENED
- 1 TEASPOON VANILLA EXTRACT
- ¾ CUP (165G) CASTER SUGAR (SUPERFINE SUGAR)
- 3 EGGS
- 1½ CUPS (225G) SELF-RAISING FLOUR
- ¼ CUP (60ML) SPARKLING WINE
- PINK SANDING SUGAR AND PINK SOFT SUGAR PEARLS, TO DECORATE

CHAMPAGNE BUTTER CREAM

- 250G (8 OUNCES) BUTTER, SOFTENED
- 3 CUPS (480G) ICING SUGAR (CONFECTIONERS' SUGAR)
- ¼ CUP (60ML) SPARKLING WINE

1 Preheat oven to 180°C/350°F. Line four 12-hole (1-tablespoon/20ml) mini muffin pans with paper cases.

2 Beat butter, extract, sugar, eggs, sifted flour and wine in a small bowl with an electric mixer on low speed until ingredients are combined. Increase speed to medium; beat until mixture has changed to a paler colour. Drop 2 level teaspoons of mixture into each paper case.

3 Bake cupcakes about 12 minutes. Leave cakes in pan for 5 minutes before turning, top-side up, onto wire racks to cool.

4 Make champagne butter cream.

5 Spoon butter cream into a large piping bag fitted with a large fluted tube. Pipe swirls of butter cream on top of cooled cakes. Sprinkle with sanding sugar and sugar pearls.

CHAMPAGNE BUTTER CREAM

Beat butter in a small bowl with an electric mixer until as white as possible. Beat in sifted icing sugar and wine, in two batches.

tips If you don't have four mini muffin pans, simply bake the cakes in batches, washing the pan in cool water and drying well after each batch.

Sanding sugar is a decorating sugar that adds colour and sparkle, and it also holds its shape and colour after baking. It is available in a range of colours from specialist food and cake decorating stores and some major supermarkets.

Uniced cakes can be made a day ahead or frozen for up to 3 months.

EDITOR'S
Favourite

Grapefruit & orange
COCKTAIL

- 4 MEDIUM RUBY GRAPEFRUIT (1.7KG)
- ½ CUP (125ML) ORANGE JUICE
- 2 TABLESPOONS DRY SHERRY
- 4 SPRIGS FRESH MINT

1 Segment 2 grapefruit; place in a small bowl with combined juice and sherry. Cover; refrigerate for 30 minutes or until ready to serve.

2 Cut remaining grapefruit in half in a zigzag pattern, place into serving glasses.

3 Spoon segments onto each grapefruit half with some of the liquid; top with mint.

tip To segment the grapefruit, cut the top and bottom off each fruit; cut down the side following the curve of the fruit to remove the rind and white pith. Cut between the membranes to release the grapefruit segments.

MILK JUG COVER

MATERIALS

- 5 TEA BAGS
- PURCHASED CROCHETED WHITE DOILY
- A VARIETY OF BEADS AND SEED BEADS
- COTTON THREAD
- FINE NEEDLE
- NARROW SATIN RIBBON

1 Soak tea bags in 2 cups of boiling water until the water turns cold and dark. Squeeze and remove tea bags.

2 Place the doily into the tea and leave for 2-4 hours or until it is the colour you want. Remove the doily from the tea, rinse and dry.

3 Thread a fine needle with double thread; sew it into the edge of the doily to attach it firmly, then thread it through the larger beads. When you get to the last bead, thread the needle through a small seed bead then thread the needle back through the larger beads. Re-attach the thread firmly in the doily edge before cutting. Repeat right around the doily.

4 When you have added all the beads, thread a length of satin ribbon through the eyelets in the doily and finish off with a bow.

tip Choose beads and a ribbon that will complement the tea-dyed doily.

STEP 1
Soak 5 tea bags in 2 cups of boiling water until the water turns cold and dark. Remove the tea bags.

STEP 2
Soak the doily in the tea for 2-4 hours or until it is the colour you want. Rinse, then dry the doily completely.

STEP 3
Pass the double thread through the beads, ending with a seed bead. Thread the needle back through the beads; attach to doily.

STEP 4
Thread a length of narrow satin ribbon through the eyelets in the doily and finish off with a bow.

Mulberry cream
POWDER PUFFS

- 2 EGGS
- ⅓ CUP (75G) CASTER SUGAR (SUPERFINE SUGAR)
- 2 TABLESPOONS CORNFLOUR (CORNSTARCH)
- 2 TABLESPOONS PLAIN FLOUR (ALL-PURPOSE FLOUR)
- 2 TABLESPOONS SELF-RAISING FLOUR
- 1 TABLESPOON ICING SUGAR (CONFECTIONERS' SUGAR)

MULBERRY CREAM

- ½ CUP (125ML) THICKENED (HEAVY) CREAM
- 1 TABLESPOON ICING SUGAR (CONFECTIONERS' SUGAR)
- ½ CUP (70G) FINELY CHOPPED FRESH MULBERRIES

1 Preheat oven to 180°C/350°F. Butter and flour two 12-hole (1-tablespoon/20ml) shallow round-based patty pans.

2 Beat eggs and caster sugar in a small bowl with an electric mixer for 5 minutes or until thick and creamy. Combine and sift all flours twice onto baking paper, then sift a third time over egg mixture; fold flour into egg mixture. Drop level tablespoons of mixture into pan holes.

3 Bake cakes about 12 minutes; immediately turn onto wire racks to cool.

4 Make mulberry cream.

5 Just before serving, sandwich cooled cakes with mulberry cream; dust with sifted icing sugar.

MULBERRY CREAM Beat cream and sifted icing sugar in a small bowl with an electric mixer until soft peaks form; fold in berries.

tips Use any fresh berries you like in this recipe.

If you only have one patty pan, bake the first batch, then wash the pan in cool water, dry well and butter and flour the pan again before baking the next batch.

Classic PUFFS

- ½ CUP (125ML) WATER
- 60G (2 OUNCES) BUTTER, CHOPPED FINELY
- 1 TABLESPOON CASTER SUGAR (SUPERFINE SUGAR)
- ½ CUP (75G) BAKER'S FLOUR
- 3 EGGS
- 1 TABLESPOON ICING SUGAR (CONFECTIONERS' SUGAR)

CRÈME PÂTISSIÈRE

- 3 CUPS (750ML) MILK
- ⅔ CUP (150G) CASTER SUGAR (SUPERFINE SUGAR)
- 1 TEASPOON VANILLA EXTRACT
- 6 EGG YOLKS
- ⅓ CUP (50G) CORNFLOUR (CORNSTARCH)

1 Make crème pâtissière.

2 Preheat oven to 220°C/425°F. Grease oven trays.

3 To make choux pastry, combine the water, butter and caster sugar in a medium saucepan; bring to the boil. Add flour; beat with a wooden spoon over medium heat until the mixture comes away from the base of the pan. Transfer the pastry to a medium bowl; beat in two of the eggs, one at a time. Whisk remaining egg with a fork; beat enough of the egg into the pastry until it becomes smooth and glossy but still holds its shape.

4 Drop level tablespoons of the pastry, about 5cm (2 inches) apart, onto trays.

5 Bake puffs for 10 minutes. Reduce oven temperature to 180°C/350°F; bake for 15 minutes. Cut a small opening into the base of each puff; bake for a further 10 minutes or until puffs are dry. Cool on trays.

6 Spoon crème pâtissière into a piping bag fitted with a 5mm (¼-inch) plain tube; pipe through cuts into cooled puffs. Dust puffs with sifted icing sugar to serve.

CRÈME PÂTISSIÈRE Bring milk, sugar and extract to the boil in a medium saucepan. Meanwhile, whisk the egg yolks and sifted cornflour in a medium heatproof bowl. Gradually add hot milk mixture to egg mixture. Return mixture to pan; stir over medium heat until it boils and thickens. Cover surface with plastic wrap. Refrigerate for 4 hours.

tips Crème pâtissière can be made a day ahead; store, covered, in the refrigerator. It will need to be softened before piping; beat it with an electric mixer until smooth.

Baker's flour is a strong flour – it has more gluten (protein) than regular plain flour, so gives baked goods shape and structure, which is why we've used it to make the puffs. Baker's flour is available from most supermarkets, however, you can use plain (all-purpose) flour.

APPLE GINGER CAKES
with lemon icing

You need one large apple (200g) for this recipe.

- 250G (8 OUNCES) BUTTER, SOFTENED
- 1½ CUPS (330G) FIRMLY PACKED DARK BROWN SUGAR
- 3 EGGS
- ¼ CUP (90G) GOLDEN SYRUP OR TREACLE
- 2 CUPS (300G) PLAIN FLOUR (ALL-PURPOSE FLOUR)
- 1½ TEASPOONS BICARBONATE OF SODA (BAKING SODA)
- 2 TABLESPOONS GROUND GINGER
- 1 TABLESPOON GROUND CINNAMON
- 1 CUP (170G) COARSELY GRATED APPLE
- ⅔ CUP (160ML) HOT WATER

LEMON ICING

- 2 CUPS (320G) ICING SUGAR (CONFECTIONERS' SUGAR)
- 2 TEASPOONS BUTTER, SOFTENED
- ⅓ CUP (80ML) LEMON JUICE

1 Preheat oven to 180°C/350°F. Grease two 6-hole (¾-cup/180ml) mini fluted tube pans or texas muffin pans.

2 Beat butter and sugar in a small bowl with an electric mixer until light and fluffy. Beat in eggs, one at a time, then beat in syrup.

3 Transfer mixture to a medium bowl; stir in sifted dry ingredients, apple and the water. Divide mixture between pan holes; smooth tops.

4 Bake cakes about 25 minutes. Leave cakes in pans for 5 minutes before turning, top-side up, onto a wire rack to cool.

5 Make lemon icing. Drizzle lemon icing over cooled cakes.

LEMON ICING Sift icing sugar into a medium heatproof bowl; stir in butter and juice to form a paste. Stir over a medium saucepan of simmering water until icing is of a pouring consistency.

tip Store cakes in an airtight container for up to 3 days. Uniced cakes are suitable to freeze for up to 3 months.

FRICKLES
with sriracha mayonnaise

- 1 CUP (150G) SELF-RAISING FLOUR
- ¼ CUP (40G) INSTANT POLENTA
- 2 TEASPOONS ONION POWDER
- 2 EGGS
- 1 CUP (250ML) ICE-COLD WATER
- VEGETABLE OIL, FOR DEEP-FRYING
- 680G (1¼-POUND) JAR WHOLE SWEET AND SOUR PICKLED CUCUMBERS, DRAINED, QUARTERED LENGTHWAYS
- 520G (1-POUND) JAR SLICED BREAD AND BUTTER PICKLES

SRIRACHA MAYONNAISE

- 1 CUP (300G) WHOLE-EGG MAYONNAISE
- 2 TABLESPOONS SRIRACHA CHILLI SAUCE
- 2 TABLESPOONS LEMON JUICE
- 1 CLOVE GARLIC, CRUSHED

1 Make sriracha mayonnaise.

2 Combine flour, polenta and onion powder in a medium bowl. Season. Add eggs and the water; whisk until just combined.

3 Fill a large saucepan or deep fryer one-third full with vegetable oil; heat to 180°C/350°F (or until a cube of bread turns golden in 10 seconds).

4 Pat pickles dry with paper towel. Working in batches, dip pickles in batter, shake off excess; deep-fry for 2 minutes or until golden.

5 Remove frickles with a slotted spoon; drain on paper towel. Serve frickles with sriracha mayonnaise.

SRIRACHA MAYONNAISE

Combine ingredients in a small bowl.

tips Sriracha is a medium-hot chilli sauce available from Asian food stores and some major supermarkets. Use a mild chilli sauce if you prefer. You can make the sriracha mayonnaise 2 days ahead; refrigerate, covered, until ready to use.

Orange raspberry
SHERBET FLOAT

*Due to the freezing time, it's best
to start this recipe the day before.*

- 1½ CUPS (330G) CASTER SUGAR
  (SUPERFINE SUGAR)
- 2 CUPS (500ML) FRESHLY
  SQUEEZED ORANGE JUICE
- 1 CUP FRESH OR THAWED
  FROZEN RASPBERRIES
- ½ CUP (125ML) POURING CREAM
- 1 TABLESPOON FINELY GRATED
  ORANGE RIND
- 2 LITRES (8 CUPS) LEMON-
  FLAVOURED SOFT DRINK
- 65G (2 OUNCES) FRESH OR
  FROZEN RASPBERRIES, EXTRA

1 Stir sugar and juice in a medium
saucepan over medium heat until
sugar dissolves. Bring to the boil.
Reduce heat and simmer mixture
for 1 minute. Cool.

2 Process or blend raspberries,
cream and rind until smooth. Stir
in cooled juice mixture.

3 Churn mixture in an ice-cream
machine, following manufacturer's
instructions, until firm (see tip).
Transfer to an airtight container;
freeze for 4 hours or overnight
until firm.

4 Pour soft drink into eight glasses;
top each with a scoop of the frozen
sherbet and extra raspberries. Stir
to combine.

tip If you don't have an ice-cream
machine, pour the mixture into a
shallow, freezer-proof container;
freeze until just set. Chop the
mixture and then process until
combined; return to the container
and freeze overnight.

BANANA SPLIT

- 1 CUP (250ML) THICKENED (HEAVY) CREAM
- 4 MEDIUM BANANAS (800G), HALVED LENGTHWAYS
- 4 SCOOPS (240ML) CHOCOLATE ICE-CREAM
- 4 SCOOPS (240ML) VANILLA ICE-CREAM
- 4 SCOOPS (240ML) STRAWBERRY ICE-CREAM
- 4 MARASCHINO CHERRIES
- 1 TABLESPOON HUNDREDS AND THOUSANDS

1 Beat cream in a small bowl with an electric mixer until firm peaks form. Spoon mixture into a piping bag fitted with a large fluted tube.

2 Place two banana halves in each of four dishes; place a scoop of chocolate, vanilla and strawberry ice-cream between banana halves in each dish.

3 Pipe cream on top of ice-cream scoops; top with cherries, sprinkle with hundreds and thousands.

tip For ice-cream sundae topping ideas, see pages 132-133.

Sundae TOPPINGS

These toppings use the Wafer Roll Biscuits found on page 134.

CLASSIC SUNDAE

Half-dip wafer roll biscuits in melted milk chocolate, then coat in hundreds and thousands; leave to set. Serve wafers with scoops of vanilla ice-cream, topped with strawberry topping, extra hundreds and thousands and maraschino cherries.

GINGER & PECAN

Half-dip wafer roll biscuits in melted dark chocolate, then coat in finely chopped glacé ginger; leave to set. Serve wafers with scoops of vanilla ice-cream, topped with ginger syrup and chopped roasted pecans.

ROCKY ROAD

Half-dip wafer roll biscuits in melted
dark chocolate, then coat in chopped roasted
peanuts; leave to set. Serve wafers with
scoops of vanilla ice-cream, topped with
chocolate sauce, mini marshmallows and
extra chopped peanuts.

CARAMEL SPLIT

Half-dip wafer roll biscuits in melted
milk chocolate, then coat in chopped
vienna almonds; leave to set. Serve wafers
with scoops of vanilla ice-cream topped with
sliced banana, caramel sauce and
extra chopped almonds.

WAFER ROLL BISCUITS

*Cook one tray of wafer rolls at
a time for easy handling.*

- 2 EGG WHITES
- ⅓ CUP (75G) CASTER SUGAR
  (SUPERFINE SUGAR)
- ¼ CUP (35G) PLAIN FLOUR
  (ALL-PURPOSE FLOUR)
- ¼ TEASPOON MIXED SPICE
- ¼ TEASPOON GROUND GINGER
- 40G (1½ OUNCES) BUTTER,
  MELTED
- 1 TEASPOON CINNAMON SUGAR

1 Preheat oven to 180°C/350°F.
Grease two oven trays. Mark four
8.5cm (3½-inch) circles on two
sheets of baking paper; place on
trays, marked-side down.

2 Beat egg whites in a small bowl
with an electric mixer until soft
peaks form. Gradually add sugar,
beating until dissolved after each
addition. Fold in sifted flour and
spices, then butter.

3 Drop rounded teaspoons of the
mixture into marked circles, spread
evenly to fill circles. Sprinkle circles
with a pinch of cinnamon sugar.

4 Bake one tray of biscuits at a time
for 4 minutes or until browned lightly.
Working quickly with one circle at
a time, slide a metal spatula under
circle then roll around a plastic
chopstick; leave until firm. Repeat
with remaining circles.

tips Wafer rolls are best made on
the day of serving. For ideas on
using wafer roll biscuits, see Sundae
Toppings on pages 132-133.

Cinnamon sugar is available in the
spice section of most supermarkets.
To make your own cinnamon sugar,
combine ½ cup caster sugar with
1 teaspoon cinnamon. Store in an
airtight container in the cupboard.

MEDALLION

MEDALLION 5 Way TOPPING CHOCOLATE

 SummerTime Hit

5 WAY TOPPING LIFTS EVERY DESSERT

IN ALL FLAVOURS

STRAWBERRY

PINEAPPLE

RASPBERRY

PASSIONFRUIT

LIME

Use Medallion Topping 5 ways—

1. Ice cream topping.   2. Milk drinks.

3. Milk and ice blocks.   4. Cake icing and filling.   5. As a flavour.

Ask your grocer!

Here's another cool treat — Medallion Fruit Juice Cordials

EDITOR'S Favourite

Juicy lucy BURGER

- 1KG (2 POUNDS) MINCED (GROUND) BEEF (SEE TIPS)
- 2 TABLESPOONS WORCESTERSHIRE SAUCE
- 4 CLOVES GARLIC, CRUSHED
- 1¼ CUPS (125G) COARSELY GRATED MOZZARELLA
- ¾ CUP (80G) COARSELY GRATED CHEDDAR
- 1 TABLESPOON OLIVE OIL
- 8 BURGER BUNS, SPLIT, TOASTED
- ⅓ CUP (95G) DIJON MUSTARD
- 8 SMALL BUTTER (BOSTON) LETTUCE LEAVES
- 2 LARGE TOMATOES (440G), SLICED THINLY
- ⅓ CUP (120G) TOMATO SAUCE (KETCHUP)
- 4 GHERKINS, SLICED THINLY LENGTHWAYS
- 1 SMALL BROWN ONION (80G), HALVED, SLICED THINLY

1 Combine beef, worcestershire sauce and garlic in a large bowl; season. Divide mixture into 16 equal portions. Using oiled or damp hands, form each portion into a thin 9cm (3¾-inch) pattie. Combine cheeses in a bowl. Place ¼ cup cheese over eight patties, leaving a 1cm (½-inch) border. Place remaining patties on top; pinch edges to seal in cheese. (Patties will now be 10cm/4 inches.)

2 Heat oil in a large frying pan over medium heat; cook patties, in batches, for 3 minutes one side and 2 minutes the other side, or until cooked through.

3 Spread buns with mustard; fill with lettuce, tomato, patties, tomato sauce, gherkin and onion.

tips For the best tasting burger, avoid lean minced beef or the burgers will be dry.

Burger patties can be prepared to the end of step 1 a day ahead; refrigerate, separated by layers of baking paper.

You can use pizza cheese instead of the mozzarella, if you like.

Candied bacon MAC & CHEESE

- 8 RINDLESS BACON SLICES (500G)
- ⅔ CUP (150G) FIRMLY PACKED BROWN SUGAR
- 1 TEASPOON CAYENNE PEPPER
- 500G (1 POUND) MACARONI
- 500G (1 POUND) CREAM CHEESE, CHOPPED
- 1 TEASPOON SEA SALT
- 2 TABLESPOONS DIJON MUSTARD
- 1 LITRE (4 CUPS) MILK
- 300ML POURING CREAM
- 1½ CUPS (180G) GRATED VINTAGE CHEDDAR
- 1½ CUPS (150G) GRATED MOZZARELLA

PRETZEL CRUMB

- 200G (6½ OUNCES) PRETZELS
- 80G (2½ OUNCES) BUTTER, MELTED
- 1½ CUPS (150G) GRATED MOZZARELLA
- ½ CUP (60G) GRATED VINTAGE CHEDDAR

1 For candied bacon, preheat oven to 220°C/425°F. Lightly grease two large wire racks; place on two large oven trays lined with foil. Combine bacon, sugar and cayenne in a large bowl until bacon is well coated. Place bacon on racks. Bake for 15 minutes or until bacon is caramelised. Cool slightly, then chop coarsely. Reduce oven temperature to 200°C/400°F.

2 Meanwhile, cook macaroni in a large saucepan of boiling water for 2 minutes less than the cooking time on the packet. Drain; return to pan.

3 Make pretzel crumb.

4 Process cream cheese, salt and mustard until smooth. Add half the milk; process until smooth. Transfer mixture to a large bowl; stir in remaining milk, cream, cheeses, candied bacon and warm macaroni until combined well. (Mixture will be very wet, but will thicken on cooking.)

5 Spoon macaroni mixture into a lightly oiled 4-litre (16-cup) ovenproof dish. Top with pretzel crumb; bake for 20 minutes or until golden.

PRETZEL CRUMB Place pretzels in a large ziptop bag; crush roughly with a rolling pin. Combine pretzels, butter and cheeses in a medium bowl.

CHILLI DOGS

- 8 FRANKFURTERS (640G)
- 8 SOFT HOT DOG BUNS, SPLIT, WARMED
- 2 TABLESPOONS MILD AMERICAN MUSTARD
- 1 SMALL BROWN ONION (80G), CHOPPED FINELY
- ⅔ CUP (50G) FINELY GRATED PECORINO OR PARMESAN

CHILLI CON CARNE

- 1 TABLESPOON OLIVE OIL
- 1 SMALL BROWN ONION (80G), CHOPPED FINELY
- 2 CLOVES GARLIC, CRUSHED
- 300G (9½ OUNCES) MINCED (GROUND) BEEF
- 2 CHIPOTLE CHILLIES IN ADOBO SAUCE (SEE TIPS), CHOPPED
- 2 TEASPOONS GROUND CUMIN
- ½ CUP (100G) CANNED KIDNEY BEANS, RINSED, DRAINED
- 400G (12½ OUNCES) CANNED DICED TOMATOES
- 1½ CUPS (375ML) BEEF STOCK
- 1 TABLESPOON BROWN SUGAR

1 Make chilli con carne.

2 Cook frankfurters in a large saucepan of simmering water over medium heat for 5 minutes or until warmed through.

3 Spread buns with mustard. Top with frankfurters, chilli con carne, onion and pecorino.

CHILLI CON CARNE Heat oil in a large frying pan over high heat; cook onion, garlic, beef, chilli and cumin, stirring, for 5 minutes or until beef is browned. Stir in beans, tomatoes, stock and sugar; bring to the boil. Reduce heat to low; simmer, uncovered, for 12 minutes or until mixture is thickened, stirring occasionally. Season to taste.

tips Chipotle chillies in adobo sauce are sold in small cans from delicatessens and specialist food stores; they have a medium-hot smoky taste. Any leftover chillies will keep with their sauce in a small screw-top jar in the fridge for up to 3 months. Substitute with a teaspoon of smoked paprika and a pinch of chilli powder.

You can use grated mozzarella or cheddar instead of the pecorino, if you prefer.

You can make the chilli con carne ahead of time; refrigerate, covered. Gently reheat before serving; you may need to add a little extra stock as it may thicken while refrigerated.

Old-fashioned MILKSHAKES

Chocolate MILKSHAKE

PREP TIME 5 MINUTES **SERVES** 1

Blend 1 cup (250ml) milk, 1 scoop chocolate ice-cream and 2 tablespoons rich chocolate sauce until combined. Place 2 scoops chocolate ice-cream into a glass; pour milkshake over ice-cream. Top with whipped cream, grated chocolate and a maraschino cherry.

Strawberry MILKSHAKE

PREP TIME 5 MINUTES **SERVES** 1

Blend 1 cup (250ml) milk, 1 scoop vanilla ice-cream, 4 fresh strawberries and 1 tablespoon strawberry topping until combined. Place 2 scoops vanilla ice-cream into a glass; pour milkshake over ice-cream. Top with whipped cream and a fresh strawberry.

Vanilla MILKSHAKE

PREP TIME 5 MINUTES **SERVES** 1

Blend 1 cup (250ml) milk, 1 scoop vanilla ice-cream
and 1 teaspoon vanilla extract until combined.
Place 2 scoops vanilla ice-cream into a glass;
pour milkshake over ice-cream. Top with whipped
cream, coloured sprinkles and a maraschino cherry.

Caramel MILKSHAKE

PREP TIME 5 MINUTES **SERVES** 1

Blend 1 cup (250ml) milk, 1 scoop vanilla ice-cream
and 2 tablespoons canned caramel top 'n' fill
until combined. Place 2 scoops vanilla ice-cream
into a glass; pour milkshake over ice-cream.
Top with whipped cream and chopped peanuts.

Pan-fried SANDWICHES

- 1 CUP (160G) FINELY CHOPPED COOKED CHICKEN
- ½ TRIMMED CELERY STALK (50G) CHOPPED FINELY
- 2 GREEN ONIONS (SCALLIONS), CHOPPED FINELY
- ½ TEASPOON FRENCH MUSTARD
- 2 TABLESPOONS WHOLE-EGG MAYONNAISE
- 8 SLICES WHITE BREAD (360G)
- 120G (4 OUNCES) BUTTER, CHOPPED

1 Combine chicken, celery, onion, mustard and mayonnaise in a small bowl; season.

2 Sandwich chicken mixture between bread slices.

3 Melt a quarter of the butter in a medium frying pan over medium heat; cook sandwiches, one at a time, until golden on both sides, adding butter as needed. Serve sandwiches cut into triangles.

serving suggestion Thin-cut fries.

Turkey, bacon & avocado
CLUB SANDWICH

- 4 RINDLESS BACON SLICES (260G)
- 12 SLICES WHITE BREAD (480G)
- ⅓ CUP (100G) MAYONNAISE
- 2 TABLESPOONS DIJON MUSTARD
- 1 MEDIUM AVOCADO (250G), SLICED THINLY
- 150G (4½ OUNCES) SHAVED TURKEY
- 75G (2½ OUNCES) ICEBERG LETTUCE LEAVES, SHREDDED FINELY

1 Cook bacon in a heated large frying pan until crisp; drain on paper towel. Tear bacon into coarse pieces.

2 Toast bread until browned lightly.

3 Spread 8 slices of toast with mayonnaise. Spread remaining toast with mustard.

4 Top four mayonnaise toast slices with bacon, avocado, then mustard toast slices, mustard-side down. Top with turkey, lettuce, then remaining toast, mayonnaise-side down.

Onion CHEESE BALL

- 500G (1 POUND) CREAM CHEESE
- 1 MEDIUM BROWN ONION (150G), CHOPPED FINELY
- 6 GREEN ONIONS (SCALLIONS), CHOPPED FINELY
- 2 TABLESPOONS FINELY CHOPPED FRESH FLAT-LEAF PARSLEY
- 1 TEASPOON WORCESTERSHIRE SAUCE
- ¼ CUP (70G) TOMATO SAUCE (KETCHUP)
- 4 GHERKINS, CHOPPED FINELY
- 1 CLOVE GARLIC, CRUSHED
- 1 CUP (50G) DEHYDRATED ONION FLAKES

1 Beat cream cheese in a small bowl with an electric mixer until smooth. Stir in onions, parsley, sauces, gherkins and garlic until well combined; season.

2 Sprinkle onion flakes on a sheet of baking paper. Divide cream cheese mixture in half, shape into balls; roll in onion flakes to coat. Cover with plastic wrap; refrigerate for 2 hours or overnight.

tip Dehydrated onion flakes are available from the spice section of the supermarket.

serving suggestion Accompany with potato chips for dipping.

TEST
... KITCHEN ...
Classic

WAFFLES
with maple syrup

- 1¾ CUPS (260G) PLAIN FLOUR (ALL-PURPOSE FLOUR)
- ¼ CUP (35G) SELF-RAISING FLOUR
- ¼ CUP (55G) CASTER SUGAR (SUPERFINE SUGAR)
- 2 EGGS, SEPARATED
- 1½ CUPS (375ML) MILK
- 60G (2 OUNCES) BUTTER, MELTED
- 2 TABLESPOONS WATER
- 2 TABLESPOONS ICING SUGAR (CONFECTIONERS' SUGAR)
- 5 SCOOPS (625ML) VANILLA ICE-CREAM
- ½ CUP (125ML) PURE MAPLE SYRUP

1 Sift flours and caster sugar into a small bowl; make a well in the centre. Gradually stir in combined egg yolks and milk, then butter and the water until smooth.

2 Beat egg whites in a small bowl with an electric mixer until soft peaks form. Fold into batter mixture, in two batches.

3 Drop ⅓-cup of mixture onto a lightly greased, preheated waffle iron. Close iron; cook for 2 minutes or until golden brown. Repeat with remaining mixture.

4 Serve waffles dusted with sifted icing sugar, topped with ice-cream and drizzled with syrup.

tips You will need a waffle iron for this recipe; they are available from kitchenware stores and some department stores.

Pure maple syrup is best to use on waffles rather than maple-flavoured syrup; maple-flavoured syrup is made from sugar cane and is not an adequate substitute for the real thing.

For other waffle topping ideas, see pages 156-157.

Waffle TOPPINGS

These toppings will be delicious additions to your waffle repertoire (see page 154).

CHOCOLATE & HAZELNUTS

Serve waffles topped with a scoop of vanilla ice-cream, chocolate sauce and chopped roasted hazelnuts. Dust with sifted icing (confectioners') sugar.

BLUEBERRY & WALNUTS

Serve waffles topped with a scoop of vanilla ice-cream, warmed blueberry jam, fresh blueberries and chopped toasted walnuts. Dust with sifted icing (confectioners') sugar.

BANANA, PECAN & CARAMEL

Serve waffles topped with a scoop of vanilla ice-cream, sliced banana, caramel sauce and chopped roasted pecans. Dust with sifted icing (confectioners') sugar.

STRAWBERRIES & ICE-CREAM

Serve waffles topped with a scoop of vanilla ice-cream, strawberry topping and halved fresh strawberries. Dust with sifted icing (confectioners') sugar.

EDITOR'S
Favourite

BANOFFEE PIE

- 2 X 395G (12½ OUNCES) CANNED SWEETENED CONDENSED MILK
- 150G (4½ OUNCES) BUTTER, CHOPPED
- 1 CUP (220G) FIRMLY PACKED BROWN SUGAR
- ⅓ CUP (115G) GOLDEN SYRUP
- 2 LARGE BANANAS (460G), SLICED THINLY
- 300ML THICKENED (HEAVY) CREAM, WHIPPED

PASTRY
- 1½ CUPS (225G) PLAIN FLOUR (ALL-PURPOSE FLOUR)
- 1 TABLESPOON ICING SUGAR (CONFECTIONERS' SUGAR)
- 140G (4½ OUNCES) COLD BUTTER, CHOPPED
- 1 EGG YOLK
- 2 TABLESPOONS COLD WATER

1 Make pastry.

2 Grease a 24cm (9½-inch) round loose-based fluted flan pan. Roll pastry between sheets of baking paper until large enough to line pan. Ease pastry into pan; press into base and side. Trim edge; prick base all over with a fork. Cover; refrigerate for 30 minutes.

3 Preheat oven to 200°C/400°F.

4 Place pan on an oven tray; line pastry with baking paper, fill with dried beans or rice. Bake for 10 minutes. Carefully remove paper and beans; bake for a further 10 minutes. Cool.

5 Meanwhile, place condensed milk, butter, sugar and syrup in a medium saucepan over medium heat; cook, stirring continuously, for 15 minutes or until mixture is caramel-coloured. Stand for 5 minutes.

6 Pour filling into cooled pastry case; cool. Just before serving, arrange banana slices on caramel; top with cream. Sprinkle with ground nutmeg, if you like.

PASTRY Process flour, sugar and butter until crumbly; add egg yolk and the water, process until ingredients just come together. Knead dough on a floured surface until smooth. Wrap in plastic wrap; refrigerate for 30 minutes.

FAMILY Meals

Cooked ENGLISH BREAKFAST

- 50G (1½ OUNCES) BUTTER
- 300G (9½ OUNCES) BUTTON MUSHROOMS, HALVED
- 8 CHIPOLATA SAUSAGES (240G)
- 4 RINDLESS BACON SLICES (260G)
- 2 MEDIUM TOMATOES (300G), HALVED
- 1 TABLESPOON VEGETABLE OIL
- 8 EGGS

1 Heat butter in a medium saucepan over medium-high heat; cook mushrooms, stirring, about 5 minutes or until tender. Season to taste; cover to keep warm.

2 Cook sausages and bacon in a heated oiled large frying pan, over medium-high heat, for 8 minutes or until bacon is crisp and sausages are browned and cooked through. Remove from pan; cover to keep warm. Discard fat from pan.

3 Preheat grill (broiler).

4 Place tomato, cut-side up, on an oven tray; grill tomato until browned lightly.

5 Meanwhile, heat oil in same large frying pan; cook eggs until done to your liking.

6 Serve mushrooms, sausages, bacon, tomato and eggs. Accompany with toast, if you like.

TEST
··· KITCHEN ···
Classic

Italian MEATBALLS

- 375G (12 OUNCES) MINCED (GROUND) BEEF
- 250G (8 OUNCES) LEAN MINCED (GROUND) PORK
- 1 SMALL BROWN ONION (80G), CHOPPED FINELY
- 2 CUPS (150G) FRESH BREADCRUMBS
- ½ CUP (250ML) MILK
- 1 EGG
- ½ SMALL GREEN CAPSICUM (BELL PEPPER) (75G), CHOPPED FINELY
- 2 TABLESPOONS FINELY CHOPPED FRESH FLAT-LEAF PARSLEY
- 1 CLOVE GARLIC, CRUSHED
- ¼ CUP (60ML) OLIVE OIL
- 1 TABLESPOON OLIVE OIL, EXTRA
- 1 CLOVE GARLIC, EXTRA, CRUSHED
- ¼ CUP (60ML) DRY WHITE WINE
- 400G (12½ OUNCES) CANNED DICED TOMATOES
- ½ CUP (140G) TOMATO PASTE
- 1½ CUPS (375ML) CHICKEN STOCK
- 2 TABLESPOONS FINELY CHOPPED FRESH FLAT-LEAF PARSLEY, EXTRA
- 375G (12 OUNCES) SPAGHETTI

1 Combine beef, pork, onion, breadcrumbs, milk, egg, capsicum, flat-leaf parsley and garlic in a large bowl; season. Roll mixture into 24 balls.

2 Heat oil in a large frying pan; cook meatballs, in batches, for 5 minutes or until browned all over. Drain on paper towel.

3 Heat extra oil in a large saucepan over medium heat; cook extra garlic, stirring until fragrant. Add wine, tomatoes, paste and stock; bring to the boil. Reduce heat to low; cook, covered, for 15 minutes. Add meatballs; simmer, covered, for 25 minutes. Stir in extra flat-leaf parsley; season to taste.

4 Meanwhile, cook spaghetti in a large saucepan of boiling water until tender; drain.

5 Serve spaghetti topped with meatballs; garnish with curly-leaf parsley sprigs, if you like.

tips Meatballs can be prepared a day ahead; cover, refrigerate. Meatballs in sauce can be frozen for up to 3 months.

Devilled LAMB CUTLETS

- 1 TABLESPOON OLIVE OIL
- 2 TEASPOONS CASTER SUGAR (SUPERFINE SUGAR)
- 1½ TEASPOONS MUSTARD POWDER
- ¼ CUP (80G) FRUIT CHUTNEY
- 1½ TEASPOONS CURRY POWDER
- 8 FRENCH-TRIMMED LAMB CUTLETS (400G)

1 Preheat grill (broiler) to medium-high.

2 Combine oil, sugar, mustard, chutney and curry powder in a small bowl.

3 Brush cutlets on one side with half the chutney mixture. Cook cutlets under grill for 4 minutes, turn, brush with remaining chutney mixture; grill for another 4 minutes or until cooked to your liking.

serving suggestion Steamed peas, baby carrots and mashed potato.

TEST
... KITCHEN ...
Classic

DUCK A L'ORANGE

- 2KG (4-POUND) WHOLE DUCK
- 30G (1 OUNCE) BUTTER, MELTED
- 1 LARGE ORANGE (300G)
- 1 TABLESPOON CASTER SUGAR (SUPERFINE SUGAR)
- 1 TABLESPOON WHITE VINEGAR
- 2 TEASPOONS LEMON JUICE
- 2 CUPS (500ML) CHICKEN STOCK
- 2 TEASPOONS ARROWROOT
- 1 TABLESPOON WATER
- ½ CUP (125ML) ORANGE-FLAVOURED LIQUEUR

1 Preheat oven to 180°C/350°F.

2 Rinse duck under cold water; pat dry inside and out with paper towel. Tie legs together with kitchen string; tuck wings under duck. Place duck in an oiled large baking dish; brush butter all over duck, season. Roast for 1 hour, basting occasionally.

3 Meanwhile, peel orange thinly. Discard any white pith from peel; cut peel into thin strips. Juice orange; reserve ½ cup juice.

4 Combine rind, orange juice, sugar, vinegar, lemon juice and stock in a medium saucepan; bring to the boil. Boil, uncovered, without stirring, until liquid is reduced by half. Gradually stir in blended arrowroot and the water; cook, stirring, until the sauce almost boils and thickens. Remove from heat; stir in liqueur.

5 Remove baking dish from oven; drain pan juices from dish. Pour orange sauce over duck; roast for a further 30 minutes, basting with sauce occasionally, until duck is tender and well-glazed.

6 Serve duck with orange sauce.

serving suggestion Steamed beans, potatoes and carrots.

SHEPHERD'S PIE

- 30G (1 OUNCE) BUTTER
- 1 MEDIUM BROWN ONION (150G), CHOPPED FINELY
- 1 MEDIUM CARROT (120G), CHOPPED FINELY
- ½ TEASPOON DRIED MIXED HERBS
- 4 CUPS (750G) FINELY CHOPPED COOKED LAMB
- ¼ CUP (70G) TOMATO PASTE
- ¼ CUP (60ML) TOMATO SAUCE (KETCHUP)
- 2 TABLESPOONS WORCESTERSHIRE SAUCE

- 2 CUPS (500ML) BEEF STOCK
- 2 TABLESPOONS PLAIN FLOUR (ALL-PURPOSE FLOUR)
- ⅓ CUP (80ML) WATER

POTATO TOPPING

- 5 MEDIUM POTATOES (1KG), CHOPPED COARSELY
- 60G (2 OUNCES) BUTTER, CHOPPED COARSELY
- ¼ CUP (60ML) MILK

1 Preheat oven to 200°C/400°F. Oil a deep 2.5-litre (10-cup) ovenproof dish.

2 Make potato topping.

3 Heat butter in a large saucepan; cook onion and carrot, stirring, until vegetables are tender. Add mixed herbs and lamb; cook, stirring, for 2 minutes. Stir in paste, sauces and stock, then blended flour and the water; cook, stirring, until mixture boils and thickens. Season. Pour mixture into dish.

4 Spoon potato topping into a piping bag fitted with a large fluted tube; pipe over lamb mixture.

5 Bake pie for 20 minutes or until browned lightly.

POTATO TOPPING Boil, steam or microwave potato until tender; drain. Mash potato in a medium bowl with butter and milk until smooth; season to taste.

STEAK DIANE

- 1 TABLESPOON OLIVE OIL
- 4 X 150G (4½-OUNCE) BEEF FILLET STEAKS
- ⅓ CUP (80ML) BRANDY
- 2 CLOVES GARLIC, CRUSHED
- ¼ CUP (60ML) WORCESTERSHIRE SAUCE
- 1 CUP (250ML) POURING CREAM
- 1 TABLESPOON FINELY CHOPPED FRESH FLAT-LEAF PARSLEY

1 Heat oil in a large frying pan; cook steaks until cooked as desired. Remove steaks from pan; cover to keep warm.

2 Add brandy to pan; bring to the boil. Add garlic, sauce and cream; cook, stirring, for 3 minutes or until sauce thickens slightly.

3 Remove pan from heat; stir in parsley, season to taste.

4 Serve steaks with sauce.

serving suggestion Thin-cut fries and a leafy green salad.

CORNED BEEF
with parsley sauce

- 1.5KG (3-POUND) PIECE BEEF CORNED SILVERSIDE
- 6 BLACK PEPPERCORNS
- 2 DRIED BAY LEAVES
- 1 LARGE BROWN ONION (200G), QUARTERED
- 1 LARGE CARROT (180G), CHOPPED COARSELY
- 1 TABLESPOON MALT VINEGAR
- ¼ CUP (50G) BROWN SUGAR

PARSLEY SAUCE

- 30G (1 OUNCE) BUTTER
- ¼ CUP (35G) PLAIN FLOUR (ALL-PURPOSE FLOUR)
- 2½ CUPS (625ML) MILK
- ⅓ CUP (40G) COARSELY GRATED CHEDDAR CHEESE
- ⅓ CUP FINELY CHOPPED FRESH FLAT-LEAF PARSLEY
- 1 TABLESPOON MILD MUSTARD

1 Place beef, peppercorns, bay leaves, onion, carrot, vinegar and half the sugar in a large saucepan. Add enough water to just cover beef; simmer, covered, about 2 hours or until beef is tender. Cool the beef in the liquid for 1 hour.

2 Remove beef from pan; discard liquid. Sprinkle a sheet of foil with remaining sugar, wrap beef in foil; stand 20 minutes then slice thinly.

3 Meanwhile, make parsley sauce.

4 Serve sliced corned beef with parsley sauce.

PARSLEY SAUCE Heat butter in a small saucepan, add flour; cook, stirring, for 2 minutes or until mixture thickens and bubbles. Gradually stir in milk; cook, stirring, for 5 minutes or until sauce boils and thickens. Remove from heat; stir in cheese, parsley and mustard. Season to taste.

serving suggestion Roasted potatoes and steamed beans.

MACARONI CHEESE

- 185G (6 OUNCES) MACARONI
- 2 RINDLESS BACON SLICES (130G), CHOPPED COARSELY
- 30G (1 OUNCE) BUTTER
- ¼ CUP (35G) PLAIN FLOUR (ALL-PURPOSE FLOUR)
- ¼ TEASPOON MUSTARD POWDER
- 2¼ CUPS (560ML) MILK
- 2 CUPS (240G) COARSELY GRATED CHEDDAR
- 30G (1 OUNCE) BUTTER, EXTRA, MELTED
- ½ CUP (50G) PACKAGED BREADCRUMBS

1 Cook macaroni in a large saucepan of boiling water until just tender; drain.

2 Preheat oven to 200°C/400°F. Grease a 1.5 litre (6-cup) ovenproof dish well.

3 Cook bacon in a medium frying pan, over high heat, stirring, until crisp; drain on paper towel.

4 Melt butter in same pan, add flour and mustard; cook, stirring for 1 minute. Gradually add milk; cook, stirring, until mixture boils and thickens. Cool 2 minutes. Stir in 1½ cups of the cheese; season.

5 Combine pasta, cheese sauce and bacon in a large bowl; transfer mixture to dish. Top with combined melted butter and breadcrumbs; sprinkle with remaining cheese.

6 Bake for 30 minutes or until top is browned lightly.

tip You can swap the packaged breadcrumbs for stale or panko (japanese) breadcrumbs if you like.

EDITOR'S
Favourite

TEA TOWEL

MATERIALS

- BAKING PAPER
- WATER-SOLUBLE FABRIC PEN
- PLAIN TEA TOWEL
- THICK COTTON THREAD (SUCH AS COTTON KNITTING YARN)
- LARGE EMBROIDERY NEEDLE
- SMALL AMOUNT OF DOUBLE-SIDED IRON-ON APPLIQUÉ WEBBING (VLIESOFIX)
- SCRAP OF COTTON PRINT FABRIC
- EMBROIDERY THREAD AND NEEDLE

1 Write the word 'baking' in large simple running writing onto the baking paper. Using a light box (from craft shops) or a well-lit window, trace the word onto the lower edge of the tea towel using a water-soluble fabric marker.

2 Thread a length of thick cotton thread into a large embroidery needle and stitch over the traced letters in simple running stitch. Any remaining visible marker can be sponged away with a damp cloth.

3 Draw a small heart on the paper side of the Vliesofix, then iron the Vliesofix onto the wrong side of the cotton print fabric and cut out.

4 Peel away the backing paper and iron the heart, right side of fabric up, onto the tea towel above the 'i' in your embroidered word. Using the embroidery thread, work a line of simple stitches around the edge of the heart.

STEP 1

Write 'baking' in running writing on baking paper; place tea towel on top of paper and trace 'baking' onto tea towel.

STEP 2

Stitch over the traced letters in simple running stitch using thick cotton thread. Any visible marker can be sponged away.

STEP 3

Draw a small heart on the paper side of the Vliesofix; iron onto the wrong side of the cotton print fabric and cut out.

STEP 4

Peel away backing paper; and iron the heart onto the tea towel above the 'i'. Sew simple stitches around edge of heart.

Pressure cooker
PEA & HAM SOUP

- 1 TABLESPOON OLIVE OIL
- 1 LARGE BROWN ONION (200G), CHOPPED COARSELY
- 2 CLOVES GARLIC, CRUSHED
- 2 STALKS CELERY (300G), TRIMMED, CHOPPED COARSELY
- 1 MEDIUM CARROT (120G), CHOPPED COARSELY
- 1 HAM HOCK (750G)
- 2 DRIED BAY LEAVES
- 2 LITRES (8 CUPS) WATER
- 1½ CUPS (225G) FROZEN BROAD BEANS (FAVA BEANS), PEELED
- 1½ CUPS (300G) GREEN SPLIT PEAS, RINSED, DRAINED
- 2 TABLESPOONS FRESH SMALL MINT LEAVES

CROÛTONS

- 3 SLICES WHITE BREAD (135G)
- 2 TABLESPOONS VEGETABLE OIL

1 Heat oil in a 6-litre (24-cup) pressure cooker; cook onion, garlic, celery and carrot, stirring, for 3 minutes or until vegetables soften. Add ham hock, bay leaves and the water; secure lid. Bring cooker to high pressure. Reduce heat to stabilise pressure; cook for 20 minutes.

2 Release pressure using the quick release method (see glossary entry under 'Pressure Cookers', page 486); remove lid. Add beans and peas to cooker; secure lid. Bring cooker to high pressure, then reduce the heat to stabilise pressure; cook for 20 minutes. Release pressure using the quick release method; remove lid. Discard bay leaves. Remove ham. Cool soup for 10 minutes.

3 Meanwhile, discard skin, fat and bone from ham; shred meat coarsely.

4 Blend or process soup, in batches, until smooth. Return soup to cooker; stir in ham. Simmer, uncovered, until hot; season to taste.

5 Meanwhile, make croûtons.

6 Serve bowls of soup topped with croûtons and mint.

CROÛTONS Discard crusts from bread, then cut bread into cubes. Heat oil in a medium frying pan; cook bread for 3 minutes, turning, until golden. Drain on paper towel.

tip If you have an electric pressure cooker you won't need to reduce the heat to stabilise pressure, your cooker will automatically stabilise itself. Before using your appliance, you should always check the manufacturer's instructions.

SCOTCH EGGS
with herb mayonnaise

- 7 EGGS
- 1 TABLESPOON PLAIN FLOUR (ALL-PURPOSE FLOUR)
- 1 TABLESPOON MILK
- ⅔ CUP (70G) PACKAGED BREADCRUMBS
- 500G (1 POUND) SAUSAGE MINCE
- VEGETABLE OIL, FOR DEEP-FRYING

HERB MAYONNAISE

- ½ CUP (150G) MAYONNAISE
- 1 TABLESPOON LEMON JUICE
- 1 TABLESPOON FINELY CHOPPED FRESH CHIVES
- 1 TABLESPOON FINELY CHOPPED FRESH OREGANO

1 Boil six of the eggs in a medium saucepan of water for 6 minutes or until hard-boiled. Drain. Cool, then shell eggs.

2 Make herb mayonnaise.

3 Place flour in a small shallow bowl. Beat remaining egg and milk in a small bowl until combined. Place breadcrumbs in a small shallow bowl.

4 Toss hard-boiled eggs in flour; shake off excess.

5 Divide sausage mince into six equal portions; using floured hands, shape mince around each egg. Dip in egg mixture, then in breadcrumbs.

6 Heat oil in a deep, wide saucepan; deep-fry eggs, in batches, until browned and cooked through. Drain on paper towel. Serve with herb mayonnaise.

HERB MAYONNAISE

Combine ingredients in a small bowl; season to taste.

ROAST TURKEY
with forcemeat stuffing

- 4.5KG (9-POUND) WHOLE TURKEY
- 1 CUP (250ML) WATER
- 80G (2½ OUNCES) BUTTER, MELTED
- ¼ CUP (35G) PLAIN FLOUR (ALL-PURPOSE FLOUR)
- 3 CUPS (750ML) CHICKEN STOCK
- ½ CUP (125ML) DRY WHITE WINE

FORCEMEAT STUFFING

- 40G (1½ OUNCES) BUTTER
- 3 MEDIUM BROWN ONIONS (450G), CHOPPED FINELY
- 2 RINDLESS BACON SLICES (130G), CHOPPED COARSELY
- 1 CUP (70G) STALE BREADCRUMBS
- ½ CUP COARSELY CHOPPED FRESH FLAT-LEAF PARSLEY
- 250G (8 OUNCES) MINCED (GROUND) PORK
- 250G (8 OUNCES) MINCED (GROUND) CHICKEN

1 Preheat oven to 180°C/350°F.

2 Make forcemeat stuffing.

3 Discard neck from turkey. Rinse turkey under cold water; pat dry inside and out with paper towel. Fill neck cavity loosely with forcemeat; secure skin over opening with small skewers. Fill large cavity loosely with forcemeat; tie legs together with kitchen string. Tuck wings under turkey.

4 Place turkey on an oiled wire rack in a large shallow flameproof baking dish; pour the water into the dish. Brush turkey all over with half the butter; season. Cover turkey tightly with two layers of greased foil. Roast for 2 hours.

5 Uncover turkey; brush with remaining butter. Roast turkey, uncovered, for 1 hour or until cooked through. Remove turkey from dish, cover loosely with foil; stand for 20 minutes.

6 Pour juice from dish into a large jug; skim 1 tablespoon of fat from juice, return fat to same dish. Skim and discard fat from remaining juice; reserve juice. Add flour to dish; cook, over medium-high heat, stirring, for 2 minutes or until mixture bubbles and is well-browned. Gradually stir in stock, wine and reserved juice; cook, stirring, for 3 minutes or until gravy boils and thickens. Strain gravy into jug; serve with turkey.

FORCEMEAT STUFFING Melt butter in a medium frying pan; cook onion and bacon, stirring, over low heat, until onion softens. Cool. Combine onion mixture and remaining ingredients in a large bowl; season.

tip To test if the turkey is cooked, insert a skewer sideways into the thickest part of the thigh, then remove and press flesh to release the juices. If the juice runs clear, the turkey is cooked. Alternatively, insert a meat thermometer into the thickest part of the thigh, without touching the bone; the turkey is cooked when the thermometer reaches 90°C/195°F.

GUARD OF HONOUR

- ½ CUP FIRMLY PACKED FRESH FLAT-LEAF PARSLEY
- ½ CUP FIRMLY PACKED FRESH MINT LEAVES
- ¼ CUP LOOSELY PACKED FRESH OREGANO LEAVES
- 4 CLOVES GARLIC, CHOPPED COARSELY
- ⅓ CUP (80ML) OLIVE OIL
- 2 X 8 FRENCH-TRIMMED LAMB CUTLET RACKS (720G)
- 1KG (2 POUNDS) BABY NEW POTATOES

1 Preheat oven to 200°C/400°F.

2 Blend or process herbs, garlic and half the oil until smooth; season to taste. Place lamb racks in a large oiled baking dish, leaning against one another, interlacing cutlet bones, so racks stand upright. Press herb mixture onto each rack.

3 Boil, steam or microwave potatoes until just tender; drain. Cut potatoes in half, place on an oiled oven tray; drizzle with remaining oil, season.

4 Roast lamb and potatoes for 35 minutes or until lamb is cooked as desired. Remove lamb from oven, cover; rest for 10 minutes. Roast potatoes for a further 10 minutes or until browned lightly.

5 Serve lamb with potatoes.

tips Use skewers or toothpicks to help keep the guard of honour secure if you like. Wrap the ends of the cutlet bones with small pieces of foil to stop them burning during roasting. If you want to decorate the racks with 'paper booties', put them on after removing lamb racks from the oven.

serving suggestion Steamed vegetables of your choice.

Just five simple ingredients
and Leggo's Tomato Paste

...makes the tastiest Spaghetti* this side of Napoli

Whenever a recipe says "tomatoes", then you need Leggo's Tomato Paste — a five times concentrate of the pick of glowing, sun ripe tomatoes. Ready to use ... smooth, no messy skin or seeds, and easy to blend into whatever dish you're making. A small 5-oz. tin equals 2 lbs. of tomatoes. Use it to add richer, fuller flavour to soups, sauces, casseroles; and for some real cooking fun, try continental dishes using Leggo's Tomato Paste, like the easy to prepare, easy-on-the-pocket Spaghetti Marinara here ...

Spaghetti Marinara *

First cook your spaghetti in boiling water (about 18 minutes). When cooked, wash immediately in a colander under running water. Strain, heat again, and place in warm shallow dish.

SAUCE: Cut 1 clove of garlic and 1 onion very finely and fry in cooking oil. Add 1 small tin sardines and cook all together for 3 or 4 minutes. Dissolve 3 teaspoons of Leggo's Tomato Paste in ½ cup of water. Salt and pepper to taste. Add to other ingredients, bring all to boil and simmer 4 to 5 minutes. If necessary, extra cooking oil may be added when cooked. Pour over spaghetti and serve.

Leggo's
make meals *magic!*

For cheerier eating — choose from the good things in Leggo's Pantry. Tomato Sauce, Savory Relish, Pickles, Spaghetti Sauce, Tomato Juice, Soup.

Made at the new modern factory of —
H. M. LEGGO & CO. LTD., OAK AVENUE, MENTONE. TELEPHONE XF 1266

Set off by
was a lone
You
despe

Illustration featured in *The Australian Women's Weekly* magazine, circa 1953

EGG & BACON PIE

- 3 SHEETS PUFF PASTRY
- 4 RINDLESS BACON SLICES (250G), CHOPPED COARSELY
- 6 EGGS
- 2 TABLESPOONS COARSELY CHOPPED FRESH FLAT-LEAF PARSLEY
- 1 EGG YOLK
- 1 TEASPOON WATER

1 Grease a 20cm (8-inch) pie dish.

2 Cut one sheet of pastry in half. Join pieces to sides of another pastry sheet. Lift pastry into dish, ease into base and side; trim edges. Refrigerate for 15 minutes.

3 Meanwhile, cook bacon in a small frying pan, over medium heat, for 3 minutes or until browned. Cool.

4 Place half the bacon over pastry; break eggs over the bacon, one at a time, being careful not to break the yolks. Sprinkle with the remaining bacon, then the parsley; season.

5 Cover pie with remaining pastry sheet, press edges together to seal; trim excess pastry. Brush top with combined egg yolk and the water. Refrigerate for 15 minutes.

6 Meanwhile, preheat oven to 200°C/400°F.

7 Bake pie for 15 minutes. Reduce oven temperature to 180°C/350°F; bake for a further 15 minutes.

serving suggestion A simple garden salad and chips.

Garlic PRAWNS

- 1KG (2 POUNDS) UNCOOKED MEDIUM KING PRAWNS (SHRIMP)
- 2 CUPS (500ML) OLIVE OIL
- 4 CLOVES GARLIC, CRUSHED
- 2 FRESH SMALL RED THAI (SERRANO) CHILLIES, CHOPPED FINELY
- 2 TABLESPOONS COARSELY CHOPPED FRESH FLAT-LEAF PARSLEY

1 Preheat oven to 200°C/400°F.

2 Shell and devein prawns, leaving tails intact.

3 Divide oil, garlic and chilli into four 1-cup (250ml) cast-iron dishes. Place dishes on an oven tray; cover. Bake for 20 minutes or until oil is bubbling.

4 Carefully remove dishes from oven; divide prawns among dishes. Bake, covered, for a further 10 minutes or until prawns are tender.

5 Serve prawns topped with parsley.

EDITOR'S
Favourite

Pressure cooker
STEAK & KIDNEY PIE

- ¼ CUP (60ML) OLIVE OIL
- 200G (6½ OUNCES) SWISS BROWN MUSHROOMS, QUARTERED
- 400G (12½ OUNCES) OX KIDNEY, TRIMMED, CHOPPED COARSELY
- 2 TABLESPOONS PLAIN FLOUR (ALL-PURPOSE FLOUR)
- 700G (1½ POUNDS) BEEF CHUCK STEAK, CHOPPED COARSELY
- 1 MEDIUM BROWN ONION (150G), CHOPPED FINELY
- 1 LARGE CARROT (180G), CHOPPED FINELY
- 1 STALK CELERY (150G), TRIMMED, CHOPPED FINELY
- 2 SPRIGS FRESH THYME
- 1 DRIED BAY LEAF
- ⅓ CUP (80ML) WATER
- 1 SHEET PUFF PASTRY
- 1 EGG, BEATEN LIGHTLY

1 Heat 2 teaspoons of the oil in a 6-litre (24-cup) pressure cooker; cook mushrooms until browned. Remove from cooker.

2 Heat 2 teaspoons of the oil in cooker; cook kidney until browned. Remove from cooker.

3 Season flour in a large bowl; add beef, toss to coat in flour. Shake off excess flour. Heat half the remaining oil in cooker; cook beef, in batches, until browned. Remove from cooker.

4 Heat remaining oil in cooker; cook onion, carrot and celery until tender. Return beef to cooker with thyme, bay leaf and the water; secure lid. Bring cooker to high pressure. Reduce heat to stabilise pressure; cook 25 minutes.

5 Meanwhile, preheat oven to 210°C/415°F.

6 Release pressure using the quick release method (see glossary entry under 'Pressure Cookers', page 486); remove lid. Discard thyme and bay leaf. Stir in mushrooms and kidney; season to taste. Spoon hot steak and kidney mixture into a 1.5-litre (6-cup) deep ovenproof pie dish. Place pastry over filling, trim edge; make two small cuts in centre of pastry. Brush pastry with egg. Bake for 25 minutes or until well browned.

tips If you have an electric pressure cooker you won't need to reduce the heat to stabilise pressure, your cooker will automatically stabilise itself. Before using your appliance, you should always check the manufacturer's instructions. The steak and kidney filling is suitable to freeze.

ROAST BALSAMIC CHICKEN
with garlic bread sauce

- 1.8KG (3½-POUND) WHOLE CHICKEN
- ⅓ CUP (80ML) BALSAMIC VINEGAR
- 1 TABLESPOON DIJON MUSTARD
- 1 TABLESPOON OLIVE OIL
- 2 SPRIGS FRESH ROSEMARY
- 500G (1 POUND) CHERRY TRUSS TOMATOES
- 2 SPRIGS FRESH THYME

GARLIC BREAD SAUCE
- 4 CLOVES GARLIC, BRUISED
- 2 FRESH BAY LEAVES
- 1¾ CUPS (430ML) MILK
- 1½ CUPS (110G) STALE BREADCRUMBS
- 30G (1 OUNCE) BUTTER
- ½ CUP (125ML) POURING CREAM

1 Rinse chicken under cold water. Pat dry inside and out with paper towel. Combine vinegar, mustard and oil in a large bowl, add chicken; turn to coat chicken in marinade. Cover; refrigerate for 3 hours.

2 Preheat oven to 200°C/400°F.

3 Place chicken in a large baking dish; reserve marinade. Place one rosemary sprig into chicken cavity. Tie legs together with kitchen string; season. Roast for 1½ hours or until cooked through, basting with reserved marinade. Add tomatoes to the dish for the last 10 minutes of the cooking time.

4 Meanwhile, make garlic bread sauce.

5 Tuck remaining rosemary and thyme between drumsticks; serve chicken with sauce and tomatoes.

GARLIC BREAD SAUCE Bring garlic, bay leaves and milk to the boil in a small saucepan. Remove from heat, stand for 30 minutes. Strain milk mixture, discard solids; return milk mixture to same pan. Stir in breadcrumbs and butter; cook, stirring, over low heat, for 10 minutes or until thick. Add cream, stir until heated through; season to taste.

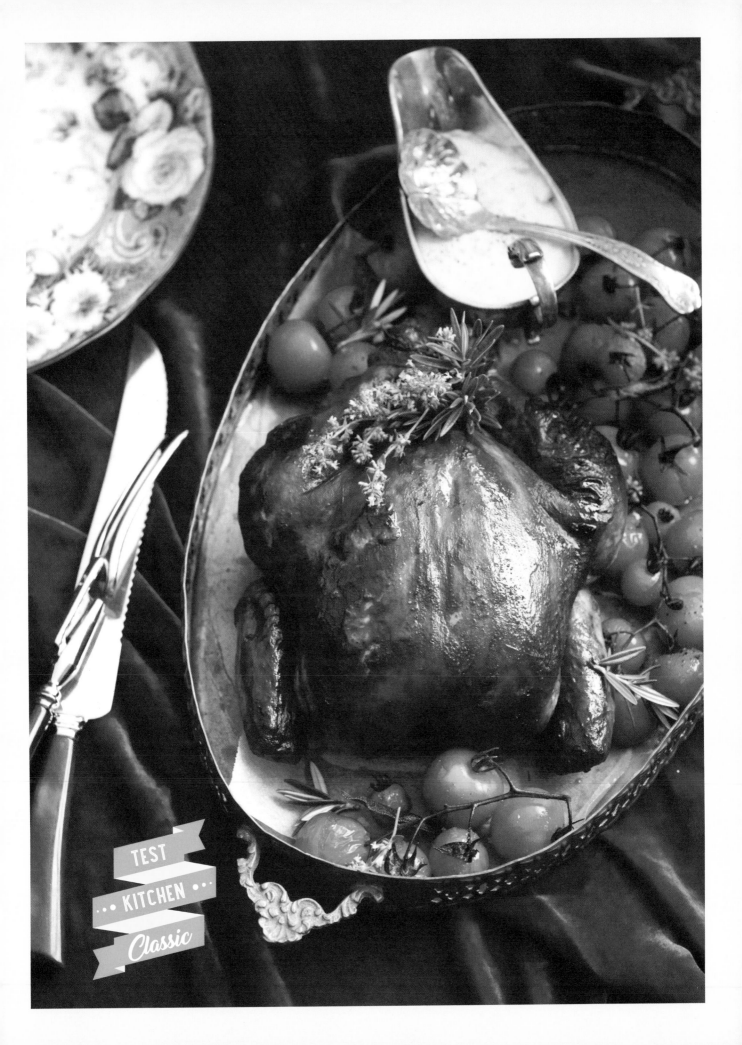

TEST ... KITCHEN ... Classic

Pressure cooker shredded beef &
SILVER BEET SOUP

- 1 TABLESPOON OLIVE OIL
- 1 MEDIUM BROWN ONION (150G), CHOPPED FINELY
- 2 CLOVES GARLIC, CRUSHED
- 2 TABLESPOONS TOMATO PASTE
- ¼ CUP (60ML) DRY RED WINE
- 1 LITRE (4 CUPS) WATER
- 410G (13 OUNCES) CANNED CRUSHED TOMATOES
- 500G (1-POUND) PIECE BEEF SKIRT STEAK
- 2 DRIED BAY LEAVES
- 3 MEDIUM SILVER BEET LEAVES (SWISS CHARD) (240G), TRIMMED, SHREDDED COARSELY

1 Heat oil in a 6-litre (24-cup) pressure cooker; cook onion and garlic, stirring, until onion softens. Add paste to cooker; cook, stirring, for 2 minutes. Add wine; simmer, uncovered, until liquid reduces by half. Add the water, tomatoes, beef and bay leaves; secure lid. Bring cooker to high pressure. Reduce heat to stabilise pressure; cook for 25 minutes.

2 Release pressure using the quick release method (see glossary entry under 'Pressure Cookers', page 486); remove lid. Discard bay leaves. Remove beef; when cool enough to handle, cut beef in half. Shred beef using two forks.

3 Return beef to soup along with silver beet; simmer, uncovered, until silver beet wilts. Season to taste.

tip If you have an electric pressure cooker you won't need to reduce the heat to stabilise pressure, your cooker will automatically stabilise itself. Before using your appliance, you should always check the manufacturer's instructions.

BEEF WELLINGTON

- 800G (1½-POUND) PIECE BEEF FILLET
- 1 TABLESPOON OLIVE OIL
- 25G (¾ OUNCE) BUTTER
- 1 SMALL BROWN ONION (80G), CHOPPED FINELY
- 125G (4 OUNCES) BUTTON MUSHROOMS, CHOPPED FINELY
- 150G (4½ OUNCES) CHICKEN OR DUCK LIVER PÂTÉ
- 2 SHEETS PUFF PASTRY
- 1 EGG, BEATEN LIGHTLY

1 Tie beef securely with kitchen string. Heat oil in a large frying pan over medium-high heat; cook beef for 10 minutes, turning, until browned all over. Wrap beef in foil; cool.

2 Heat butter in same pan over medium heat; cook onion and mushrooms, stirring, for 5 minutes or until tender. Cool.

3 Preheat oven to 240°C/425°F. Line oven tray with baking paper.

4 Stir pâté in a medium bowl until soft. Remove string from beef. Spread pâté all over beef; season.

5 Roll out pastry on a lightly floured surface into a rectangle large enough to enclose beef; moisten edges with water. Place mushroom mixture down centre of pastry; place beef on top of mushroom mixture. Fold pastry over beef to enclose; trim excess pastry and press edges to seal. Place beef, seam-side down, on tray; brush with egg then make small cuts into top of pastry.

6 Bake beef for 10 minutes. Reduce oven temperature to 200°C/400°F; bake for a further 20 minutes or until browned lightly. Serve beef, sliced thickly.

tips It is important to trim the excess pastry when covering the beef. Don't have the pastry too thick at the joins or the pastry will not cook through. To decorate, cut small leaves from pastry scraps and secure them to the beef wellington with a little of the egg before baking.

serving suggestion Steamed vegetables of your choice.

Southern
FRIED CHICKEN

- 8 CHICKEN DRUMSTICKS (1.2KG)
- 1 MEDIUM BROWN ONION (150G), CHOPPED COARSELY
- 1 TEASPOON COOKING SALT
- 1 CUP (100G) PACKAGED BREADCRUMBS
- 1 TEASPOON CURRY POWDER
- 1 TABLESPOON FINELY CHOPPED FRESH FLAT-LEAF PARSLEY
- ¼ TEASPOON MUSTARD POWDER
- ½ TEASPOON DRIED MIXED HERBS
- ⅓ CUP (50G) PLAIN FLOUR (ALL-PURPOSE FLOUR)
- 1 EGG, BEATEN LIGHTLY
- VEGETABLE OIL, FOR SHALLOW-FRYING

1 Place chicken, onion and salt in a large saucepan; cover with cold water. Bring to the boil over high heat. Reduce heat to low; simmer for 5 minutes. Drain; cool.

2 Combine breadcrumbs, curry powder, parsley, mustard and herbs in a shallow bowl; season.

3 Coat chicken in flour; shake off excess. Dip chicken, one piece at a time, into egg; coat in breadcrumb mixture. Place on a tray, cover; refrigerate for 30 minutes.

4 Heat oil in a medium frying pan; shallow-fry chicken, in batches, for 5 minutes, turning until golden brown all over. Drain on paper towel. Serve chicken hot or cold.

serving suggestion A simple garden salad.

CLASSIC BAKED BEANS
with ham hock

- 1½ CUPS (300G) DRIED HARICOT (NAVY) BEANS
- 1 LARGE HAM HOCK (1.5KG)
- 1 TABLESPOON OLIVE OIL
- 1 LARGE BROWN ONION (200G), CHOPPED COARSELY
- 3 CLOVES GARLIC, CHOPPED FINELY
- ¼ CUP (70G) TOMATO PASTE
- 1 TABLESPOON WORCESTERSHIRE SAUCE
- 2 TEASPOONS DIJON MUSTARD
- 2 TABLESPOONS PURE MAPLE SYRUP

1 Place beans in a large bowl. Cover with cold water; stand overnight. Rinse beans; drain.

2 Place beans and ham hock in a large saucepan; cover with cold water. Bring to the boil, then simmer, uncovered, for 1 hour. Remove ham hock. Reserve 2 cups of the cooking liquid. Drain beans. Discard skin, fat and bone from ham; pull meat apart into large chunks.

3 Preheat oven to 150°C/300°F.

4 Heat oil in a large flameproof dish over medium-high heat; cook onion and garlic, stirring, for 5 minutes or until onion softens. Add tomato paste, reserved cooking liquid, sauce, mustard, beans and ham. (Don't add salt at this stage, it can make the beans tough.)

5 Bake, covered, in oven, for 2 hours or until beans are tender, stirring twice during cooking. Add more water if needed to keep the beans moist but not wet. Stir in maple syrup. Season to taste.

tip This recipe can be prepared the day before and reheated gently in a saucepan.

Pressure cooker
PICKLED PORK

- 1.5KG (3-POUND) PIECE BONELESS ROLLED SHOULDER OF PICKLED PORK
- 2 DRIED BAY LEAVES
- 8 BLACK PEPPERCORNS
- 4 WHOLE CLOVES
- 1 MEDIUM BROWN ONION (150G), CHOPPED COARSELY
- 1 STALK CELERY (150G), TRIMMED, CHOPPED COARSELY
- 2 TABLESPOONS BROWN SUGAR
- 2 TABLESPOONS MALT VINEGAR
- 3 LITRES (12 CUPS) WATER, APPROXIMATELY

1 Combine pork, bay leaves, peppercorns, cloves, onion, celery, sugar, vinegar and enough of the water to barely cover pork in an 8-litre (32-cup) pressure cooker; secure lid. Bring cooker to high pressure. Reduce heat to stabilise pressure; cook for 30 minutes.

2 Release pressure using the quick release method (see glossary entry under 'Pressure Cookers', page 486); remove lid. Cool pork in cooking liquid in cooker, covered loosely with lid. Serve pork warm or cold.

tips If you have an electric pressure cooker you won't need to reduce the heat to stabilise pressure, your cooker will automatically stabilise itself. Before using your appliance, you should always check the manufacturer's instructions.

Pickled pork is a little old-fashioned, so you may need to order it from the butcher. The shoulder cut used here is also called a 'hand' of pickled pork.

serving suggestion Mashed potato, cabbage and steamed vegies.

The CAKE STALL

Apple pie SLICE

This is my version of my Mum's recipe; even though it's not exactly the same, it's still known fondly as Jeannie's apple pie slice.

- 8 MEDIUM APPLES (1.5KG)
- ⅔ CUP (150G) CASTER SUGAR (SUPERFINE SUGAR)
- ½ CUP (125ML) WATER
- 2 TABLESPOONS WHITE SUGAR (GRANULATED SUGAR), OPTIONAL

PASTRY

- 3 CUPS (450G) SELF-RAISING FLOUR
- ¼ CUP (40G) ICING SUGAR (CONFECTIONERS' SUGAR)
- 125G (4 OUNCES) COLD BUTTER, CHOPPED COARSELY
- 1 EGG, BEATEN LIGHTLY
- ½ CUP (125ML) MILK, APPROXIMATELY

PASSIONFRUIT ICING

- 1½ CUPS (240G) ICING SUGAR (CONFECTIONERS' SUGAR)
- ¼ CUP (60ML) PASSIONFRUIT PULP, APPROXIMATELY

1 Peel, quarter and core apples; slice thickly. Place apples, caster sugar and the water in a large saucepan; cover, bring to the boil. Reduce heat; simmer for 10 minutes or until apples are just tender. Gently turn apple mixture into a large strainer to drain; cool.

2 Preheat oven to 200°C/400°F. Grease a 20cm x 30cm (8-inch x 12-inch) rectangular pan; line base and long sides with baking paper, extending the paper 5cm (2 inches) above the sides.

3 Make pastry.

4 Roll two-thirds of the pastry on a floured surface until large enough to line base and sides of pan, with 1cm (½ inch) extending over the sides. Lift pastry into pan. Spread cooled apple mixture into pastry case; brush edges with a little extra milk. Roll remaining pastry until large enough to generously cover pie. Place over filling; press edges together to seal. Trim away excess pastry. Brush top with a little milk; sprinkle with white sugar. Make about six cuts into top of pastry.

5 Bake slice for 45 minutes. Stand slice in pan for 10 minutes before turning, top-side up, onto a wire rack to cool.

6 Make passionfruit icing. Spread icing over pastry. Cut slice into eight rectangles to serve.

PASTRY Sift flour and icing sugar into a large bowl; rub in butter. Make a well in the centre. Using a knife, 'cut' combined egg and enough milk through flour mixture to make a soft dough. Wrap pastry in plastic wrap; refrigerate for 30 minutes.

PASSIONFRUIT ICING Sift icing sugar into a medium heatproof bowl, stir in enough of the passionfruit pulp to make a thick paste. Place bowl over a saucepan of simmering water; stir until icing is spreadable.

tip You will need approximately two large passionfruit.

PRIZE WINNING

Lemon MERINGUE PIE

- ½ CUP (75G) CORNFLOUR (CORNSTARCH)
- 1 CUP (220G) CASTER SUGAR (SUPERFINE SUGAR)
- ½ CUP (125ML) LEMON JUICE
- 1¼ CUPS (310ML) WATER
- 2 TEASPOONS FINELY GRATED LEMON RIND
- 60G (2 OUNCES) UNSALTED BUTTER, CHOPPED
- 3 EGGS, SEPARATED (SEE TIPS)
- ⅓ CUP (150G) CASTER SUGAR (SUPERFINE SUGAR), EXTRA

PASTRY

- 1½ CUPS (225G) PLAIN FLOUR (ALL-PURPOSE FLOUR)
- 1 TABLESPOON ICING SUGAR (CONFECTIONERS' SUGAR)
- 140G (4½ OUNCES) COLD BUTTER, CHOPPED
- 1 EGG, SEPARATED (SEE TIPS)
- 2 TABLESPOONS COLD WATER

1 Make pastry.

2 Grease a 24cm (9½-inch) round loose-based fluted flan pan. Roll pastry between sheets of baking paper until large enough to line pan. Ease pastry into pan, press into base and side; trim edge. Cover; refrigerate for 30 minutes.

3 Preheat oven to 200°C/400°F.

4 Place pan on an oven tray. Line pastry case with baking paper; fill with dried beans or rice. Bake for 15 minutes. Remove paper and beans; bake for a further 10 minutes. Cool pastry case (turn oven off).

5 Meanwhile, combine cornflour and sugar in a medium saucepan. Gradually stir in juice and the water until smooth; cook, stirring, until mixture boils and thickens. Reduce heat; simmer, stirring, for 1 minute. Remove from heat; stir in rind, butter and egg yolks. Cool for 10 minutes.

6 Spread filling into pie shell. Cover; refrigerate for 2 hours.

7 Preheat oven to 240°C/475°F.

8 Beat egg whites (including the reserved egg white from the pastry) in a small bowl with an electric mixer until soft peaks form; gradually add extra sugar, beating until sugar dissolves between each addition.

9 Roughen surface of filling with a fork before spreading with meringue mixture. Bake pie for 2 minutes or until meringue is browned lightly.

PASTRY Process flour, icing sugar and butter until crumbly. Add egg yolk and the water; process until ingredients just come together. Knead dough on a floured surface until smooth. Wrap pastry in plastic wrap; refrigerate for 30 minutes.

tips You only need to use the egg yolk in the pastry; reserve the egg white and add it to the meringue mixture in step 8.

This pie is best eaten on the day it is made.

Butterfly CAKES

- 125G (4 OUNCES) BUTTER, SOFTENED
- 1 TEASPOON VANILLA EXTRACT
- ⅔ CUP (150G) CASTER SUGAR (SUPERFINE SUGAR)
- 3 EGGS
- 1½ CUPS (225G) SELF-RAISING FLOUR
- ¼ CUP (60ML) MILK
- 1 CUP (250ML) THICKENED (HEAVY) CREAM
- ½ CUP (160G) JAM
- 2 TEASPOONS ICING SUGAR (CONFECTIONERS' SUGAR)

1 Preheat oven to 180°C/350°F. Line two 12-hole (2-tablespoon/40ml) deep flat-based patty pans with paper cases.

2 Beat butter, extract, sugar, eggs, sifted flour and milk in a small bowl with an electric mixer, on low speed, until ingredients are just combined. Increase speed to medium; beat for 3 minutes or until mixture is smooth and paler in colour. Drop rounded tablespoons of mixture into paper cases.

3 Bake cakes for 20 minutes. Stand cakes in pans for 5 minutes before turning, top-side up, onto wire racks to cool.

4 Beat cream in a small bowl with an electric mixer until soft peaks form.

5 Using a small sharp pointed knife, cut a circle from the top of the cooled cakes; cut circle in half to make two 'wings'. Fill cavities with jam and cream. Place wings on top of cakes. Just before serving, dust with sifted icing sugar.

tips Store unfilled cakes in an airtight container for up to 2 days. Fill cakes just before serving. Use your favourite jam, or curd, to fill the cakes (see pages 245 and 267 for our jam and curd recipes).

APPLE CAKE
with apricot glaze

- 185G (6 OUNCES) BUTTER, SOFTENED
- 2 TEASPOONS GRATED LEMON RIND
- ⅔ CUP (150G) CASTER SUGAR (SUPERFINE SUGAR)
- 3 EGGS
- 1 CUP (150G) SELF-RAISING FLOUR
- ½ CUP (75G) PLAIN FLOUR (ALL-PURPOSE FLOUR)
- ⅓ CUP (80ML) MILK
- 2 MEDIUM APPLES (300G)
- 1 TEASPOON POWDERED GELATINE
- 2 TABLESPOONS WATER
- 2 TABLESPOONS APRICOT JAM, SIEVED

1 Preheat oven to 180°C/350°F. Grease a 20cm (8-inch) (base measurement) springform pan.

2 Beat butter, rind and sugar in a small bowl with an electric mixer until light and fluffy. Beat in eggs, one at a time, until combined. Transfer mixture to a large bowl; stir in sifted flours and milk, in two batches. Spread mixture into pan.

3 Peel apples; cut into quarters, remove cores. Make lengthways cuts into rounded sides of apple quarters, cutting about three-quarters of the way through. Arrange quarters, rounded side up, around edge of cake mixture.

4 Bake cake for 1 hour or until a skewer inserted into the centre comes out clean.

5 Sprinkle gelatine over the water in a small heatproof jug, stand jug in a small saucepan of simmering water, stirring until the gelatine dissolves. Stir in jam.

6 Spread half the jam mixture over hot cake; cool cake in pan. Remove cake from pan, brush with remaining warmed jam mixture.

tip This cake will keep in an airtight container at room temperature for up to 2 days.

Toffee APPLES

- 10 MEDIUM GREEN APPLES (1.5KG)
- 10 X 20CM (8-INCH) LONG WOODEN STICKS
- 4 CUPS (880G) CASTER SUGAR (SUPERFINE SUGAR)
- 1 CUP (250ML) WATER
- ⅓ CUP (115G) GLUCOSE SYRUP
- RED FOOD COLOURING

1 Line two baking trays with baking paper.

2 Wash apples under cold water; stand on a wire rack until completely dry (do not rub apples with a cloth). Push a wooden stick three-quarters of the way through each apple from the stem end.

3 Stir sugar, the water, glucose and colouring in a large saucepan over low heat until sugar dissolves. Bring to the boil; boil, uncovered, for 10 minutes or until mixture reaches 154°C (309°F) on a sugar thermometer (or until a small amount of mixture 'cracks' when dropped into a cup of cold water).

4 Remove pan from heat; allow bubbles to subside. Tilt pan slightly to one side and carefully dip an apple into toffee, twisting slowly to coat the apple completely. Remove apple slowly (air bubbles will form if the apples are dipped too quickly), twirling around a few times over the pan to drain excess toffee; place apples on tray. Repeat until all apples are coated. Stand apples at room temperature until set.

tips Use enough of the colouring to tint the toffee red.

Toffee apples are best eaten on the day they are made. However, they will keep for a day in an airtight container at room temperature.

EDITOR'S
Favourite

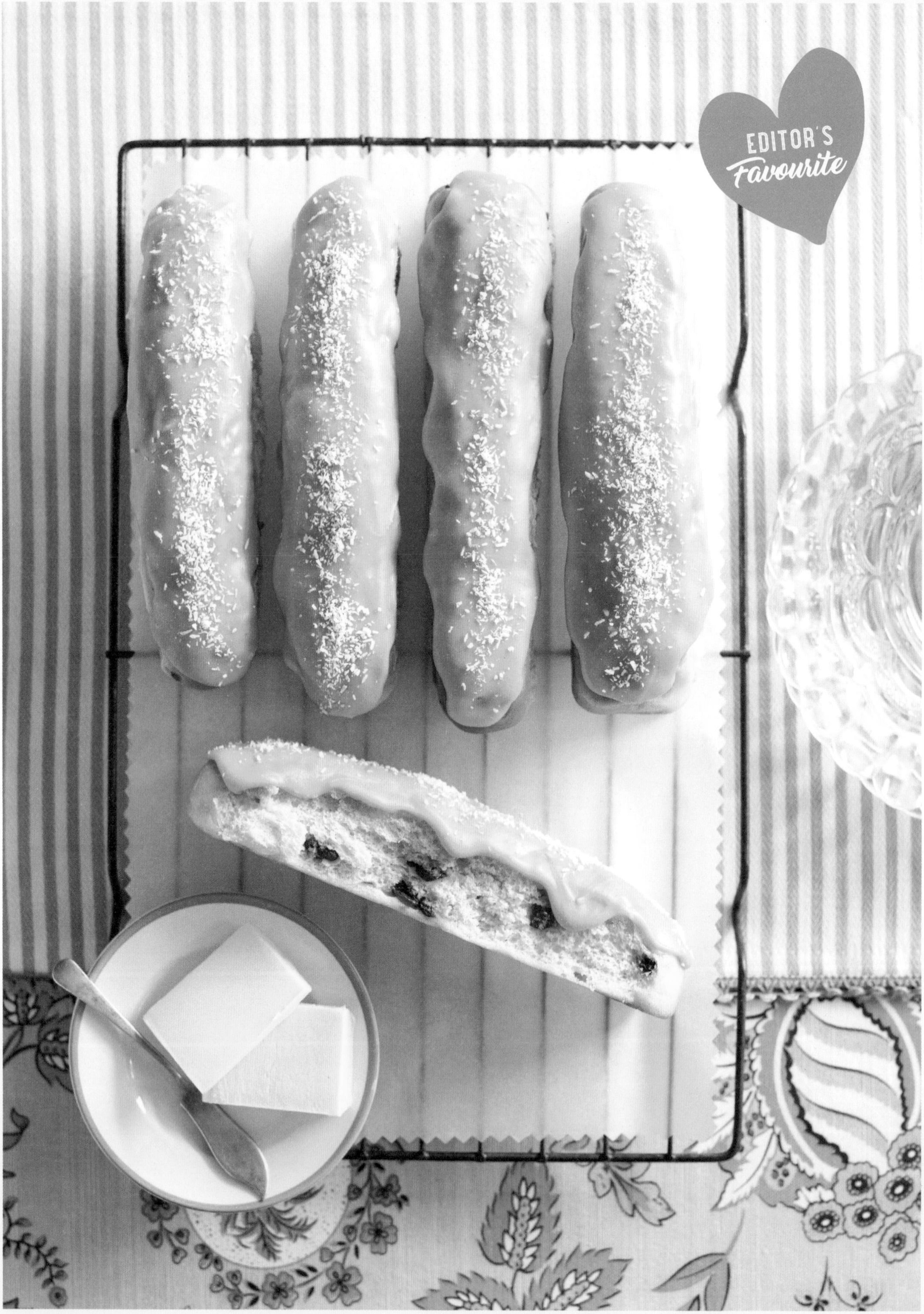
EDITOR'S
Favourite

Pink iced FINGER BUNS

- 4 TEASPOONS (14G) DRY YEAST
- ¼ CUP (55G) CASTER SUGAR (SUPERFINE SUGAR)
- 1½ CUPS (375ML) WARM MILK
- 4 CUPS (600G) PLAIN FLOUR (ALL-PURPOSE FLOUR)
- 60G (2 OUNCES) BUTTER, CHOPPED
- 1 EGG, BEATEN LIGHTLY
- ½ CUP (80G) SULTANAS
- ¼ CUP (40G) DRIED CURRANTS
- ¼ CUP (20G) DESICCATED COCONUT

BUN GLAZE

- 1 TABLESPOON CASTER SUGAR (SUPERFINE SUGAR)
- 1 TEASPOON POWDERED GELATINE
- 1 TABLESPOON HOT WATER

GLACÉ ICING

- 1 CUP (160G) ICING SUGAR (CONFECTIONERS' SUGAR)
- 10G (½ OUNCE) BUTTER, MELTED
- 1 TABLESPOON MILK, APPROXIMATELY
- PINK FOOD COLOURING

1 Combine yeast, sugar and milk in a small bowl. Cover; stand in a warm place for 10 minutes or until frothy.

2 Sift flour into a large bowl; rub in butter. Stir yeast mixture, egg and fruit into flour mixture; mix to a soft dough. Cover; stand in a warm place for 45 minutes or until dough is doubled in size.

3 Preheat oven to 220°C/425°F. Grease two 20cm x 30cm (8-inch x 12-inch) rectangular pans.

4 Knead dough on a floured surface for 5 minutes or until smooth and elastic. Divide dough into 16 portions; shape into buns 15cm (6-inches) long. Place eight buns into each pan; cover loosely with lightly oiled plastic wrap. Stand in a warm place for 10 minutes or until buns are well risen.

5 Bake buns for 8 minutes. Cover loosely with foil; bake for a further 5 minutes or until golden brown.

6 Meanwhile, make bun glaze. Turn buns, top-side up, onto a wire rack; brush with hot glaze. Cool.

7 Make icing. Spread icing on cold buns; sprinkle with coconut.

BUN GLAZE Stir ingredients in a small saucepan over low heat, without boiling, until sugar and gelatine have dissolved.

GLACÉ ICING Sift icing sugar into a small heatproof bowl, stir in butter and enough milk to make a firm paste; tint pink. Place bowl over a small saucepan of simmering water; stir until icing is spreadable.

Dark GINGERBREAD CAKE

- 125G (4 OUNCES) BUTTER, SOFTENED
- ½ CUP (110G) FIRMLY PACKED DARK BROWN SUGAR
- 2 EGGS
- 1⅔ CUPS (250G) PLAIN FLOUR (ALL-PURPOSE FLOUR)
- ½ TEASPOON BICARBONATE OF SODA (BAKING SODA)
- 2 TEASPOONS GROUND GINGER
- 1 CUP (360G) TREACLE
- 2 TABLESPOONS MILK
- ¼ CUP (55G) FINELY CHOPPED GLACÉ GINGER
- ⅓ CUP (55G) FINELY CHOPPED RAISINS
- STRIPS OF LEMON RIND AND SLICED CRYSTALLISED GINGER, TO DECORATE

LEMON GLACÉ ICING

- 2 CUPS (320G) ICING SUGAR (CONFECTIONERS' SUGAR)
- 20G (¾ OUNCE) BUTTER, SOFTENED
- 2 TABLESPOONS LEMON JUICE

1 Preheat oven to 180°C/350°F. Grease a 20cm x 30cm (8-inch x 12-inch) rectangular cake pan; line base and sides with baking paper, extending the paper 5cm (2 inches) above the sides.

2 Beat butter and sugar in a small bowl with an electric mixer until light and fluffy. Beat in eggs, one at a time. Transfer mixture to a large bowl; stir in sifted flour, soda and ground ginger, treacle, milk, glacé ginger and raisins. Spread mixture into pan.

3 Bake cake about 45 minutes. Leave cake in pan for 5 minutes before turning, top-side up, onto a wire rack to cool.

4 Make lemon glacé icing.

5 Spread cold cake with icing; stand until icing is set. Sprinkle with strips of rind and crystallised ginger before cutting.

LEMON GLACÉ ICING Sift icing sugar into a medium bowl. Stir in butter and juice until icing is smooth and spreadable.

tip Iced cake will keep in an airtight container for up to 3 days. Uniced cake can be frozen for up to 3 months.

PRIZE
WINNING

TEST

... KITCHEN ...

Classic

COCONUT ICE

- 4 CUPS (880G) CASTER SUGAR (SUPERFINE SUGAR)
- 1 CUP (250ML) MILK
- 2 TABLESPOONS GLUCOSE SYRUP
- 3 CUPS (240G) DESICCATED COCONUT
- PINK FOOD COLOURING

1 Grease a deep 19cm (8-inch) square cake pan; line base and sides with baking paper.

2 Stir sugar, milk and glucose in a medium saucepan, over low heat, until sugar dissolves. Bring to the boil; boil, uncovered, for 5 minutes or until mixture reaches 112°C (235°F) on a sugar thermometer (or until a small amount of mixture, dropped into cold water, forms a soft ball when rolled between your fingers).

3 Remove pan from heat; pour mixture into a heatproof bowl. Stir in coconut until thick and creamy. Spoon half the mixture into another heatproof bowl; work in colouring. Press pink mixture firmly over base of cake pan. Press white mixture evenly over pink layer.

4 Refrigerate for 3 hours or until firm before cutting into squares.

tip Coconut ice can be made a week ahead; store in an airtight container in the refrigerator.

Boiled FRUIT CAKE

- 2¾ CUPS (500G) MIXED DRIED FRUIT
- 1 CUP (220G) FIRMLY PACKED BROWN SUGAR
- 125G (4 OUNCES) BUTTER, CHOPPED
- ½ CUP (125ML) WATER
- 1 TEASPOON MIXED SPICE
- ½ TEASPOON BICARBONATE OF SODA (BAKING SODA)
- ½ CUP (125ML) SWEET SHERRY
- 1 EGG
- 1 CUP (150G) PLAIN FLOUR (ALL-PURPOSE FLOUR)
- 1 CUP (150G) SELF-RAISING FLOUR
- ⅓ CUP (55G) BLANCHED ALMONDS
- 2 TABLESPOONS SWEET SHERRY, EXTRA

1 Stir fruit, sugar, butter, the water, mixed spice and soda in a large saucepan over low heat, without boiling, until sugar dissolves and butter melts; bring to the boil. Reduce heat; simmer, covered, for 5 minutes. Remove from heat; stir in sherry. Cool to room temperature.

2 Preheat oven to 160°C/325°F. Grease a deep 20cm (8-inch) round cake pan; line base and side with two layers of baking paper, extending the paper 5cm (2 inches) above the side.

3 Stir egg and sifted flours into fruit mixture. Spread mixture into pan; decorate with almonds.

4 Bake cake about 1½ hours. Brush top of hot cake with extra sherry. Cover cake with foil; cool in pan.

tips Cover the cake loosely with foil during baking if it starts to over-brown. If the cake is browning unevenly, give it quarter turns several times during baking.

The cake can be made up to 1 month ahead. Store in an airtight container in a cool, dry place; refrigerate the cake if the weather is humid.

Little JAM TARTS

- 2 CUPS (300G) PLAIN FLOUR (ALL-PURPOSE FLOUR)
- ¼ CUP (40G) ICING SUGAR (CONFECTIONERS' SUGAR)
- 185G (6 OUNCES) COLD BUTTER, CHOPPED COARSELY
- 1 EGG YOLK
- 1 TABLESPOON ICED WATER, APPROXIMATELY
- ⅓ CUP (110G) STRAWBERRY JAM
- ⅓ CUP (110G) BLACK CHERRY JAM
- ⅓ CUP (110G) APRICOT JAM
- ⅓ CUP (110G) RASPBERRY JAM
- 1 TABLESPOON ICING SUGAR (CONFECTIONERS' SUGAR), EXTRA

1 Process flour, icing sugar and butter until crumbly. With motor operating, add egg yolk and enough of the water to make ingredients come together. Knead dough on a floured surface until smooth. Divide dough in half; roll one half between sheets of baking paper until 3mm (⅛-inch) thick. Repeat with remaining half. Place on trays; refrigerate for 30 minutes.

2 Grease 36 holes of four 12-hole (1-tablespoon/20ml) shallow round-based patty pans.

3 Using a 6cm (2½-inch) round cutter, cut 18 rounds from each piece of pastry; re-roll pastry scraps as necessary. Press pastry rounds into pan holes. Prick pastry cases well with a fork. Refrigerate 30 minutes.

4 Preheat oven to 220°C/425°F.

5 Bake pastry cases about 5 minutes. Using all four jams, drop slightly rounded teaspoons of jam into cases (one type of jam per case).

6 Bake tarts about 10 minutes. Cool. Just before serving, dust with extra sifted icing sugar.

tips If you don't have four patty pans, simply bake the tarts in batches; wash the pans in cool water and dry well between each batch.

You can use just one type of jam for this recipe if you like, but we like using different jams for the variety in colour and taste. Keep it all homemade and use the berry jam on page 245, if you like.

Blackberry swirl
LEMONADE CUPCAKES

- 125G (4 OUNCES) BUTTER, SOFTENED
- ½ CUP (110G) CASTER SUGAR (SUPERFINE SUGAR)
- 1 TABLESPOON FINELY GRATED LEMON RIND
- 2 EGGS
- 1½ CUPS (225G) SELF-RAISING FLOUR
- ½ CUP (125ML) LEMONADE (SEE TIP)

BLACKBERRY SWIRL FROSTING

- ¼ CUP (35G) FROZEN BLACKBERRIES, THAWED
- 500G (1 POUND) CREAM CHEESE, SOFTENED
- 2 CUPS (320G) ICING SUGAR (CONFECTIONERS' SUGAR)
- 1 TABLESPOON LEMONADE
- 2 TEASPOONS FINELY GRATED LEMON RIND

1 Preheat oven to 180°C/350°F. Line a 12-hole (⅓-cup/80ml) muffin pan with paper cases.

2 Make blackberry swirl frosting.

3 Beat butter, sugar and rind in a small bowl with an electric mixer until light and fluffy. Beat in eggs, one at a time. Transfer mixture to a large bowl; stir in sifted flour and lemonade, in two batches. Spoon mixture evenly into paper cases.

4 Bake cupcakes about 20 minutes. Stand cakes in pan for 5 minutes before turning, top-side up, onto wire racks to cool.

5 Just before serving, using a small ice-cream scoop, scoop frosting onto the cupcakes.

BLACKBERRY SWIRL FROSTING Crush blackberries very well with a fork. Beat cream cheese, sifted icing sugar, lemonade and rind in a small bowl with an electric mixer until smooth. Lightly fold crushed berries through cream cheese mixture to create a swirled effect (don't over-mix or you will lose the swirl). Place frosting in the freezer for a few hours or until firm.

tip Use a clear, carbonated lemonade for this recipe.

Here comes the Queen of Hearts
with delicious

CHOCOLATE CRACKLES

You'll be Queen of Hearts in your kitchen too, when you run up a batch of delicious Chocolate Crackles*. Your children will love them, father too will be in for his share — and what's more Chocolate Crackles are so easy to make. Have a look at the simple, no-cooking recipe below. Try it today — you'll love them.

HERE'S THE FAMOUS RECIPE

No cooking... made in minutes!

8 OZS. COPHA†. 8 OZS. ICING SUGAR,
3 HEAPED TABLESPOONS CADBURY'S BOURNVILLE COCOA‡.
1 CUP COCONUT, 4 CUPS KELLOGG'S RICE BUBBLES§.

1. Combine all the dry ingredients in a good-sized mixing bowl.
2. Melt Copha gently. Pour on to dry ingredients and mix well.
3. Spoon into paper cake containers and allow to set. (Keep in cool place, or the refrigerator, in hot weather.)

NEW, DELIGHTFUL VARIATIONS...

CHOCOLATE MINT CRACKLES — add 1 cup crushed pink-and-white bull's-eyes.
CHOCOLATE CRACKLE NESTS — Shape mixture into little nests and fill with jellybeans.
ORANGE CRACKLES — Add the thinly-grated rind of one large orange to the dry ingredients.
FRUIT CRACKLES — Stir in 1 cup crushed fruit drops or boiled sweets.

Copha . . . for your most important cooking! Copha is a pure white vegetable shortening. Copha is ideal for all your cakes, biscuits and pastries. Try it, too, for frying—Copha fries foods wonderfully crisp and light.

Hear them Snap! Crackle! Pop! with goodness. Just add milk to Kellogg's Rice Bubbles—crispest cereal that ever came out of a packet and they'll Snap! Crackle! Pop! with goodness! With hot milk or cold, Kellogg's Rice Bubbles are a delicious breakfast for the whole family.

A cup of Cadbury's Bournville Cocoa every day . . . keeps you healthy, warm and gay. It's the ideal drink for the whole family. Everybody loves its smooth chocolate flavour. Serve it for supper tonight!

* Registered Trade Mark. † Registered trade mark of World Brands Pty. Ltd.

MUFFIN WRAP

MATERIALS

- BAKING PAPER
- ASSORTED FABRICS
- PINKING SHEARS
- SMALL, ROUND PAPER DOILIES
- PEARL-HEADED PINS
- RIBBONS
- GIFT TAGS, OPTIONAL

1 Prepare muffin recipe of your choice. Lightly grease muffin tin, but instead of using muffin paper cases, cut baking paper into 15cm squares; use pinking shears to create a zig-zag edge. Push paper squares into muffin pan holes; drop muffin mixture into cases. Bake muffins as per recipe.

2 Cut fabric into 16cm squares; use pinking shears for a zig-zag edge.

3 Place a paper doily in centre of fabric square (this will stop the moist muffin from marking the fabric). Position muffin on the doily; fold up the points of the fabric and secure with the pins.

4 Tie ribbon around the fabric-wrapped muffin and make a bow to secure. Remove the pins. Add a tag with a greeting, if it's for a gift.

STEP 1

Cut baking paper into 15cm squares; push squares into pan holes. Spoon in muffin mix and bake as the recipe directs.

STEP 2

Cut the fabric into 16cm squares; use pinking shears to cut a zig-zag edging (this stops the fabric from fraying).

STEP 3

Place a paper doily in the centre of a fabric square to stop the moist muffin from marking the fabric. Place muffin on doily.

STEP 4

Fold up fabric points and pin to secure. Tie ribbon around the fabric-wrapped muffin; make a bow to secure. Remove pins.

GINGERNUTS

- 90G (3 OUNCES) BUTTER
- ⅓ CUP (75G) FIRMLY PACKED BROWN SUGAR
- ⅓ CUP (115G) GOLDEN SYRUP OR TREACLE
- 1⅓ CUPS (200G) PLAIN FLOUR (ALL-PURPOSE FLOUR)
- ¾ TEASPOON BICARBONATE OF SODA (BAKING SODA)
- 1 TABLESPOON GROUND GINGER
- 1 TEASPOON GROUND CINNAMON
- ¼ TEASPOON GROUND CLOVES

1 Preheat oven to 180°C/350°F. Grease oven trays; line trays with baking paper.

2 Stir butter, sugar and syrup in a medium saucepan over low heat until smooth. Remove from heat; stir in sifted dry ingredients. Cool for 10 minutes.

3 Roll rounded teaspoons of mixture into balls. Place about 3cm (1¼ inches) apart on trays; flatten slightly.

4 Bake biscuits about 10 minutes; cool on trays.

tip These biscuits will keep in an airtight container at room temperature for up to a week.

Berry JAM

- 125G (4 OUNCES) BLACKBERRIES
- 125G (4 OUNCES) BLUEBERRIES
- 250G (8 OUNCES) RASPBERRIES
- 500G (1 POUND) STRAWBERRIES, HULLED
- ⅓ CUP (80ML) LEMON JUICE
- 4 CUPS (880G) WHITE SUGAR (GRANULATED SUGAR)

1 Stir ingredients in a large saucepan over high heat, without boiling, until sugar dissolves. Bring to the boil, then reduce heat; simmer, uncovered, without stirring, for 30 minutes or until jam jells when tested (see tips).
2 Pour hot jam into hot sterilised jars (see tips); seal immediately. Label and date jars when cold.

tips For information on testing that jam has jelled, see glossary entry under 'Jelling', page 484.

For information on sterilising jars, see glossary entry under 'Sterilising Jars', page 487.

Use any combination of berries you like to give a total weight of 1kg (2 pounds).

Store jam in a cool, dark place for up to 12 months. Once opened, store in the fridge for up to 3 months. If any mould appears on the jam, it should be thrown away.

This berry jam can be used in any recipe in this book that has jam as an ingredient or accompaniment, such as:
Buttermilk scones, page 31
Victoria sponge sandwich, page 60
Sponge roll, page 68
Mini jam drops, page 276
Little jam tarts, page 235

Lumberjack CAKE

- 2 LARGE APPLES (400G), PEELED, CORED, CHOPPED FINELY
- 1 CUP (150G) FINELY CHOPPED SEEDED DRIED DATES
- 1 TEASPOON BICARBONATE OF SODA (BAKING SODA)
- 1 CUP (250ML) BOILING WATER
- 125G (4 OUNCES) BUTTER, SOFTENED
- 1 TEASPOON VANILLA EXTRACT
- 1 CUP (220G) CASTER SUGAR (SUPERFINE SUGAR)

- 1 EGG
- 1½ CUPS (225G) PLAIN FLOUR (ALL-PURPOSE FLOUR)
- FLAKED FRESH COCONUT, TO DECORATE (OPTIONAL)

COCONUT TOPPING

- 60G (2 OUNCES) BUTTER, CHOPPED
- ½ CUP (110G) FIRMLY PACKED BROWN SUGAR
- ½ CUP (125ML) MILK
- ⅔ CUP (50G) SHREDDED COCONUT

1 Preheat oven to 180°C/350°F. Grease a deep 23cm (9-inch) square cake pan; line base and sides with baking paper.

2 Place apple, dates and soda in a large bowl, stir in the water. Cover with plastic wrap; stand for 10 minutes.

3 Meanwhile, beat butter, extract, sugar and egg in a small bowl with an electric mixer until light and fluffy. Add butter mixture to apple mixture; stir to combine. Stir in sifted flour until combined.

4 Pour cake mixture into pan; bake about 50 minutes.

5 Meanwhile, make coconut topping.

6 Remove cake from oven; using a metal spatula, carefully spread warm coconut topping evenly over cake. Return to oven; bake for a further 20 minutes or until topping is browned. Leave cake in pan for 5 minutes before turning, top-side up, onto a wire rack to cool. Just before serving, sprinkle with flaked coconut.

COCONUT TOPPING Stir ingredients in a medium saucepan over low heat until butter melts and sugar dissolves.

tip The cake can be made 3 days ahead; store in an airtight container. The cake can also be frozen for up to 3 months.

Save Money

This bottle makes more than

2 dozen brimming glasses

of Mynor Fruit Cup!

..it costs you *less than* **2d. a glass**

MADE FROM ORANGES AND BLENDED FRUITS

EXPORT QUALITY

MYNOR FRUIT CUP

FRUIT JUICE CORDIAL

THIS BOTTLE ALWAYS REMAINS

MOTHERS! Here's the most healthy drink you can give those thirsty children of yours! Pure, delicious Mynor, rich in all those essential vitamins A, B, C and D contained in the fresh juices of oranges, lemons, pineapples and passionfruit. And, just imagine what these would cost you to buy at present-day prices! Pour a little Mynor Fruit Cup into a glass, fill it with pure, wholesome water, and let the children drink as much as they want. Just think . . . all this costs *less than 2d.* a glass!

MYNOR MEANS FRUIT JUICE

MYNOR
FRUIT CUP

P.S.: 2d. refund on undamaged Mynor bottles returned to your supplier in Sydney metropolitan

Chocolate hazelnut SLICE

- 250G (8 OUNCES) PLAIN CHOCOLATE BISCUITS (SEE TIPS)
- 60G (2 OUNCES) BUTTER, MELTED
- 4 EGGS, SEPARATED (SEE TIPS)
- ¾ CUP (165G) CASTER SUGAR (SUPERFINE SUGAR)
- ½ CUP (50G) GROUND HAZELNUTS
- 2 TABLESPOONS PLAIN FLOUR (ALL-PURPOSE FLOUR)
- 1 TABLESPOON COCOA POWDER

CHOCOLATE TOPPING

- 200G (6½ OUNCES) DARK (SEMI-SWEET) CHOCOLATE
- 125G (4 OUNCES) BUTTER, SOFTENED
- ½ CUP (110G) CASTER SUGAR (SUPERFINE SUGAR)
- 4 EGG YOLKS (FROM THE SEPARATED EGGS USED IN THE BISCUIT BASE)
- 1 TABLESPOON ORANGE JUICE

1 Preheat oven to 180°C/350°F. Grease a 20cm x 30cm (8-inch x 12-inch) rectangular pan; line base and long sides with baking paper, extending the paper 5cm (2 inches) above the sides.

2 Process biscuits until fine. Combine 1 cup of the biscuit crumbs with butter in a medium bowl; press over base of pan. Refrigerate for 10 minutes.

3 Beat egg whites in a small bowl with an electric mixer until soft peaks form. Gradually add sugar, beating until dissolved after each addition; fold in the hazelnuts, remaining biscuit crumbs and sifted flour. Spread mixture over biscuit base.

4 Bake base about 20 minutes. Cool for 20 minutes.

5 Reduce oven temperature to 160°C/325°F.

6 Make chocolate topping.

7 Spread topping over slice; bake slice for a further 20 minutes. Cool in pan. Refrigerate until firm. Dust with sifted cocoa before cutting into 24 pieces.

CHOCOLATE TOPPING Melt chocolate in a medium heatproof bowl over a medium saucepan of simmering water (don't let water touch base of bowl); stir until chocolate is smooth. Remove bowl from pan to prevent chocolate from overheating. Beat butter, sugar, egg yolks and juice in a small bowl with an electric mixer until light and fluffy. Stir in melted chocolate.

tips Buy plain chocolate biscuits for this recipe, that is, without filling, icing or chocolate coating.

For this recipe, the egg whites are used in the base, while the egg yolks are used to make the chocolate topping.

The slice can be stored in an airtight container in the fridge for up to 1 week.

GINGERBREAD PEOPLE

- 125G (4 OUNCES) BUTTER
- ½ CUP (110G) FIRMLY PACKED BROWN SUGAR
- 1 EGG, SEPARATED (SEE TIPS)
- 2½ CUPS (375G) PLAIN FLOUR (ALL-PURPOSE FLOUR)
- 1 TEASPOON BICARBONATE OF SODA (BAKING SODA)
- 3 TEASPOONS GROUND GINGER
- ½ CUP (125ML) GOLDEN SYRUP

ROYAL ICING

- 1 EGG WHITE (SEE TIPS)
- 1½ CUPS (240G) PURE ICING SUGAR (CONFECTIONERS' SUGAR), APPROXIMATELY
- FOOD COLOURINGS, OPTIONAL

1 Preheat oven to 180°C/350°F. Grease oven trays.

2 Beat butter, sugar and egg yolk in a small bowl with an electric mixer until smooth. Stir in sifted dry ingredients and syrup to make a soft dough. Knead dough on a floured surface until smooth. Roll dough between sheets of baking paper until 3mm (⅛-inch) thick. Refrigerate for 1 hour.

3 Using a 13cm (5¼-inch) gingerbread-man cutter, cut out shapes from dough; place on trays about 3cm (1¼ inches) apart.

4 Bake gingerbread for 10 minutes or until browned lightly. Cool on trays.

5 Meanwhile, make royal icing.

6 Spoon icing into a piping bag fitted with a small plain tube; decorate shapes as desired.

ROYAL ICING Beat egg white in a small bowl with an electric mixer, on low speed, until just broken up; gradually beat in enough sifted icing sugar to give the mixture a piping consistency. Tint with colourings if desired. Keep royal icing covered with a damp tea towel to prevent icing drying out.

tips You need one whole egg for this recipe: the egg yolk is used in the dough, while the egg white is used in the royal icing.

When making the royal icing, you don't want to beat air bubbles into the mixture, so beat the egg white and icing sugar on low speed to get a smooth mixture.

If you don't have a piping bag and tube, simply snip a tiny hole into a corner of a ziptop bag and use this to pipe on the decorations.

Gingerbread men cutters are available from kitchenware shops.

Crunchy
RASPBERRY MUFFINS

- 2 CUPS (300G) SELF-RAISING FLOUR
- ½ TEASPOON GROUND CINNAMON
- ⅓ CUP (75G) CASTER SUGAR (SUPERFINE SUGAR)
- 1 EGG, BEATEN LIGHTLY
- 60G (2 OUNCES) BUTTER, MELTED
- 1 CUP (250ML) BUTTERMILK
- 200G (6½ OUNCES) FRESH OR FROZEN RASPBERRIES

CRUNCHY NUT TOPPING

- 2 TABLESPOONS CASTER SUGAR (SUPERFINE SUGAR)
- ⅓ CUP (40G) FINELY CHOPPED WALNUTS OR PECANS
- ¼ TEASPOON GROUND CINNAMON
- ¼ TEASPOON GROUND NUTMEG

1 Preheat oven to 200°C/400°F. Grease 10 holes of a 12-hole (⅓-cup/80ml) muffin pan.

2 Make crunchy nut topping.

3 Sift flour, cinnamon and sugar into a large bowl. Stir in combined egg, butter and buttermilk, then raspberries; mix until just combined. Spoon mixture into pan holes, then sprinkle with the topping.

4 Bake muffins about 20 minutes. Serve warm or cooled.

CRUNCHY NUT TOPPING

Combine ingredients in a small bowl.

tip Don't thaw frozen berries before adding to the mixture, as their colour will bleed into the muffin mixture.

Boiled CHOCOLATE CAKE

- 3 CUPS (660G) CASTER SUGAR (SUPERFINE SUGAR)
- 250G (8 OUNCES) BUTTER, CHOPPED
- ⅓ CUP (35G) COCOA POWDER
- 1 TEASPOON BICARBONATE OF SODA (BAKING SODA)
- 2 CUPS (500ML) WATER
- 3 CUPS (450G) SELF-RAISING FLOUR
- 4 EGGS

FUDGE FROSTING

- 90G (3 OUNCES) BUTTER, CHOPPED
- ⅓ CUP (80ML) WATER
- ½ CUP (110G) CASTER SUGAR (SUPERFINE SUGAR)
- 1½ CUPS (240G) ICING SUGAR (CONFECTIONERS' SUGAR)
- ⅓ CUP (35G) COCOA POWDER

1 Preheat oven to 180°C/350°F. Grease a deep 26.5cm x 33cm (10½-inch x 13¼-inch), 3.5-litre (14-cup) baking dish; line base with baking paper.

2 Stir sugar, butter, sifted cocoa and soda, and the water in a medium saucepan over high heat, without boiling, until sugar dissolves. Bring to the boil. Reduce heat to low; simmer, uncovered, for 5 minutes. Transfer mixture to a large bowl; cool to room temperature.

3 Add flour and eggs to chocolate mixture; beat with an electric mixer until mixture is smooth and paler in colour. Pour mixture into pan.

4 Bake cake about 50 minutes. Leave cake in pan for 10 minutes before turning, top-side up, onto a wire rack to cool.

5 Meanwhile, make fudge frosting. Spread cold cake with frosting.

FUDGE FROSTING Stir butter, the water and caster sugar in a small saucepan over low heat, without boiling, until sugar dissolves. Sift icing sugar and cocoa into a small bowl, then gradually stir in hot butter mixture. Cover; refrigerate for 20 minutes or until frosting thickens. Beat with a wooden spoon until spreadable.

tip Store cake in an airtight container for up to 4 days. This cake is also suitable to freeze, uniced, for up to 2 months.

Master ORANGE MARMALADE

- 1KG (2 POUNDS) ORANGES
- 1.5 LITRES (6 CUPS) WATER
- 1KG (2 POUNDS) WHITE SUGAR (GRANULATED SUGAR), APPROXIMATELY

1 Peel oranges, removing rind and white pith separately; slice rind thinly, reserve half the pith. Quarter oranges; slice flesh thinly, reserve any seeds. Tie reserved pith and seeds in a muslin cloth. Place rind, flesh, muslin bag and the water in a large saucepan; bring to the boil. Reduce heat; simmer, covered, for 1 hour or until rind is soft. Discard muslin bag.

2 Measure fruit mixture, allow 1 cup sugar for each cup of fruit mixture; place in same pan, stir over high heat, without boiling, until sugar dissolves. Bring to the boil; boil, uncovered, without stirring, for 30 minutes or until marmalade jells when tested (see tips). Pour hot marmalade into hot sterilised jars (see tips); seal jars immediately. Label and date jars when cold.

tips For information on testing that jam has jelled, see glossary entry under 'Jelling', page 484.

For information on sterilising jars, see glossary entry under 'Sterilising Jars', page 487.

Store marmalade in a cool, dark place for up to 12 months. Once opened, store in the fridge for up to 3 months. If any mould should appear on the marmalade, throw it away.

6 oz. granulated sugar
¼ pint water
4 oz. butter or substitute
4 oz. finest semolina
2 oz. ground almonds

¼ teaspoon almond essence
¼ teaspoon vanilla essence
coconut
nuts
glacé cherries

Boil the sugar and water together until thick and syrupy but remove from heat before it changes colour. Melt the butter, stir in semolina and brown lightly, then add ground almonds and essences. Add this mixture to the

syrup, stirring over low
for 3 minutes. Leave to
4 portions and colour to
red colouring, but leave 1 p
quickly so that the mixture
assorted shapes. Roll some
with blanched almonds, waln
dragées and glacé cherries. Tr
recipe makes a delicious sweet
than using all marzipan.

Home made sweets are not difficult to make, if the following rules are remembered:

1) Always make sure the sugar has dissolved by stirring the mixture well
2) To prevent the ingredients drying against the sides of the pan brush with a pastry brush dipped in plenty of cold water. Do this quite often during the cooking period
3) Test quite early — if you make a lot of sweets it is worth while investing in a sugar thermometer
4) Use a really strong saucepan, since sweet mixtures reach a very high temperature

835 COCONUT ICE

1 coconut
eetened

12 oz. icing sugar
1 drop cochineal

eetened condensed milk and icing
ut (the mixture should be very
wo parts. Tint one half of the
ochineal. Shape the mixture into
s firmly together. Dust a plate
leave the coconut ice on this

836 MAGIC FONDANTS

8 oz. icing sugar

2 tablespoons sweetened
condensed milk

Sift icing sugar and blend in sweetened condensed milk until smooth and creamy. Flavour with peppermint, vanilla, fruit flavouring or soluble coffee powder. Add suitable vegetable colourings. Roll into balls and coat with coconut, grated chocolate or chopped pistachio or roasted nuts. Pres half walnuts or almonds into balls of fondant. Press into sweet moulds, leave to set. Remove and serve.

thick and cook gently
tly, then divide into
a green, yellow and
ural. Working fairly
warm, form into
r: decorate others
hazel nuts, silver
aper cases. This
ore economical

SWEETS

MARSHMALLOW TREATS

- 200G (6½ OUNCES) BUTTER
- 395G (12½ OUNCES) CANNED SWEETENED CONDENSED MILK
- 1 CUP (220G) FIRMLY PACKED BROWN SUGAR
- ¼ CUP (25G) COCOA POWDER
- 2 TEASPOONS VANILLA EXTRACT
- 3¾ CUPS (375G) PLAIN SWEET BISCUIT CRUMBS
- 300G (9½ OUNCES) PINK AND WHITE MARSHMALLOWS
- 1½ CUPS (135G) DESICCATED COCONUT

1 Stir butter, condensed milk, sugar, sifted cocoa and extract in a medium saucepan over low heat until smooth. Remove from heat; stir in biscuit crumbs.

2 Using damp hands, roll 3 heaped teaspoons of mixture around each marshmallow, pressing firmly to enclose marshmallows.

3 Place coconut in a small shallow bowl; roll balls in coconut, place on trays. Refrigerate until firm.

tip Store in an airtight container in the refrigerator up to 2 weeks.

TOFFEE BRITTLE

- 250G (8 OUNCES) BUTTER, CHOPPED COARSELY
- 1 CUP (220G) CASTER SUGAR (SUPERFINE SUGAR)
- 2 TEASPOONS WATER
- 1 TEASPOON VANILLA EXTRACT
- 180G (5½ OUNCES) DARK (SEMI-SWEET) CHOCOLATE
- ⅔ CUP (90G) ROASTED UNSALTED SHELLED PISTACHIOS, CHOPPED FINELY

1 Stir butter, sugar and the water in a medium heavy-based saucepan over low heat until sugar is dissolved and butter melted.

2 Bring mixture to the boil, stirring occasionally, until toffee mixture reaches 155°C (310°F) on a sugar thermometer. Remove pan from heat; allow bubbles to subside. Stir in extract. Drop tablespoonfuls of toffee mixture onto baking-paper-lined trays. Stand until set.

3 Melt the chocolate in a medium heatproof bowl over a medium saucepan of simmering water (don't let the water touch the base of the bowl); stir until chocolate is smooth. Remove bowl from pan. Dip toffee into chocolate, then in nuts; return to trays. Refrigerate toffee until chocolate is set.

Curd BUTTERS

PASSIONFRUIT BUTTER

- 4 EGGS, BEATEN LIGHTLY, STRAINED
- 185G (6 OUNCES) UNSALTED BUTTER, CHOPPED
- ¾ CUP (165G) CASTER SUGAR (SUPERFINE SUGAR)
- ⅓ CUP (80ML) LEMON JUICE
- 1 CUP (250ML) PASSIONFRUIT PULP

LIME BUTTER

- 4 EGGS, BEATEN LIGHTLY, STRAINED
- 185G (6 OUNCES) UNSALTED BUTTER, CHOPPED
- 1½ CUPS (330G) CASTER SUGAR (SUPERFINE SUGAR)
- ½ CUP (125ML) LIME JUICE
- ¼ CUP (60ML) LEMON JUICE
- 1 TABLESPOON FINELY GRATED LIME RIND
- GREEN FOOD COLOURING

BLOOD ORANGE BUTTER

- 4 EGGS, BEATEN LIGHTLY, STRAINED
- 185G (6 OUNCES) UNSALTED BUTTER, CHOPPED
- ¾ CUP (165G) CASTER SUGAR (SUPERFINE SUGAR)
- 1 CUP (250ML) BLOOD ORANGE JUICE
- 1 TABLESPOON FINELY GRATED BLOOD ORANGE RIND

1 For passionfruit butter, combine ingredients in a medium heatproof bowl over a medium saucepan of simmering water. Stir until mixture thickly coats the back of a wooden spoon. Remove from heat. Stand bowl in a sink of cold water, stirring occasionally, for 10 minutes. Pour into hot sterilised jars; seal.

2 For lime butter, combine the ingredients, except the rind and colouring, in a medium heatproof bowl; cook as per passionfruit butter. Stir in rind and colouring before pouring into sterilised jars.

3 For blood orange butter, combine the ingredients, except the rind, in a medium heatproof bowl; cook as per passionfruit butter. Stir in rind before pouring into sterilised jars.

tips For information on sterilising jars, see glossary entry under 'Sterilising Jars', page 487.

These butters will keep for up to 4 weeks in the refrigerator.

CANISTERS

MATERIALS

- PINKING SHEARS
- COTTON PRINT FABRICS
- SET OF CLEAN CANISTERS
- DECORATIVE LACE, RICK RACK AND BRAID OF VARYING WIDTHS
- SEWING NEEDLE AND COTTON
- SPRAY ADHESIVE
- DOUBLE-SIDED IRON-ON APPLIQUÉ WEBBING (VLIESOFIX)
- FELT SQUARES
- SMALL SHARP SCISSORS
- TACKY CRAFT GLUE

1 Using pinking shears (these will prevent the cut edges from fraying), cut fabric piece to fit around canister, overlapping a little. Cut lace (or rick rack or braid) the same length as the fabric. Pin to fabric edge and sew it in place with needle and thread.

2 Spray the back of the fabric with the spray adhesive; wrap the fabric around the canister.

3 Print the name of the canister (tea, sugar) in an appropriate size on plain paper. Trace each letter, back to front, onto the paper side of the Vliesofix, then iron it onto a piece of felt. (Place a cloth on top of the felt, if it's not pure wool, before ironing as it may scorch.)

4 Use small sharp scissors to cut out letters. Peel away backing paper and glue the letters onto the canister using tacky craft glue.

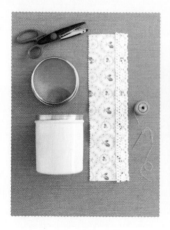   

STEP 1
Cut fabric to fit around canister; cut lace (or rick rack) the same length. Sew lace in place with a needle and thread.

STEP 2
Spray back of fabric with spray adhesive (lay it on a piece of paper to protect the surface); wrap around the canister.

STEP 3
Trace the name of the canister, back to front, onto the paper side of the Vliesofix; stick onto the felt and cut out the letters.

STEP 4
Peel away the backing paper, then glue the felt letters onto the canisters using tacky craft glue.

THE Biscuit Tin

Sugar 'n' spice BISCUITS

- 125G (4 OUNCES) BUTTER, SOFTENED
- ½ TEASPOON VANILLA EXTRACT
- ⅓ CUP (75G) RAW SUGAR
- 1 EGG
- 2 TABLESPOONS WHEATGERM
- 1 CUP (160G) WHOLEMEAL PLAIN (ALL-PURPOSE) FLOUR
- 2 TABLESPOONS WHOLEMEAL SELF-RAISING FLOUR
- ⅓ CUP (75G) RAW SUGAR, EXTRA
- 1 TEASPOON GROUND CINNAMON

1 Preheat oven to 180°C/350°F. Grease oven trays.

2 Beat butter, extract, sugar and egg in a small bowl with an electric mixer until smooth. Stir in wheatgerm and sifted flours.

3 Roll rounded teaspoons of mixture into balls; toss in combined extra sugar and cinnamon.

4 Place balls on trays about 3cm (1¼ inches) apart; flatten with a floured fork.

5 Bake biscuits for 12 minutes or until browned lightly. Leave on trays for 5 minutes before transferring to wire racks to cool.

tips These biscuits can be stored in an airtight container for up to 1 week.

The 'germ' is the part of the plant that germinates to form the sprout that becomes wheat. It has a nutty flavour and is very oily, which causes it to turn rancid (and is the reason why it is removed during processing of wheat into flour). Wheatgerm is available from health-food stores and most major supermarkets. Store it in the fridge so it doesn't go off.

EDITOR'S
Favourite

FRUIT CHEW SQUARES

- 90G (3 OUNCES) BUTTER, CHOPPED
- ⅓ CUP (75G) FIRMLY PACKED BROWN SUGAR
- 1¼ CUPS (185G) PLAIN FLOUR (ALL-PURPOSE FLOUR)
- 1 EGG YOLK

FRUIT AND NUT TOPPING

- 2 EGGS
- 1 CUP (220G) FIRMLY PACKED BROWN SUGAR
- ⅓ CUP (50G) SELF-RAISING FLOUR
- ½ CUP (85G) RAISINS
- ¾ CUP (120G) SULTANAS
- 1¼ CUPS (185G) ROASTED UNSALTED PEANUTS
- 1 CUP (80G) DESICCATED COCONUT

1 Preheat oven to 180°C/350°F. Grease a 20cm x 30cm (8-inch x 12-inch) rectangular pan; line base and long sides with baking paper, extending the paper 5cm (2 inches) above the sides.

2 Stir butter and sugar in a medium saucepan over medium heat until butter is melted. Stir in sifted flour and egg yolk. Press mixture over base of pan.

3 Bake for 10 minutes or until browned lightly; cool (keep oven on).

4 Make fruit and nut topping.

5 Spread topping over cooled base; bake for a further 30 minutes or until browned lightly. Cool in pan before cutting into 24 pieces.

FRUIT AND NUT TOPPING

Beat eggs and sugar in a small bowl with an electric mixer until changed to a lighter colour and thickened slightly; fold in sifted flour. Transfer mixture to a large bowl; stir in remaining ingredients.

tips Brown sugar gives this nutty slice the colour and taste of caramel.

This slice can be stored in an airtight container for up to 1 week.

Mini JAM DROPS

- 125G (4 OUNCES) BUTTER, SOFTENED
- ½ TEASPOON VANILLA EXTRACT
- ½ CUP (110G) CASTER SUGAR (SUPERFINE SUGAR)
- 1 CUP (120G) GROUND ALMONDS
- 1 EGG
- 1 CUP (150G) PLAIN FLOUR (ALL-PURPOSE FLOUR)
- ⅓ CUP (110G) RASPBERRY JAM
- ⅓ CUP (110G) APRICOT JAM
- 1 TEASPOON FINELY GRATED LEMON RIND

1 Preheat oven to 180°C/350°F. Line oven trays with baking paper.

2 Beat butter, extract, sugar and ground almonds in a small bowl with an electric mixer until light and fluffy. Beat in egg, then stir in sifted flour.

3 Roll tablespoons of mixture into balls; place on trays about 5cm (2 inches) apart. Press a floured spoon or your thumb into the centre of each ball to make a hole.

4 Place raspberry and apricot jams into two small bowls. Divide rind between jams; mix well. Spoon jams into biscuit holes.

5 Bake biscuits about 15 minutes. Cool on trays.

tips You can use any fruit jam you like, strawberry would also work well, or use the homemade berry jam on page 245, if you like.

Jam drops will keep in an airtight container for up to 2 days.

MELTING MOMENTS

- 250G (8 OUNCES) BUTTER, SOFTENED
- 1 TEASPOON VANILLA EXTRACT
- ½ CUP (80G) ICING SUGAR (CONFECTIONERS' SUGAR)
- 1½ CUPS (225G) PLAIN FLOUR (ALL-PURPOSE FLOUR)
- ½ CUP (75G) CORNFLOUR (CORNSTARCH)

BUTTER CREAM

- 90G (3 OUNCES) BUTTER, SOFTENED
- ¾ CUP (120G) ICING SUGAR (CONFECTIONERS' SUGAR)
- 1 TEASPOON FINELY GRATED LEMON RIND
- 1 TEASPOON LEMON JUICE

1 Preheat oven to 160°C/325°F. Line oven trays with baking paper.

2 Beat butter, extract and sifted icing sugar in a small bowl with an electric mixer until light and fluffy. Transfer mixture to a large bowl; stir in combined sifted flours, in two batches.

3 With floured hands, roll rounded teaspoons of mixture into balls; place on trays about 2.5cm (1 inch) apart. Flatten slightly with a floured fork.

4 Bake biscuits about 15 minutes. Leave biscuits on trays for 5 minutes before lifting onto wire racks to cool.

5 Meanwhile, make butter cream.

6 Sandwich cooled biscuits with butter cream. Just before serving, dust with a little extra sifted icing sugar, if you like.

BUTTER CREAM Beat butter, sifted icing sugar and rind in a small bowl with an electric mixer until pale and fluffy; beat in juice.

tip Unfilled biscuits will keep in an airtight container for up to 1 week. Filled biscuits will keep for a few days in an airtight container in the fridge.

Milk Shakes
The Unique Sweet

SWEETACRES Milk Shakes

Made **FROM PURE CONDENSED MILK AND GLUCOSE**

Made only by James Stedman Henderson's Sweets Ltd., "Sweetacres," Rosebery, N.S.W., and Auckland, N.Z.

Chocolate chip COOKIES

- 250G (8 OUNCES) BUTTER, SOFTENED
- 1 TEASPOON VANILLA EXTRACT
- ¾ CUP (165G) CASTER SUGAR (SUPERFINE SUGAR)
- ¾ CUP (165G) FIRMLY PACKED BROWN SUGAR
- 1 EGG
- 2¼ CUPS (335G) PLAIN FLOUR (ALL-PURPOSE FLOUR)
- 1 TEASPOON BICARBONATE OF SODA (BAKING SODA)
- 375G (12 OUNCES) DARK CHOCOLATE MELTS, CHOPPED COARSELY

1 Preheat oven to 180°C/350°F. Grease oven trays; line with baking paper.

2 Beat butter, extract, sugars and egg in a small bowl with an electric mixer until light and fluffy. Transfer mixture to a large bowl; stir in sifted flour and soda, in two batches. Stir in chocolate.

3 Roll tablespoons of mixture into balls; place on trays about 5cm (2 inches) apart.

4 Bake cookies for 15 minutes or until golden. Cool on trays.

tips For a more indulgent and intense chocolate taste, use a chocolate with 70% cocoa solids.

For a chewier cookie, bake for 12 minutes.

The cookies can be stored in an airtight container for up to 1 week.

VARIATIONS

MILK CHOC Replace the dark chocolate Melts with either milk or white chocolate Melts.

CHOC NUT Replace a third of the chocolate with roasted coarsely chopped nuts such as hazelnuts, walnuts, pecans or macadamias.

Monte carlo BISCUITS

- 180G (5½ OUNCES) BUTTER, SOFTENED
- 1 TEASPOON VANILLA EXTRACT
- ½ CUP (110G) FIRMLY PACKED BROWN SUGAR
- 1 EGG
- 1¼ CUPS (185G) SELF-RAISING FLOUR
- ¾ CUP (105G) PLAIN FLOUR (ALL-PURPOSE FLOUR)
- ¼ TEASPOON BICARBONATE OF SODA (BAKING SODA)
- ⅔ CUP (50G) DESICCATED COCONUT
- ⅓ CUP (110G) RASPBERRY JAM

VIENNA CREAM

- 60G (2 OUNCES) BUTTER, SOFTENED
- ½ TEASPOON VANILLA EXTRACT
- ¾ CUP (120G) ICING SUGAR (CONFECTIONERS' SUGAR)
- 2 TEASPOONS MILK

1 Preheat oven to 200°C/400°F. Grease oven trays; line with baking paper.

2 Beat butter, extract and sugar in a small bowl with an electric mixer until just combined. Beat in egg. Stir in sifted flours, soda and coconut, in two batches.

3 Roll 2 level teaspoons of mixture into ovals; place on trays about 5cm (2 inches) apart. Flatten slightly; use the back of a fork to roughen surface.

4 Bake biscuits about 7 minutes. Lift biscuits onto a wire rack to cool.

5 Meanwhile, make vienna cream.

6 Sandwich cooled biscuits with vienna cream and jam.

VIENNA CREAM Beat butter, extract and sifted icing sugar in a small bowl with an electric mixer until fluffy; beat in milk.

Apricot choc-chip
MUESLI BARS

- 125G (4 OUNCES) BUTTER, CHOPPED
- ½ CUP (110G) FIRMLY PACKED BROWN SUGAR
- 2 TABLESPOONS HONEY
- 1½ CUPS (135G) ROLLED OATS
- ¼ CUP (40G) SUNFLOWER SEEDS
- ⅓ CUP (25G) DESICCATED COCONUT
- ½ TEASPOON GROUND CINNAMON
- ½ CUP (75G) FINELY CHOPPED DRIED APRICOTS
- 2 TABLESPOONS DARK CHOC BITS

1 Preheat oven to 180°C/350°F. Grease a deep 20cm (8-inch) square cake pan; line base and sides with baking paper, extending the paper 5cm (2 inches) above the sides.

2 Stir butter, sugar and honey in a medium saucepan over low heat until sugar is dissolved. Stir in oats, sunflower seeds, coconut, cinnamon and apricots. Press mixture into pan.

3 Bake slice for 30 minutes or until firm to touch. Sprinkle with Choc Bits; bake for a further 5 minutes. Mark into 15 bars while warm; cool in pan. Cut when cold.

tip Muesli bars can be stored in an airtight container for up to 1 week.

COOKIE JAR

MATERIALS

- 1 LITRE (4-CUP) JAR WITH LID
- DRY COOKIE INGREDIENTS (SEE TIPS)
- PINKING SHEARS
- FABRIC
- TWINE
- HOME-MADE GIFT TAG
- HOLE PUNCH
- RIBBON

1 Using your favourite cookie recipe (we're using white chocolate macadamia cookies, page 320), measure out the dry ingredients.

2 Spoon the dry ingredients into the jar, keeping ingredients as level as possible. The sugar should be packed firmly so other ingredients don't run through it.

3 Using pinking shears for a zig-zag edge, cut a fabric square larger than the lid diameter.

4 Tighten lid on jar and cover with the fabric square. Wind the twine tightly around fabric to secure. Make a gift tag out of coloured cardboard with the name of the recipe. Punch a hole in the tag, thread through the ribbon; tie with a bow.

tips Don't forget to include the recipe along with the cookie jar. If you like, choose a recipe where all the dry ingredients are mixed together at the same time, then the jar can just be emptied into the bowl in one hit.

STEP 1
Measure out all the dry ingredients for the recipe. Carefully spoon ingredients into the jar, keeping each layer as level as possible.

STEP 2
The sugar should be packed in firmly so the other ingredients don't run through it and mix with the other layers.

STEP 3
Cut a fabric square larger than the lid diameter; using pinking shears creates a zig-zag edge, and stops fraying.

STEP 4
Make a gift tag from cardboard with the name of the recipe. Punch a hole in the tag, thread with ribbon; tie with a bow.

Dream BARS

- 90G (3 OUNCES) BUTTER, SOFTENED
- ⅓ CUP (75G) FIRMLY PACKED BROWN SUGAR
- 1 CUP (150G) PLAIN FLOUR (ALL-PURPOSE FLOUR)
- 2 TABLESPOONS ICING SUGAR (CONFECTIONERS' SUGAR)

TOPPING

- 2 EGGS, BEATEN LIGHTLY
- 1 TEASPOON VANILLA EXTRACT
- ½ CUP (110G) FIRMLY PACKED BROWN SUGAR
- 1 TABLESPOON PLAIN FLOUR (ALL-PURPOSE FLOUR)
- ½ TEASPOON BAKING POWDER
- 1½ CUPS (135G) DESICCATED COCONUT
- 1 CUP (320G) BOTTLED FRUIT MINCE

1 Preheat oven to 180°C/350°F. Grease a 20cm x 30cm (8-inch x 12-inch) rectangular pan; line base and long sides with baking paper, extending the paper 5cm (2 inches) above the sides.

2 Beat butter and sugar in a small bowl with an electric mixer until smooth. Stir in sifted flour.

3 Press mixture over base of pan. Bake base for 10 minutes.

4 Meanwhile, make topping.

5 Spread topping over hot base; bake for a further 30 minutes or until firm. Cool slice in pan. Just before serving, cut into 16 pieces and dust with sifted icing sugar.

TOPPING Beat eggs, extract and sugar in a small bowl with an electric mixer until thick and creamy. Fold in combined sifted flour and baking powder; then coconut and fruit mince.

Coconut MACAROONS

- **2 EGG WHITES**
- **½ CUP (110G) CASTER SUGAR (SUPERFINE SUGAR)**
- **1 TEASPOON VANILLA EXTRACT**
- **¼ CUP (35G) PLAIN FLOUR (ALL-PURPOSE FLOUR)**
- **1½ CUPS (120G) DESICCATED COCONUT**

1 Preheat oven to 150°C/300°F. Grease oven trays; line with baking paper.

2 Beat egg whites in a small bowl with an electric mixer until soft peaks form. Gradually add sugar, beating until dissolved after each addition. Stir in extract, sifted flour and coconut, in two batches.

3 Drop level tablespoons of the mixture onto trays about 5cm (2 inches) apart.

4 Bake macaroons for 25 minutes. Cool on trays.

tip These macaroons will keep in an airtight container for about 1 week.

Traditional SHORTBREAD

- 250G (8 OUNCES) BUTTER, SOFTENED
- ⅓ CUP (75G) CASTER SUGAR (SUPERFINE SUGAR)
- 1 TABLESPOON WATER
- 2 CUPS (300G) PLAIN FLOUR (ALL-PURPOSE FLOUR)
- ½ CUP (100G) RICE FLOUR
- 2 TABLESPOONS WHITE SUGAR (GRANULATED SUGAR)

1 Preheat oven to 160°C/325°F. Grease two oven trays.

2 Beat butter and caster sugar in a medium bowl with an electric mixer until light and fluffy. Stir in the water and sifted flours, in two batches. Knead dough on a floured surface until smooth.

3 Divide dough in half; shape each, on separate trays, into a 20cm (8-inch) round. Mark each round into 12 wedges; prick with a fork. Pinch edges of rounds with your fingers; sprinkle with white sugar.

4 Bake shortbread about 40 minutes. Leave shortbread on trays for 5 minutes. Using a sharp knife, cut the rounds into wedges along the marked lines. Cool on trays.

tips We found that using half regular (salted) and half unsalted butter in shortbread recipes achieved the taste we liked best.

The rice flour is the ingredient that makes shortbread 'short' – a pastry that is rich, crumbly and very tender.

Shortbread should be quite pale in colour after it's cooked.

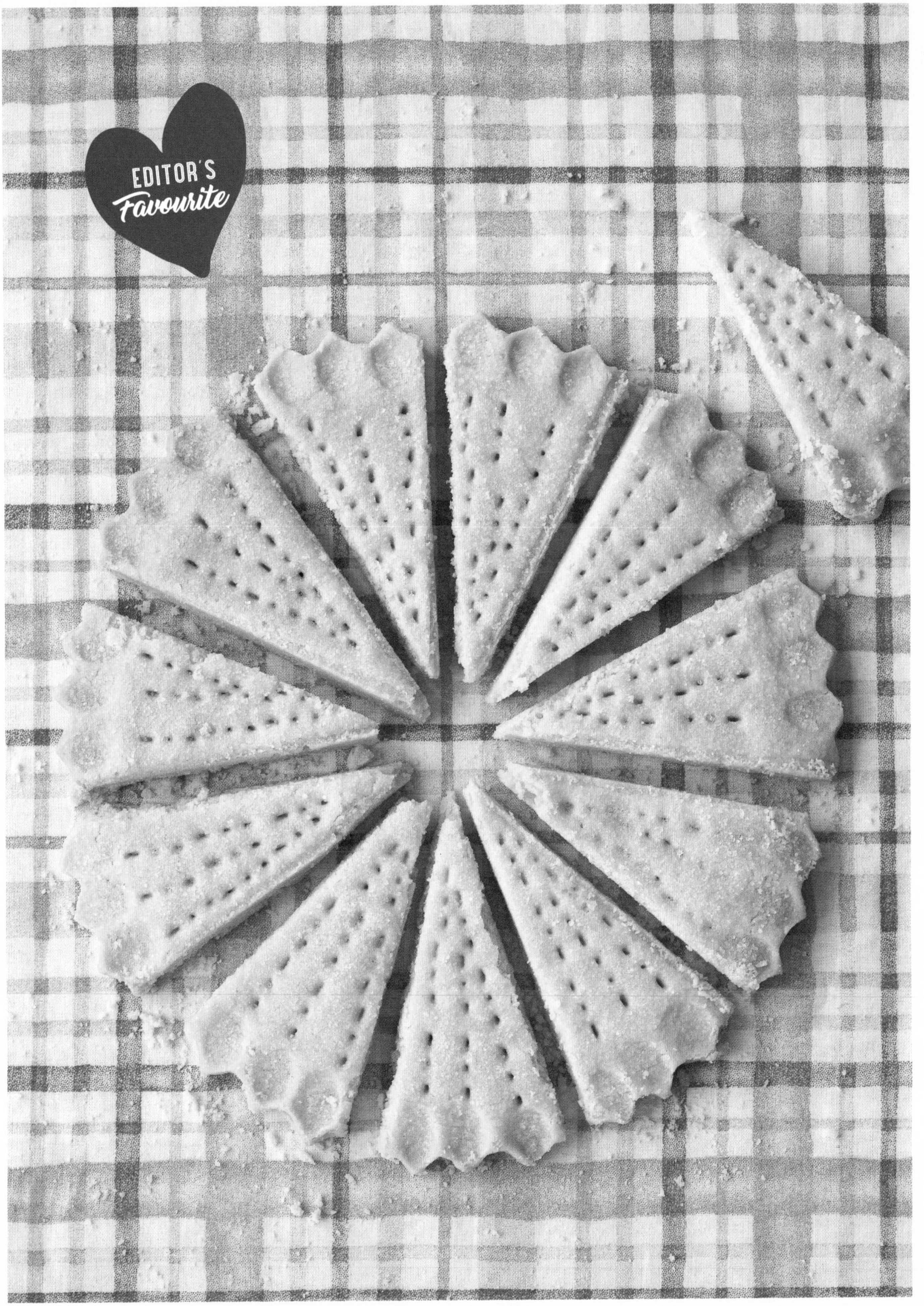
EDITOR'S
Favourite

Honey MUESLI BARS

- ¼ CUP (35G) SESAME SEEDS
- 1 CUP (130G) TOASTED MUESLI
- 3 CUPS (105G) RICE BUBBLES
- ½ CUP (40G) DESICCATED COCONUT
- ¼ CUP (35G) SUNFLOWER SEEDS

- 125G (4 OUNCES) BUTTER, CHOPPED
- ⅓ CUP (115G) HONEY
- ⅓ CUP (95G) PEANUT BUTTER
- ½ CUP (110G) RAW SUGAR

1 Preheat oven to 180°C/350°F. Grease a 20cm x 30cm (8-inch x 12-inch) rectangular pan; line base and long sides with baking paper, extending the paper 5cm (2 inches) above the sides.

2 Place sesame seeds on an oven tray, roast for 5 minutes or until golden; transfer to a large bowl with muesli, rice bubbles, coconut and sunflower seeds and stir until well combined.

3 Stir butter, honey, peanut butter and sugar in a small saucepan over medium heat, without boiling, until butter is melted and sugar is dissolved. Bring to the boil. Reduce heat; simmer, uncovered, without stirring, for 5 minutes. Pour over dry ingredients, stir to combine.

4 Press mixture firmly into pan. Cover; refrigerate until set before cutting into bars.

tip Muesli bars can be stored, covered, in the refrigerator for up to 4 days.

VANILLA BEAN THINS

- 1 VANILLA BEAN
- 30G (1 OUNCE) BUTTER, SOFTENED
- ¼ CUP (55G) CASTER SUGAR (SUPERFINE SUGAR)
- 1 EGG WHITE, BEATEN LIGHTLY
- ¼ CUP (35G) PLAIN FLOUR (ALL-PURPOSE FLOUR)

1 Preheat oven to 200°C/400°F. Grease oven trays; line with baking paper.

2 Split vanilla bean in half lengthways; scrape seeds into a medium bowl, discard pod. Add butter and sugar to the bowl; stir until combined. Stir in egg white and sifted flour.

3 Spoon mixture into a piping bag fitted with a 5mm (¼-inch) plain tube. Pipe 6cm (2½-inch) long strips (making them slightly wider at both ends) onto trays, about 5cm (2 inches) apart.

4 Bake biscuits for 5 minutes or until edges are browned lightly. Cool on trays.

STRAWBERRY CREAM TURKISH DELIGHT FRENCH NOUGAT FRUIT SUNDAE

oy

"Snack"

6 different centres

Mm-m-m make mine..
MAC. ROBERTSON'S

Mac. Robertson
MILK CHOCOLATE
"Snack"

PINEAPPLE CREAM CREAM CARAMEL STRAWBERRY CREAM TURKISH DELIGHT FRENCH NOUGAT

- **6 different centres**
- **12 novelty shaped pieces**
- *just like a box of chocolates*
- *all for only* **2/-**

ANOTHER REASON YOU'LL SAY

Mm-m-m make mine..

MacRobertson's

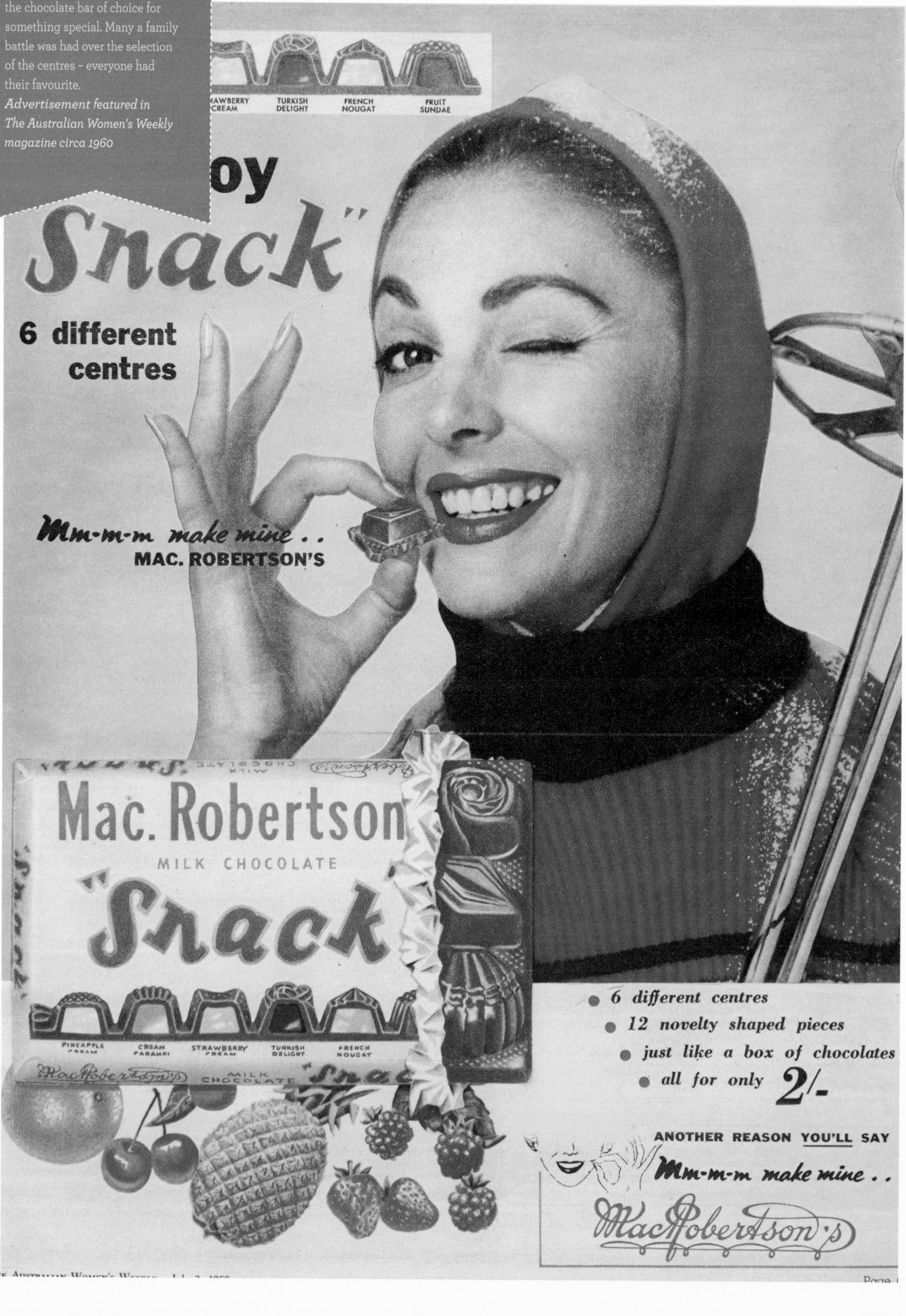

TEST
... KITCHEN ...
Classic

Anzac BISCUITS

- 1 CUP (180G) ROLLED OATS
- 1 CUP (150G) PLAIN FLOUR (ALL-PURPOSE FLOUR)
- 1 CUP (220G) CASTER SUGAR (SUPERFINE SUGAR)
- ¾ CUP (60G) DESICCATED COCONUT
- 125G (4 OUNCES) BUTTER, CHOPPED
- 2 TABLESPOONS GOLDEN SYRUP OR TREACLE
- 1 TEASPOON BICARBONATE OF SODA (BAKING SODA)
- 2 TABLESPOONS BOILING WATER

1 Preheat oven to 150°C/300°F. Grease oven trays.

2 Combine oats, sifted flour, sugar and coconut in a large bowl.

3 Stir butter and syrup in a small saucepan over low heat until butter is melted.

4 Combine soda and water, add to butter mixture; stir into dry ingredients while mixture is warm.

5 Place 3-level-teaspoon portions of mixture onto trays about 4cm (1½ inches) apart; press down lightly on biscuits.

6 Bake biscuits for 20 minutes or until golden brown. Loosen biscuits while warm; cool on trays.

tips It is best to use the traditional oats, not quick-cooking oats, in this recipe.

These biscuits can be stored in an airtight container for up to 1 week.

Honey JUMBLES

- 60G (2 OUNCES) BUTTER
- ½ CUP (110G) FIRMLY PACKED BROWN SUGAR
- ¾ CUP (270G) GOLDEN SYRUP
- 1 EGG, BEATEN LIGHTLY
- 2½ CUPS (375G) PLAIN FLOUR (ALL-PURPOSE FLOUR)
- ½ CUP (75G) SELF-RAISING FLOUR
- ½ TEASPOON BICARBONATE OF SODA (BAKING SODA)
- 1 TEASPOON GROUND CINNAMON
- ½ TEASPOON GROUND CLOVE
- 2 TEASPOONS GROUND GINGER
- 1 TEASPOON MIXED SPICE

ICING

- 1 EGG WHITE
- 1½ CUPS (240G) ICING SUGAR (CONFECTIONERS' SUGAR)
- 2 TEASPOONS PLAIN FLOUR (ALL-PURPOSE FLOUR)
- 1 TABLESPOON LEMON JUICE, APPROXIMATELY
- PINK FOOD COLOURING

1 Preheat oven to 160°C/325°F. Grease oven trays.

2 Stir butter, sugar and syrup in a medium saucepan over low heat until sugar dissolves. Cool for 10 minutes.

3 Transfer cooled mixture to a large bowl; stir in egg and sifted dry ingredients, in two batches. Knead dough on a floured surface until it loses its stickiness. Wrap in plastic wrap; refrigerate for 30 minutes.

4 Divide dough into eight portions. Roll each portion into a 2cm (¾-inch) thick sausage; cut each sausage into five 6cm (2½-inch) lengths. Place on trays about 3cm (1¼ inches) apart; round ends with lightly floured fingers, flatten slightly.

5 Bake biscuits about 15 minutes. Cool on trays.

6 Make icing. Spread cooled jumbles with pink and white icing.

ICING Beat egg white lightly in a small bowl; gradually stir in sifted icing sugar and flour, then enough juice to make icing spreadable. Place half the mixture in another small bowl; tint with pink colouring. Keep icings covered with a damp tea towel while in use.

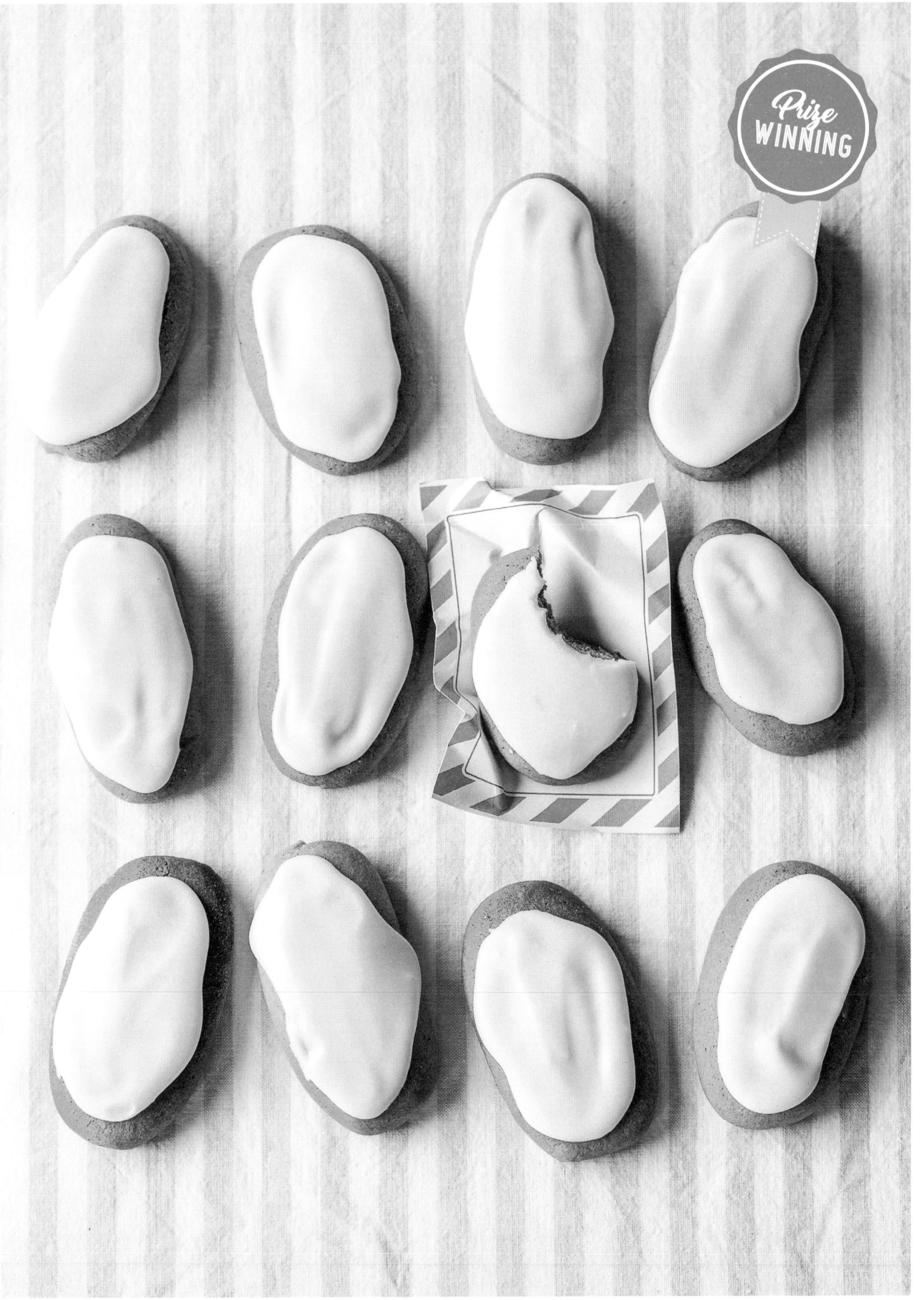
Prize
WINNING

Caramel WALNUT SLICE

- 1 CUP (150G) SELF-RAISING FLOUR
- 1 CUP (80G) DESICCATED COCONUT
- ½ CUP (110G) CASTER SUGAR (SUPERFINE SUGAR)
- 125G (4 OUNCES) BUTTER, MELTED

COCONUT WALNUT TOPPING

- 2 EGGS, BEATEN LIGHTLY
- 1 TEASPOON VANILLA EXTRACT
- 1 CUP (80G) DESICCATED COCONUT
- ¾ CUP (165G) FIRMLY PACKED BROWN SUGAR
- ½ CUP (60G) COARSELY CHOPPED WALNUTS

1 Preheat oven to 180°C/350°F. Grease a 20cm x 30cm (8-inch x 12-inch) rectangular pan; line base and long sides with baking paper, extending the paper 5cm (2 inches) above the sides.

2 Combine sifted flour, coconut and sugar in a medium bowl; stir in butter. Press mixture into pan.

3 Bake base for 15 minutes.

4 Meanwhile, make coconut walnut topping; spread over base.

5 Bake slice for a further 20 minutes. Cool slice in pan before cutting.

COCONUT WALNUT TOPPING

Combine eggs and extract in a medium bowl; stir in coconut, sugar and walnuts.

tip This slice can be stored in an airtight container for up to 4 days.

Honey lemon BISCUITS

- 60G (2 OUNCES) BUTTER
- ¼ CUP (90G) HONEY
- 1 CUP (160G) WHOLEMEAL SELF-RAISING FLOUR
- ¼ CUP (35G) WHITE PLAIN (ALL-PURPOSE FLOUR)
- ½ TEASPOON GROUND CINNAMON
- ½ TEASPOON GROUND GINGER
- ¼ CUP (15G) UNPROCESSED WHEAT BRAN

- 1 TEASPOON WATER, APPROXIMATELY

ICING

- ⅔ CUP (110G) ICING SUGAR (CONFECTIONERS' SUGAR)
- 1 TEASPOON HONEY
- 2 TEASPOONS LEMON JUICE, APPROXIMATELY

1 Preheat oven to 180°C/350°F. Grease oven trays.

2 Beat butter and honey in a small bowl with an electric mixer until smooth. Stir in sifted dry ingredients, bran and enough water to mix to a soft dough.

3 Knead dough on a floured surface until smooth. Roll dough between sheets of baking paper until 3mm (⅛-inch) thick. Using a 5cm (2-inch) round fluted cutter, cut rounds from dough; place on trays about 3cm (1¼ inches) apart.

4 Bake biscuits for 10 minutes or until browned lightly. Leave biscuits on trays for 5 minutes before transferring to wire racks to cool.

5 Make icing. Spread biscuits with icing; leave to set on wire racks.

ICING Sift icing sugar into a small heatproof bowl; stir in honey and enough juice to make a stiff paste. Place bowl over a small saucepan of simmering water; stir until icing is spreadable.

tip Wheat bran is the outer layer of the wheat kernel. It is available from health-food stores.

OVEN MITT

MATERIALS

- **DOUBLE-SIDED IRON-ON APPLIQUÉ WEBBING (VLIESOFIX)**
- **MOTIF FABRIC SUITABLE FOR APPLIQUÉ (FABRIC WITH A REPEATED PATTERN, SUCH AS THE TEAPOT USED HERE; YOU NEED ONE MOTIF PER MITT)**
- **OVEN MITTS**
- **NEEDLE**
- **EMBROIDERY AND COTTON SEWING THREADS**
- **70CM (28-INCH) LENGTH RICK RACK TO MATCH MOTIF FABRIC**

1 Cut Vliesofix slightly larger than the motif and iron it onto the wrong side of the motif fabric. (Vliesofix prevents raw edges from fraying.)

2 Cut out motif, leaving just a small margin of fabric around the motif.

3 Peel off the backing paper; iron the motif onto the mitt. Using a needle and embroidery thread, stitch around the motif edge in running stitch.

4 Measure around the oven mitt; cut rick rack the same length plus a 2cm (¾-inch) overlap. Pin onto mitt; use cotton thread to stitch in place using either running stitch or large tacking stitches.

5 Repeat on the second oven mitt.

STEP 1

Cut a piece of Vliesofix just slightly larger than the motif and iron it onto the wrong side of the motif fabric.

STEP 2

Cut out the motif, leaving just a small margin (about 1cm/½-inch) of fabric around the motif.

STEP 3

Using a needle and embroidery thread, stitch around the motif edge in running stitch to secure to the oven mitt.

STEP 4

Pin the rick rack onto the mitt, then stitch in place with running stitch or large tacking stitches.

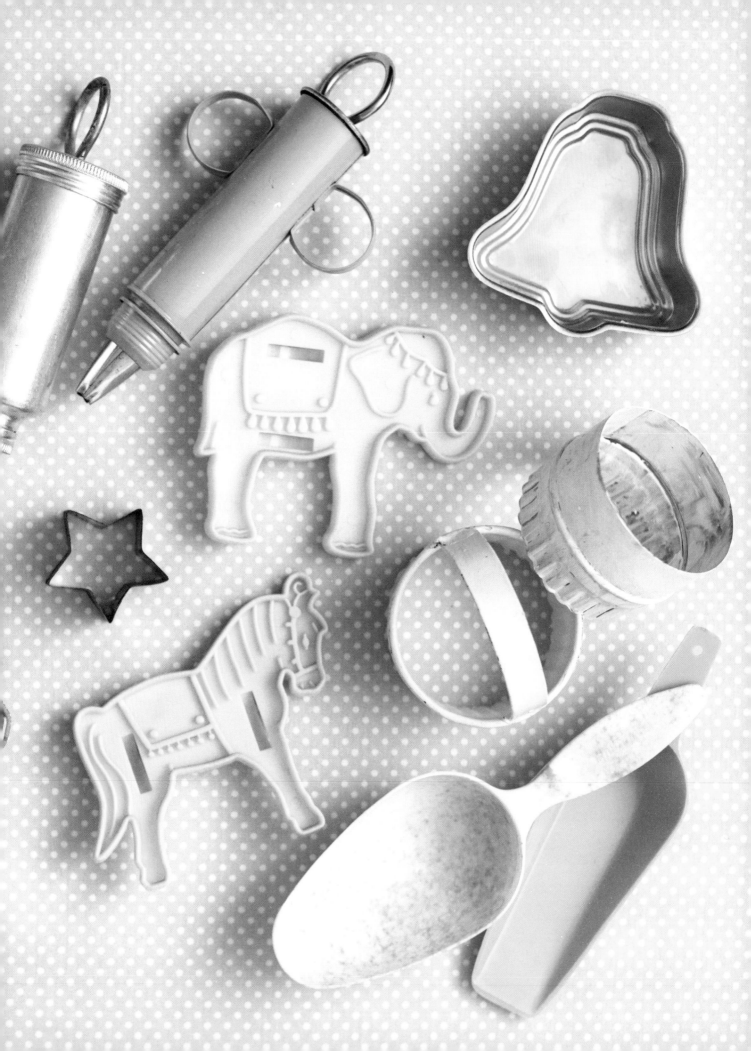

Chocolate WHEATIES

- 90G (3 OUNCES) BUTTER, SOFTENED
- ½ CUP (110G) FIRMLY PACKED BROWN SUGAR
- 1 EGG, BEATEN LIGHTLY
- ¼ CUP (20G) DESICCATED COCONUT
- ¼ CUP (25G) WHEATGERM
- ¾ CUP (120G) WHOLEMEAL PLAIN (ALL-PURPOSE) FLOUR
- ½ CUP (75G) WHITE SELF-RAISING FLOUR
- 150G (4½ OUNCES) DARK (SEMI-SWEET) CHOCOLATE

1 Preheat oven to 180°C/350°F. Grease oven trays.

2 Beat butter and sugar in a small bowl with an electric mixer until smooth. Beat in egg. Stir in coconut, wheatgerm and sifted flours.

3 Roll rounded teaspoons of mixture into balls; place on trays about 3cm (1¼ inches) apart. Flatten with a floured fork.

4 Bake biscuits for 12 minutes or until browned lightly. Cool on trays.

5 Meanwhile, stir chocolate in a small heatproof bowl over a small saucepan of simmering water (don't let the water touch the base of the bowl) until just melted.

6 Dip half of each biscuit in melted chocolate; place on wire racks, leave until set.

tips These biscuits can be stored in an airtight container for up to 1 week.

The 'germ' is the part of the plant that germinates to form the sprout that becomes wheat. It has a nutty flavour and is very oily, which causes it to turn rancid (and is the reason why it is removed during processing of wheat into flour). Wheatgerm is available from health-food stores and most major supermarkets. Store it in the fridge so it doesn't go off.

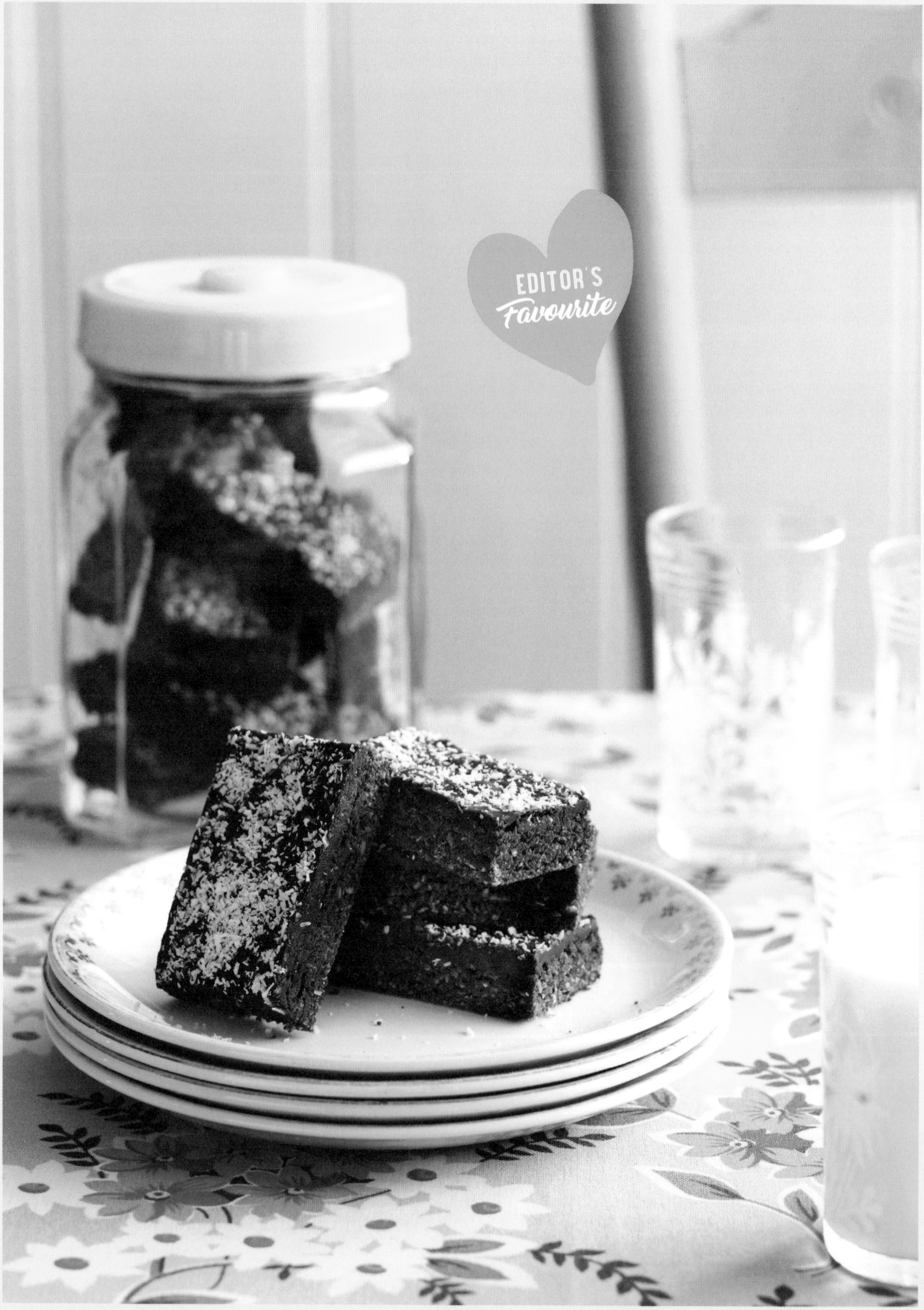
EDITOR'S
Favourite

Chewy CHOCOLATE SLICE

- 125G (4 OUNCES) BUTTER, MELTED
- 1 CUP (220G) FIRMLY PACKED BROWN SUGAR
- 1 EGG, BEATEN LIGHTLY
- 1 TEASPOON VANILLA EXTRACT
- ½ CUP (75G) PLAIN FLOUR (ALL-PURPOSE FLOUR)
- ¼ CUP (35G) SELF-RAISING FLOUR
- 2 TABLESPOONS COCOA POWDER
- ½ CUP (40G) DESICCATED COCONUT
- 1 TABLESPOON DESICCATED COCONUT, EXTRA

CHOCOLATE ICING

- 1 CUP (160G) ICING SUGAR (CONFECTIONERS' SUGAR)
- 2 TABLESPOONS COCOA POWDER
- 10G (½ OUNCE) BUTTER, MELTED
- 1½ TABLESPOONS HOT WATER, APPROXIMATELY

1 Preheat oven to 180°C/350°F. Grease a 20cm x 30cm (8-inch x 12-inch) rectangular pan; line with baking paper, extending the paper 5cm (2 inches) above the sides.

2 Combine butter, sugar, egg and extract in a medium bowl. Stir in sifted flours and cocoa, then coconut. Spread mixture over base of pan.

3 Bake about 30 minutes or until slice is firm.

4 Meanwhile, make chocolate icing.

5 Spread hot slice with chocolate icing; sprinkle with extra coconut. Cool in pan before cutting.

CHOCOLATE ICING Sift icing sugar and cocoa into a medium bowl; stir in combined butter and water until icing is spreadable.

tip Store in an airtight container for up to 1 week.

White chocolate
MACADAMIA COOKIES

- 1½ CUPS (225G) PLAIN FLOUR (ALL-PURPOSE FLOUR)
- ½ TEASPOON BICARBONATE OF SODA (BAKING SODA)
- ¼ CUP (55G) CASTER SUGAR (SUPERFINE SUGAR)
- ⅓ CUP (75G) FIRMLY PACKED BROWN SUGAR
- 125G (4 OUNCES) BUTTER, MELTED
- ½ TEASPOON VANILLA EXTRACT
- 1 EGG
- 180G (6 OUNCES) WHITE CHOC BITS
- ¾ CUP (105G) ROASTED MACADAMIAS, CHOPPED COARSELY

1 Preheat oven to 200°C/400°F. Line two oven trays with baking paper.

2 Sift flour, soda and sugars into a large bowl. Stir in butter, extract and egg, then chocolate and nuts.

3 Drop rounded tablespoons of mixture onto trays, about 5cm (2 inches) apart.

4 Bake cookies about 10 minutes. Cool on trays.

tips To roast macadamias, spread evenly on an oven tray and place in a 180°C/350°F oven for about 5 minutes. You can also stir them in a heavy-based frying pan over low heat. The natural oils will help turn them golden brown.

These cookies can be stored in an airtight container for up to 1 week.

Baking
UP A STORM

PREP + COOK TIME 1¾ HOURS SERVES 12

Mango
COCONUT CAKE

- 250G (8 OUNCES) BUTTER, SOFTENED
- 1 TEASPOON COCONUT ESSENCE
- 1½ CUPS (330G) CASTER SUGAR (SUPERFINE SUGAR)
- 4 EGGS
- ⅔ CUP (160ML) MANGO PUREE
- 2 CUPS (180G) DESICCATED COCONUT
- 2½ CUPS (375G) SELF-RAISING FLOUR
- SHREDDED COCONUT, TO DECORATE

COCONUT FROSTING

- 1 EGG WHITE
- 1¼ CUPS (200G) ICING SUGAR (CONFECTIONERS' SUGAR)
- 2 TEASPOONS MANGO PUREE
- ¾ CUP (65G) DESICCATED COCONUT
- ½ CUP (125G) MASCARPONE CHEESE

1 Preheat oven to 180°C/350°F. Grease a deep 22cm (9-inch) round cake pan; line base with baking paper.
2 Beat butter, essence and sugar in a small bowl with an electric mixer until combined. Add eggs, one at a time, beating only until combined between additions. Transfer mixture to a large bowl. Using a wooden spoon, stir in puree and desiccated coconut, then sifted flour. Spread mixture into pan.
3 Bake cake about 1¼ hours. Leave cake in pan for 5 minutes before turning, top-side up, onto a wire rack to cool.
4 Make coconut frosting.
5 Spread cooled cake with frosting. Just before serving, sprinkle with shredded coconut.

COCONUT FROSTING Beat egg white in a small bowl with an electric mixer until foamy. Gradually beat in sifted icing sugar, 1 tablespoon at a time. Using a fork, mix in puree, coconut and mascarpone. Cover frosting with plastic wrap until required, pressing plastic directly onto the surface to stop it drying out.

EDITOR'S
Favourite

Chocolate caramel SLICE

- 1 CUP (150G) PLAIN FLOUR (ALL-PURPOSE FLOUR)
- ½ CUP (110G) FIRMLY PACKED BROWN SUGAR
- ½ CUP (40G) DESICCATED COCONUT
- 125G (4 OUNCES) BUTTER, MELTED
- 60G (2 OUNCES) BUTTER, EXTRA

- 395G (12½ OUNCES) CANNED SWEETENED CONDENSED MILK
- 2 TABLESPOONS GOLDEN SYRUP OR TREACLE
- 185G (6 OUNCES) DARK (SEMI-SWEET) CHOCOLATE, CHOPPED COARSELY
- 2 TEASPOONS VEGETABLE OIL

1 Preheat oven to 180°C/350°F. Grease a 20cm x 30cm (8-inch x 12-inch) rectangular pan; line base and long sides with baking paper, extending the paper 5cm (2 inches) above the sides.

2 Combine sifted flour, sugar and coconut in a medium bowl; stir in the melted butter. Press mixture firmly over base of pan; bake about 15 minutes. Remove from oven; cool. (Leave oven on.)

3 Place extra butter, condensed milk and syrup in a medium saucepan; stir over low heat until smooth. Pour mixture over cooled base. Bake for 15 minutes or until golden brown. Cool.

4 Place chocolate and oil in a medium heatproof bowl over a medium saucepan of simmering water (make sure the water doesn't touch the base of the bowl); stir until smooth. Spread chocolate mixture over cooled slice. Refrigerate for 30 minutes or until set before cutting with a hot knife.

tip This slice will keep in an airtight container for up to 1 week. If the weather is hot, store the container in the fridge.

MARMALADE & SULTANA CAKE

You need to start this recipe the day before serving.

- 1 CUP (130G) SULTANAS
- 1 CUP (250ML) ORANGE-FLAVOURED LIQUEUR
- 1 LARGE ORANGE (300G)
- 1 CUP (250ML) WATER
- 1½ CUPS (330G) CASTER SUGAR (SUPERFINE SUGAR)
- 185G (6 OUNCES) BUTTER, SOFTENED
- 3 EGGS
- 1 CUP (120G) GROUND ALMONDS
- 1 CUP (150G) PLAIN FLOUR (ALL-PURPOSE FLOUR)
- ½ CUP (75G) SELF-RAISING FLOUR

ORANGE GLAZE

- 3 CUPS (480G) PURE ICING SUGAR (CONFECTIONERS' SUGAR)
- ¼ CUP (60ML) ORANGE JUICE, APPROXIMATELY
- ORANGE FOOD COLOURING

1 Combine sultanas and liqueur in a small bowl. Cover with plastic wrap; stand overnight.

2 Meanwhile, cut unpeeled orange into eight wedges; cut wedges thinly crossways. Place fruit and seeds (if any) in a small bowl with the water. Cover; stand overnight.

3 Transfer orange mixture to a medium saucepan; bring to the boil. Reduce heat; simmer, covered, stirring occasionally, for 40 minutes or until rind is tender.

4 Add sugar to pan; stir over high heat, without boiling, until sugar dissolves. Bring to the boil; boil, uncovered, stirring occasionally, for 20 minutes or until marmalade jells (see tips) when tested.

5 Strain marmalade through a sieve into a small heatproof bowl; reserve marmalade and rind mixtures. Cool.

6 Preheat oven to 150°C/300°F. Grease a 22cm (9-inch) baba or fluted ring pan well; sprinkle with flour, shake out excess.

7 Beat butter and marmalade in a medium bowl with an electric mixer until combined. Beat in eggs, one at a time. Stir in ground almonds, sifted flours, sultana mixture and rind mixture. Spread mixture into pan.

8 Bake cake about 1¼ hours. Leave cake in pan for 5 minutes before turning onto a wire rack to cool.

9 Make orange glaze; drizzle over cooled cake. Decorate with thin strips of orange rind, if you like.

ORANGE GLAZE Sift icing sugar into a medium bowl; stir in enough juice to make a stiff paste. Tint the mixture pale orange. Stir the mixture over a medium saucepan of simmering water until glaze is pourable.

tips For information on testing that jam has jelled, see glossary entry under 'Jelling', page 484.

The iced cake will keep in an airtight container at room temperature for up to 1 week. Uniced, the cake can be frozen for up to 3 months.

Basic WHITE BREAD

- 3 TEASPOONS (10G) DRY YEAST
- 2 TEASPOONS CASTER SUGAR (SUPERFINE SUGAR)
- ⅔ CUP (160ML) WARM WATER
- 2½ CUPS (375G) PLAIN FLOUR (ALL-PURPOSE FLOUR)
- 1 TEASPOON SALT
- 30G (1 OUNCE) BUTTER, MELTED
- ½ CUP (125ML) WARM MILK

1 Whisk yeast, sugar and the water in a small bowl until yeast dissolves. Cover; stand in a warm place for 10 minutes or until mixture is frothy.

2 Sift flour and salt into a large bowl; stir in butter, milk and yeast mixture to form a soft dough. Knead dough on a floured surface for 10 minutes or until dough is smooth and elastic. Place dough into an oiled large bowl. Cover; stand in a warm place for 1 hour or until dough has doubled in size.

3 Preheat oven to 200°C/400°F. Oil a 10cm (4-inch) deep, 9cm x 15cm (3¼-inch x 6-inch) bread tin.

4 Knead dough on a floured surface until smooth. Divide dough in half. Roll each half into a ball; place side-by-side in bread tin. Dust with a little extra flour. Cover; stand in a warm place for 20 minutes or until dough has risen.

5 Bake bread for 45 minutes or until it sounds hollow when tapped. Turn onto a wire rack to cool.

tip Bread can be frozen sliced or as a whole loaf for up to 3 months.

ICE CREAM GÂTEAU

53¹

Victoria sandwich
(Recipe No. 700)
Maraschino or canned
cherries

ice cream
long strips of angelica*
fresh oranges

* Soak angelica in a little warm water to make pliable

Cut centre out of Victoria Sandwich. This can be used
as an ingredient in a trifle or cut into small cakes. Lift on
to serving dish. Spoon a little of the syrup from the
cherries over sponge. Fill centre with ice cream. Decorate
with cherries, angelica leaves and thick half-slices of fresh
orange. Plait strips of angelica to form a handle and put
into position.

YOGHOURT MOULD

53²

½ pint yoghourt
1½ oz. raisins
3 tablespoons sugar
3 oz. mixed glacé fruit
1½ gills water

2 oz. brown sugar
½ oz. gelatine
whipped cream
juice of 1 lemon

Simmer the raisins in ½ pint of the water and 3 tablespoons sugar for about 10 minutes on low heat. Remove
from heat, add the gelatine, softened in ½ gill water, and
stir until the gelatine has thoroughly dissolved. Leave
to cool a little and mix in yoghourt with brown sugar,
half the glacé fruit, chopped finely, and the lemon juice.
When the mixture begins to set, stir just once in order
to prevent the fruit from sinking to the bottom and turn
into a buttered mould. Leave to set and turn out. Decorate with whipped cream and glacé fruit.

Pearls in Oyster

533
Make Victoria Sandwich as Recipe No. 700. When cool fill with cream and halved peaches. Top with cream and broken toasted almonds.

Sponge Mamluk

534
Bake sponge Recipe No. 729 (but using 3 eggs etc.) in fluted mould or ovenproof basin. Soak in Kirsch-flavoured syrup. Decorate with cream and grapes or cherries.

Chocolate Sponge Flan

535
Bake flan as Recipe No. 483. Fill with chocolate blanc-mange with a little cream added. Decorate with toasted almonds.

Paramé Mousse

536
Make lemon jelly using just *under* 1 pint water. Allow to cool and begin to set then whisk in 4 oz. cake crumbs, 1 oz. chopped crystallised ginger and 2 stiffly beaten egg whites. Decorate with crystallised ginger and pistachio nuts.

PATTY CAKES
with glacé icing

- 125G (4 OUNCES) BUTTER, SOFTENED
- ¾ CUP (165G) CASTER SUGAR (SUPERFINE SUGAR)
- 3 EGGS
- ½ TEASPOON VANILLA EXTRACT
- 2 CUPS (300G) SELF-RAISING FLOUR
- ¼ CUP (60ML) MILK
- 12 MARASCHINO CHERRIES

GLACÉ ICING

- 2 CUPS (320G) ICING SUGAR (CONFECTIONERS' SUGAR)
- 20G (¾ OUNCE) BUTTER, MELTED
- 2 TABLESPOONS HOT WATER, APPROXIMATELY
- PINK AND GREEN FOOD COLOURING

1 Preheat oven to 180°C/350°F. Line a 12-hole (⅓-cup/80ml) muffin pan with paper cases.

2 Beat butter, sugar, eggs, extract, flour and milk in a medium bowl with an electric mixer on low speed until ingredients are combined. Increase speed to medium; beat for 3 minutes or until mixture is smooth and paler in colour.

3 Spoon mixture into paper cases. Bake cakes about 25 minutes. Leave cakes in pan for 5 minutes before turning, top-side up, onto a wire rack to cool.

4 Meanwhile, make glacé icing.

5 Spread cooled cakes with icing; top each with a cherry.

GLACÉ ICING Sift icing sugar into a small bowl; stir in butter and enough of the water to make a firm paste. Place bowl over a small saucepan of simmering water; stir until icing is spreadable. Divide icing into two small bowls; tint one pink and the other green.

CAKE VARIATIONS

BERRY & ORANGE Stir 1 teaspoon finely grated orange rind and ½ cup dried mixed berries into the mixture at the end of step 2.

CITRUS Stir in ½ teaspoon each of finely grated lime, orange and lemon rind at the end of step 2.

PASSIONFRUIT & WHITE CHOCOLATE Stir in ½ cup white Choc Bits and ¼ cup passionfruit pulp at the end of step 2.

GLACÉ ICING VARIATIONS

COCONUT & LIME Stir in ½ teaspoon coconut essence and 1 teaspoon finely grated lime rind. Omit the food colouring.

ORANGE Stir in 1 teaspoon finely grated orange rind. Replace half the hot water with orange juice. Omit the food colouring.

PASSIONFRUIT Stir 1 tablespoon passionfruit pulp into the icing mixture. Omit the food colouring.

Caramel BUTTER CAKE

- 125G (4 OUNCES) BUTTER, SOFTENED
- 1 CUP (220G) FIRMLY PACKED BROWN SUGAR
- 1 TEASPOON VANILLA EXTRACT
- 2 EGGS
- 1 TABLESPOON GOLDEN SYRUP OR TREACLE
- 1 CUP (150G) PLAIN FLOUR (ALL-PURPOSE FLOUR)
- ½ CUP (75G) SELF-RAISING FLOUR
- 1 TEASPOON GROUND CINNAMON
- ½ CUP (125ML) MILK

CARAMEL ICING

- 1½ CUPS (330G) FIRMLY PACKED BROWN SUGAR
- 90G (3 OUNCES) BUTTER
- 2½ TABLESPOONS MILK
- 1¼ CUPS (200G) ICING SUGAR (CONFECTIONERS' SUGAR)
- 2 TEASPOONS MILK, EXTRA

1 Preheat oven to 180°C/350°F. Grease a deep 20cm (8-inch) round cake pan; line base with baking paper.

2 Beat butter, sugar and extract in a small bowl with an electric mixer until light and fluffy. Beat in eggs and golden syrup. Stir in sifted flours and cinnamon, and milk in two batches. Spread mixture into pan.

3 Bake cake about 50 minutes. Leave cake in pan for 5 minutes before turning, top-side up, onto a wire rack to cool.

4 Make caramel icing. Spread icing on cold cake before serving.

CARAMEL ICING Heat brown sugar, butter and milk in a small saucepan, stirring constantly, over medium heat, without boiling, until sugar dissolves. Bring to the boil. Reduce heat; simmer, uncovered, for 3 minutes without stirring. Remove pan from heat; stir in sifted icing sugar until combined. Stir in extra milk until icing is of a spreadable consistency.

tip This cake will keep in an airtight container for up to 3 days. The uniced cake can be frozen for up to 3 months.

CHOC BROWNIES
with sour cream frosting

- 125G (4 OUNCES) BUTTER, CHOPPED
- 185G (6 OUNCES) DARK (SEMI-SWEET) CHOCOLATE, CHOPPED COARSELY
- 1 CUP (220G) CASTER SUGAR (SUPERFINE SUGAR)
- 2 TEASPOONS VANILLA EXTRACT
- 2 EGGS, BEATEN LIGHTLY
- 1 CUP (150G) PLAIN FLOUR (ALL-PURPOSE FLOUR)
- ½ CUP (60G) COARSELY CHOPPED PECANS

SOUR CREAM FROSTING

- 100G (3 OUNCES) DARK (SEMI-SWEET) CHOCOLATE, CHOPPED COARSELY
- ¼ CUP (60G) SOUR CREAM

1 Preheat oven to 180°C/350°F. Grease a deep 19cm (8-inch) square cake pan; line base with baking paper.

2 Stir butter and chocolate in a small saucepan over low heat until melted. Transfer mixture to a large bowl; stir in sugar and extract, then egg, sifted flour and nuts. Pour mixture into pan.

3 Bake brownie about 30 minutes. Cool brownie in pan.

4 Make sour cream frosting.

5 Turn brownie out of pan; top with frosting. Refrigerate until set before cutting into pieces.

SOUR CREAM FROSTING Melt chocolate in a small heatproof bowl over a small saucepan of simmering water (make sure the water doesn't touch the base of the bowl). Add sour cream; stir constantly until mixture is smooth and glossy.

tip Store brownies, covered, in the refrigerator for up to 4 days.

Prize
WINNING

Traditional DAMPER

Damper is an iconic Australian bread substitute. It was created by early settlers as they travelled west and fresh bread wasn't available.

- 3½ CUPS (525G) SELF-RAISING FLOUR
- 1 TEASPOON SALT
- 2 TEASPOONS CASTER SUGAR (SUPERFINE SUGAR)
- 40G (1½ OUNCES) BUTTER
- ½ CUP (125ML) MILK
- 1¼ CUPS (310ML) WATER, APPROXIMATELY

1 Preheat oven to 200°C/400°F. Grease an oven tray.

2 Sift flour, salt and sugar into a large bowl; rub in butter with your fingertips. Stir in milk and enough of the water to form a sticky dough. Knead dough on a floured surface until just smooth.

3 Place dough on oven tray; press into a 16cm (6½-inch) round. Cut a cross into top of dough, about 1cm (½ inch) deep. Brush dough with a little extra milk; sprinkle with a little extra flour.

4 Bake damper about 45 minutes. Transfer, top-side up, onto a wire rack to cool.

tip Damper is best eaten warm on the day it is made, as it doesn't keep well.

serving suggestion Butter and golden syrup.

Berry & rhubarb MINI PIES

- 2 CUPS (220G) COARSELY CHOPPED RHUBARB
- ¼ CUP (55G) CASTER SUGAR (SUPERFINE SUGAR)
- 2 TABLESPOONS WATER
- 1 TABLESPOON CORNFLOUR (CORNSTARCH)
- 2 CUPS (300G) FROZEN MIXED BERRIES
- 1 EGG, BEATEN LIGHTLY
- 2 TEASPOONS DEMERARA SUGAR

PASTRY
- 1⅔ CUPS (250G) PLAIN FLOUR (ALL-PURPOSE FLOUR)
- ⅓ CUP (75G) CASTER SUGAR (SUPERFINE SUGAR)
- 150G (4½ OUNCES) COLD BUTTER, CHOPPED COARSELY
- 1 EGG YOLK
- 2 TEASPOONS WATER

1 Make pastry.

2 Place rhubarb, caster sugar and half the water in a medium saucepan; bring to the boil. Reduce heat; simmer, covered, for 3 minutes or until rhubarb is tender. Blend cornflour with the remaining water; stir into rhubarb mixture. Stir over heat until mixture boils and thickens. Remove from heat; stir in berries. Cool.

3 Grease six ¾-cup (180ml) pie tins (top measure 12.5cm/5 inches). Roll two-thirds of the pastry between sheets of baking paper until 4mm (¼ inch) thick. Cut out 6 x 12cm (4¾-inch) rounds; press rounds into base and side of tins. Refrigerate for 30 minutes.

4 Preheat oven to 200°C/400°F.

5 Roll remaining pastry between sheets of baking paper until 4mm (¼ inch) thick; cut out 6 x 9cm (3¾-inch) rounds.

6 Spoon cooled fruit mixture into pastry cases. Brush edge of 9cm (3¾-inch) rounds with a little of the egg; place over filling. Press edges firmly to seal. Brush tops with a little more egg; sprinkle with demerara sugar. (See pages 344-345 for decorating ideas.)

7 Bake pies about 30 minutes. Leave in tins for 10 minutes. Using a palette knife, loosen pies from edge of tin before lifting out. Serve warm with vanilla ice-cream, or custard, if you like.

PASTRY Process flour, sugar and butter until crumbly. Add egg yolk and the water; process until combined. Knead on a floured surface until smooth. Wrap dough in plastic wrap; refrigerate for 30 minutes.

tips You need 4 large stems of rhubarb for this recipe. If you don't have pie tins, you could use a 6-hole (¾-cup/180ml) texas muffin pan instead.

Decorating PIES

With these top decorating ideas, your pies will always look spectacular.

CUT-OUTS

Cutting shapes out of pastry not only looks good it also allows steam to escape from the pie. Using any size and shape of cookie cutter you like, dip the cutter in flour; shake off excess and cut out the shapes from shortcrust or puff pastry before the pastry is placed over the filling. Crimp the edge of the pie with a fork to seal.

LATTICE TOP

Using a floured pastry wheel, cut shortcrust pastry into narrow strips. Without stretching the pastry, 'weave' the pastry strips directly over the pie filling; trim the edge, and brush with a little water to hold the lattice strips in position. If you don't have a pastry wheel, cutting the pastry with a sharp knife looks just as good.

BEADED EDGE

Using a floured 2.5cm (1-inch) round cutter, cut out
enough rounds from shortcrust pastry to cover the edge
of the pie. Brush a little water on the edge of the pie,
then position each round on the pie edge, overlapping
slightly, until the edge is covered.

TWISTED SPIRAL TOP

Using a floured pastry wheel (or sharp knife if you don't
have one), cut narrow strips of shortcrust pastry. Position
strips on the pie in a zigzag pattern; brush the pie edge
with water to secure the strips.

Classic POUND CAKE

- 250G (8 OUNCES) BUTTER, SOFTENED
- 1 CUP (220G) CASTER SUGAR (SUPERFINE SUGAR)
- 1 TEASPOON VANILLA EXTRACT
- 4 EGGS
- ½ CUP (75G) SELF-RAISING FLOUR
- 1 CUP (150G) PLAIN FLOUR (ALL-PURPOSE FLOUR)
- 2 TEASPOONS ICING SUGAR (CONFECTIONERS' SUGAR)

1 Preheat oven to 180°C/350°F. Grease a deep 20cm (8-inch) round cake pan; line base with baking paper.

2 Beat butter, caster sugar and extract in a small bowl with an electric mixer until light and fluffy. Beat in eggs, one at a time. Transfer mixture to a large bowl; fold in sifted flours, in two batches. Spread mixture into pan.

3 Bake cake about 1 hour. Leave cake in pan for 5 minutes before turning, top-side up, onto a wire rack to cool. Dust cold cake with sifted icing sugar to serve.

serving suggestion Strawberries and whipped cream.

Lemon & poppy seed FRIANDS

- 6 EGG WHITES
- 2 TEASPOONS FINELY GRATED LEMON RIND
- 1 TABLESPOON POPPY SEEDS
- 185G (6 OUNCES) BUTTER, MELTED
- 1 CUP (120G) GROUND ALMONDS
- 1½ CUPS (240G) ICING SUGAR (CONFECTIONERS' SUGAR)
- ½ CUP (75G) PLAIN FLOUR (ALL-PURPOSE FLOUR)
- 1 TEASPOON ICING SUGAR (CONFECTIONERS' SUGAR), EXTRA

1 Preheat oven to 200°C/400°F. Grease 12 x ½-cup (125ml) oval friand pans and place on an oven tray (or grease a 12-hole (⅓-cup/80ml) muffin pan).

2 Lightly whisk egg whites in a medium bowl with a fork until combined. Add rind, seeds, butter, ground almonds and sifted icing sugar and flour; using a wooden spoon, stir until just combined. Spoon mixture into pans.

3 Bake friands about 25 minutes. Leave friands in pan for 5 minutes before turning, top-side up, onto a wire rack. Serve friands warm or at room temperature, dusted with extra sifted icing sugar.

tips You could use orange rind instead of the lemon, or use a mix of both.

Friands are at their best made on the day of serving, but can be stored in an airtight container for 2 days, or frozen for up to 3 months.

Frozen friands can be thawed, individually wrapped in foil, in a 180°C/350°F oven for about 15 minutes, or in a microwave oven, wrapped in plastic wrap, on HIGH (100%) for about 30 seconds.

HOT CROSS BUNS

- 4 TEASPOONS (14G) DRY YEAST
- ¼ CUP (55G) CASTER SUGAR (SUPERFINE SUGAR)
- 1½ CUPS (375ML) WARM MILK
- 4 CUPS (600G) PLAIN FLOUR (ALL-PURPOSE FLOUR)
- 1 TEASPOON MIXED SPICE
- ½ TEASPOON GROUND CINNAMON
- 60G (2 OUNCES) BUTTER
- 1 EGG
- ¾ CUP (120G) SULTANAS

FLOUR PASTE

- ½ CUP (75G) PLAIN FLOUR (ALL-PURPOSE FLOUR)
- 2 TEASPOONS CASTER SUGAR (SUPERFINE SUGAR)
- ⅓ CUP (80ML) WATER, APPROXIMATELY

GLAZE

- 1 TABLESPOON CASTER SUGAR (SUPERFINE SUGAR)
- 1 TEASPOON POWDERED GELATINE
- 1 TABLESPOON WATER

1 Whisk yeast, sugar and milk in a small bowl until yeast dissolves. Cover; stand in a warm place for 10 minutes or until mixture is frothy.

2 Sift flour and spices into a large bowl; rub in butter. Stir in yeast mixture, egg and sultanas; mix to a soft, sticky dough. Cover; stand in a warm place for 45 minutes or until dough has doubled in size.

3 Grease a deep 22cm (9-inch) square cake pan.

4 Knead dough on a floured surface for 5 minutes or until smooth and elastic. Divide dough into 16 equal pieces; knead into balls. Place balls into pan, cover; stand in a warm place for 10 minutes or until buns have risen two-thirds of the way up the pan.

5 Preheat oven to 220°C/425°F.

6 Make flour paste; place in a piping bag fitted with a small plain tube. Pipe crosses on buns.

7 Bake buns for 30 minutes or until they sound hollow when tapped. Turn buns, top-side up, onto a wire rack.

8 Meanwhile, make glaze; brush hot glaze onto hot buns. Cool.

FLOUR PASTE Combine flour and the sugar in a small bowl. Gradually blend in enough of the water to form a smooth firm paste.

GLAZE Stir ingredients in a small saucepan over heat, without boiling, until sugar and gelatine are dissolved.

tips Hot cross buns are best made on the day of serving. Freeze the unglazed buns for up to 3 months.

TEST
KITCHEN
Classic

Mixed berry MUFFINS

- 2½ CUPS (375G) SELF-RAISING FLOUR
- 100G (3 OUNCES) BUTTER, CHOPPED COARSELY
- 1 CUP (220G) CASTER SUGAR (SUPERFINE SUGAR)
- 1¼ CUPS (310ML) BUTTERMILK
- 1 EGG, BEATEN LIGHTLY
- 1⅓ CUPS (200G) FROZEN MIXED BERRIES

1 Preheat oven to 200°C/400°F. Line a 12-hole (⅓-cup/80ml) muffin pan with paper cases.

2 Sift flour into a large bowl; rub in butter. Stir in sugar, buttermilk and egg. Do not over-mix; mixture should be lumpy. Stir in berries. Spoon mixture into pan holes.

3 Bake muffins about 20 minutes. Leave muffins in pan for 5 minutes before turning, top-side up, onto a wire rack to cool. Dust with sifted icing sugar (confectioners' sugar) before serving, if you like.

VARIATION

MANGO BUTTERMILK Replace the berries with 1 small mango (300g), chopped finely.

tips Don't thaw the frozen berries before using as they will bleed colour into the muffin batter. This recipe works well with any frozen or fresh berries.

These muffins can be stored in an airtight container for up to 2 days.

Café-style BANANA BREAD

You need about two large over-ripe bananas (460g) to get the amount of mashed banana needed here.

- 1 CUP MASHED BANANA
- 1 CUP (220G) FIRMLY PACKED DARK BROWN SUGAR
- 2 EGGS
- 40G (1½ OUNCES) BUTTER, MELTED
- ½ CUP (125ML) BUTTERMILK
- ¼ CUP (90G) TREACLE
- 1½ CUPS (225G) PLAIN FLOUR (ALL-PURPOSE FLOUR)
- 1 CUP (150G) SELF-RAISING FLOUR
- 2 TEASPOONS MIXED SPICE
- 1 TEASPOON BICARBONATE OF SODA (BAKING SODA)

1 Preheat oven to 180°C/350°F. Grease a 14cm x 21cm (5½ inch x 8½ inch) loaf pan; line base with baking paper, extending the paper 5cm (2 inches) above the sides.

2 Combine banana, sugar, eggs, butter, buttermilk and treacle in a large bowl; stir in sifted dry ingredients. Spoon mixture into pan.

3 Bake bread about 1 hour. Leave bread in pan for 10 minutes before turning, top-side up, onto a wire rack to cool.

tips It is important the bananas are over-ripe; if they are under-ripe, the cake will be too heavy.

Dark brown sugar, though not essential to the bread's success, does improve the bread's flavour and colour.

You can use golden syrup or honey instead of the treacle, but treacle will produce the best colour and flavour. Don't over-mix the batter; lumpy is good in this case.

Serve the bread as it is, or toasted with butter.

Chocolate heart CUPCAKES

- 1 CUP (150G) SELF-RAISING FLOUR
- ½ CUP (75G) PLAIN FLOUR (ALL-PURPOSE FLOUR)
- ⅓ CUP (35G) COCOA POWDER
- ¾ CUP (165G) CASTER SUGAR (SUPERFINE SUGAR)
- 185G (6 OUNCES) BUTTER, SOFTENED
- 3 EGGS
- ½ CUP (125ML) MILK
- 1 TABLESPOON ICING SUGAR (CONFECTIONERS' SUGAR)

RASPBERRY FROSTING

- 40G (1½ OUNCES) BUTTER, SOFTENED
- ¼ CUP (40G) FROZEN RASPBERRIES, THAWED
- 1 CUP (160G) ICING SUGAR (CONFECTIONERS' SUGAR)

1 Preheat oven to 180°C/350°F. Line a 12-hole (⅓-cup/80ml) muffin pan with paper cases.

2 Sift flours and cocoa into a large bowl of an electric mixer, add caster sugar, butter, eggs and milk; beat on low speed until combined. Increase speed to medium; beat until mixture is smooth and has changed to a paler colour. Drop ¼ cups of mixture into paper cases.

3 Bake cupcakes about 20 minutes. Leave cakes in pan for 5 minutes before turning, top-side up, onto a wire rack to cool.

4 Make raspberry frosting.

5 Carefully cut the tops off cold cupcakes. Using a 4cm (1½-inch) heart-shaped cutter, cut heart shapes from cake tops; reserve cake tops. Dust heart shapes with sifted icing sugar.

6 Spread 2 teaspoons of raspberry frosting over each cake. Replace cake tops, then top with hearts, using picture as a guide.

RASPBERRY FROSTING

Process ingredients until smooth.

tips You need a 4cm (1½-inch) heart-shaped cutter.

Uniced cakes can be made a day ahead or frozen for up to 3 months. Ice cakes on the day of serving.

BLUEBERRY CAKE
with vanilla syrup

- 125G (4 OUNCES) BUTTER, SOFTENED
- ½ CUP (110G) CASTER SUGAR (SUPERFINE SUGAR)
- 2 EGGS
- 1¾ CUPS (260G) SELF-RAISING FLOUR
- ½ CUP (125ML) BUTTERMILK
- ¾ CUP (110G) FROZEN BLUEBERRIES (SEE TIP)

VANILLA SYRUP

- ½ CUP (110G) CASTER SUGAR (SUPERFINE SUGAR)
- ½ CUP (125ML) WATER
- 2 TEASPOONS VANILLA EXTRACT

1 Preheat oven to 180°C/350°F. Grease a deep 20cm (8-inch) ring pan well; line base and side with baking paper.

2 Beat butter and sugar in a small bowl with an electric mixer until light and fluffy. Beat in eggs, one at a time. Stir in flour and buttermilk, in two batches. Spread mixture into pan. Sprinkle with frozen berries, gently pressing into cake mixture.

3 Bake cake about 45 minutes. Leave cake in pan for 5 minutes before turning, top-side up, onto a wire rack over a tray.

4 Meanwhile, make vanilla syrup.

5 Drizzle hot syrup over hot cake.

VANILLA SYRUP Stir sugar and water in a small saucepan over medium heat, without boiling, until sugar dissolves. Simmer, uncovered, without stirring, for 2 minutes. Stir in extract.

tip Don't thaw frozen blueberries before using as they will bleed colour into the cake batter.

Isn't it gorgeous?

The polka dot cake you make so easily with Puffin Cake Mix!

"Everyone loves layer cake! Make it specially delicious and gay with colourful chocolate buttons!" says *Betty King*
Home Economist of World Brands

This is the kind of cake you'll be proud to bring in — a high-rising, light, rich-flavoured layer cake that stays deliciously fresh to the very last slice. You make it in minutes — without weighing, creaming or tiring beating. Only *one* bowl needed. With Puffin Cake Mix, all the *hard* work has been done for you before you open the pack!

From packet to oven in minutes with this recipe!
You just add eggs and milk to Puffin Cake Mix, and bake. Then sandwich those fine, moist-textured layers with your favourite icing and frost all over. (Four easy frostings to choose from, on the pack!) Now, press those little chocolate buttons all over (we've used Cadbury's Dairy Milk Rolls). Finished! Quickest cake you've ever made!

Special ingredients in Puffin guarantee success.
You see, Puffin contains special soft flour and enriched shortening you can't buy in any other way. These ingredients are blended accurately and smoothly with fine cane sugar and a special raising ingredient to guarantee you a gorgeous cake — or double your money back!

On cake mix box: **Puffin Cake Mix** — JUST ADD EGGS AND MILK — YOU'LL MAKE A PERFECT CAKE — *NOW Easier than ever to make!*

Golden! Light!

Scones more delicious than ever before with New Puffin Scone Mix!

Just add milk to new Puffin Scone Mix — then mix and bake. Fifteen minutes later you're looking at the highest, lightest, most handsome scones you've ever baked! *No more weighing, sifting, measuring or rubbing in the shortening.*

All the work — gone forever! Puffin Scones are made with such little effort, you'll never stop being amazed.

Puffin Scone Mix makes many other delicious recipes, too. Pikelets, pancakes, rock cakes, savoury pinwheels and tea-cakes . . . they're but a few of the delicious variety of recipes you'll make so easily and quickly with Puffin Scone Mix. All the recipes are right on the Puffin packet.

Double-money-back guarantee
— so try Puffin soon as you like.

On scone mix box: **Puffin Scone Mix** — YOU MAKE TWO DOZEN GOLDEN, LIGHT SCONES

Featherlight SPONGE

If you like, fill the sponge with your own homemade berry jam, page 245. You can serve the sponge without the icing, if you prefer; top with the fresh berries just before serving.

- **4 EGGS**
- **¾ CUP (165G) CASTER SUGAR (SUPERFINE SUGAR)**
- **⅔ CUP (150G) WHEATEN CORNFLOUR (CORNSTARCH)**
- **¼ CUP (30G) CUSTARD POWDER**
- **1 TEASPOON CREAM OF TARTAR**
- **½ TEASPOON BICARBONATE OF SODA (BAKING SODA)**
- **300ML THICKENED (HEAVY) CREAM**
- **1 TEASPOON VANILLA EXTRACT**
- **¼ CUP (80G) STRAWBERRY JAM**
- **250G (8 OUNCES) STRAWBERRIES, SLICED THINLY**
- **125G (4 OUNCES) STRAWBERRIES, EXTRA, HALVED**

ICING

- **1 CUP (160G) ICING SUGAR (CONFECTIONERS' SUGAR)**
- **10G (½ OUNCE) BUTTER, SOFTENED**
- **1½ TABLESPOONS MILK, APPROXIMATELY**

1 Preheat oven to 200°C/400°F. Grease and flour two deep 22cm (9-inch) round cake pans; shake out excess flour.

2 Beat eggs and sugar in a small bowl with an electric mixer for 7 minutes or until thick and creamy (see tips). Transfer mixture to a large bowl.

3 Sift dry ingredients twice onto a piece of baking paper. Sift flour mixture a third time evenly onto egg mixture. Using a balloon whisk or a large metal spoon, quickly and lightly fold flour mixture through egg mixture until incorporated. Pour mixture evenly into pans; tilt pans to spread mixture to the edge. Tap the sponge on the base of the pan with your fingers to remove any large air pockets.

4 Bake sponges about 20 minutes. Turn sponges immediately, top-side up, onto baking paper-covered wire racks. Cool.

5 Beat cream and extract in a small bowl with an electric mixer until firm peaks form.

6 Place one cooled sponge on a cake stand or plate, spread with jam and cream, then top with the sliced strawberries.

7 Make icing.

8 Place remaining sponge on a wire rack; spread with warm icing. Position icing-topped sponge on other sponge. Stand for 15 minutes or until icing is set. Top with halved strawberries; dust with a little icing sugar, if you like.

ICING Sift icing sugar into a medium heatproof bowl; stir in butter and enough milk to form a firm paste. (Add the milk gradually, as just a small amount can alter the consistency.) Place the bowl over a medium saucepan of simmering water; stir until icing is of a pouring consistency.

tips Use a small bowl when beating the eggs and sugar in step 2 to maximise the volume. To test if the mixture is thick and creamy, turn off mixer, then lift the beaters – the mixture should form thick ribbons.

This recipe is best made on the day of serving. The sponge can be filled several hours ahead.

HUMMINGBIRD CAKE

- 450G (14½ OUNCES) CANNED CRUSHED PINEAPPLE IN SYRUP
- 1 CUP (150G) PLAIN FLOUR (ALL-PURPOSE FLOUR)
- ½ CUP (75G) SELF-RAISING FLOUR
- ½ TEASPOON BICARBONATE OF SODA (BAKING SODA)
- ½ TEASPOON GROUND CINNAMON
- ½ TEASPOON GROUND GINGER
- 1 CUP (220G) FIRMLY PACKED BROWN SUGAR
- ½ CUP (40G) DESICCATED COCONUT
- 1 CUP MASHED BANANA (SEE TIP)
- 2 EGGS, BEATEN LIGHTLY
- ¾ CUP (180ML) VEGETABLE OIL

PINEAPPLE IN SYRUP

- 2 TABLESPOONS CASTER SUGAR (SUPERFINE SUGAR)
- ½ CUP (125ML) WATER
- 1 SMALL PINEAPPLE (900G), PEELED, HALVED, SLICED THINLY

CREAM CHEESE FROSTING

- 60G (2 OUNCES) BUTTER, SOFTENED
- 120G (4 OUNCES) CREAM CHEESE, SOFTENED
- 2 TEASPOONS VANILLA EXTRACT
- 3 CUPS (480G) ICING SUGAR (CONFECTIONERS' SUGAR)

1 Make pineapple in syrup.

2 Preheat oven to 180°C/350°F. Grease a deep 23cm (9-inch) square cake pan; line base with baking paper.

3 Drain pineapple over a medium bowl, pressing with a spoon to extract as much syrup as possible. Reserve ¼ cup of the syrup.

4 Sift flours, soda, spices and sugar into a large bowl. Stir in drained pineapple, reserved syrup, coconut, banana, egg and oil. Pour mixture into pan.

5 Bake cake about 40 minutes. Leave cake in pan for 5 minutes before turning, top-side up, onto a wire rack to cool.

6 Make cream cheese frosting; spread cooled cake with frosting. Top with pineapple slices and a little syrup.

PINEAPPLE IN SYRUP Stir sugar and the water in a small saucepan over medium heat, without boiling, until sugar dissolves. Bring to the boil; reduce heat to a simmer (do not stir). Add pineapple, in batches; cook, without stirring, for 4 minutes or until softened. Transfer to a plate to cool. Repeat with the remaining pineapple. Reserve syrup.

CREAM CHEESE FROSTING Beat butter, cream cheese and extract in a small bowl with an electric mixer until light and fluffy. Gradually beat in sifted icing sugar.

tip You need about two large over-ripe bananas (460g) to get the amount of mashed banana needed here.

Rich dark FRUIT LOAF

- 1 CUP (160G) SULTANAS
- ½ CUP (75G) DRIED CURRANTS
- ¾ CUP (110G) COARSELY CHOPPED DRIED APRICOTS
- 1½ CUPS (250G) SEEDED DRIED DATES, HALVED
- 1 CUP (250ML) WARM WATER
- 2 TEASPOONS (7G) DRY YEAST
- ¼ CUP (60ML) WARM WATER, EXTRA
- ½ CUP (75G) WHITE PLAIN (ALL-PURPOSE) FLOUR

- ½ CUP (80G) WHOLEMEAL PLAIN (ALL-PURPOSE FLOUR)
- 1½ CUPS (225G) RYE FLOUR
- 2 TEASPOONS GROUND CINNAMON
- ½ TEASPOON GROUND CARDAMOM
- ½ TEASPOON GROUND CLOVES
- ½ TEASPOON GROUND NUTMEG
- 2 TEASPOONS POPPY SEEDS

1 Combine dried fruit and the water in a medium bowl. Cover; stand for 30 minutes.

2 Combine yeast, extra water and 1 teaspoon of the white plain flour in a small bowl. Cover; stand in a warm place for 10 minutes or until frothy.

3 Sift remaining flours and spices into a large bowl; add husks left in the sifter to the mixture. Stir in undrained fruit mixture and yeast mixture; mix to a sticky dough. Knead dough on a floured surface for 5 minutes. Place dough in a large oiled bowl. Cover; stand in a warm place for 1 hour or until risen slightly.

4 Grease an oven tray. Knead dough on a floured surface for 5 minutes. Shape dough into a 15cm (6-inch) round, place on tray. Cover; stand in a warm place for 40 minutes or until risen slightly.

5 Meanwhile, preheat oven to 200°C/400°F.

6 Brush top of dough with water, then sprinkle with seeds; cover loosely with foil. Bake bread for 30 minutes; remove foil. Reduce oven temperature to 180°C/350°F; bake for a further 1¼ hours or until bread sounds hollow when tapped. (Cover bread loosely with foil if over-browning.) Turn bread, top-side up, onto a wire rack to cool.

TEA TOWEL APRON

MATERIALS

- LARGE TEA TOWEL, ABOUT 70CM (28 INCHES) IN LENGTH
- SEWING COTTON AND NEEDLE
- 2.2M (2¼ YARDS) COTTON TAPE
- 4 LARGE BUTTONS (PLAIN OR COVERED)

1 Measure 39cm (16 inches) up from bottom corner on each side of the tea towel; mark with a pin. From this point, evenly fold in both sides of the tea towel until the top edge measures 16cm (6½ inches) wide. Iron, then cut off excess fabric, leaving a 2cm border on each side.

2 Press a double hem under on both sides to match the existing hems on the tea towel and stitch in place with a slipstitch or small running stitch.

3 Cut a 60cm (24-inch) length of cotton tape; turn the raw edges under and stitch to the top corners of the apron to form the neck strap.

4 Cut the remaining tape in half and stitch on either side at waist level. Sew on a button at the four tape points.

STEP 1
Measure 39cm up from bottom of tea towel; fold in sides so the top is 16cm wide. Cut excess fabric, leaving a 2cm border.

STEP 2
Press a double hem on both sides to match the existing hems on the tea towel. Stitch in place using running stitch.

STEP 3
Cut a length of cotton tape; turn the raw edges under and stitch to top corners of the apron to form the neck strap.

STEP 4
Cut the remaining tape in half and stitch on either side at waist level for ties. Sew on the buttons at the four tape points.

Mixed grain LOAF

- ¼ CUP (45G) CRACKED BUCKWHEAT
- ½ CUP (80G) BURGHUL
- ¼ CUP (50G) KIBBLED RYE
- 3 TEASPOONS (10G) DRY YEAST
- 1 TEASPOON WHITE SUGAR (GRANULATED SUGAR)
- ¾ CUP (180ML) WARM MILK
- ¼ CUP (60ML) WARM WATER
- 2¼ CUPS (335G) WHITE PLAIN (ALL-PURPOSE) FLOUR
- ½ CUP (80G) WHOLEMEAL PLAIN (ALL-PURPOSE) FLOUR
- 1 TEASPOON SALT
- 1 TABLESPOON LINSEEDS
- 2 TEASPOONS OLIVE OIL
- 1 EGG YOLK
- 1 TEASPOON MILK, EXTRA
- 2 TEASPOONS SESAME SEEDS
- 2 TEASPOONS CRACKED BUCKWHEAT, EXTRA

1 Place buckwheat, burghul and rye in a small heatproof bowl; cover with boiling water. Cover bowl, stand for 30 minutes. Rinse well, drain well.

2 Combine yeast, sugar, milk and water in a small bowl. Cover; stand in a warm place for 10 minutes or until frothy. Sift flours and salt into a large bowl; add grain mixture and linseeds. Stir in oil and yeast mixture; mix to a soft dough.

3 Knead dough on a floured surface for 10 minutes or until dough is smooth and elastic. Place dough in a large greased bowl. Cover; stand in a warm place for 1 hour or until doubled in size.

4 Grease a 14cm x 21cm (5½-inch x 8-inch) loaf pan. Knead dough on a floured surface until smooth. Place dough in pan. Cover; stand in a warm place for 30 minutes or until well risen.

5 Meanwhile, preheat oven to 200°C/400°F.

6 Brush dough with combined egg yolk and extra milk, sprinkle with combined sesame seeds and extra cracked buckwheat.

7 Bake bread about 45 minutes. Turn bread, top-side up, onto a wire rack to cool.

Bacon & fresh herb MUFFINS

- 6 RINDLESS BACON SLICES (480G), CHOPPED FINELY
- 3 CUPS (450G) SELF-RAISING FLOUR
- 60G (2 OUNCES) BUTTER, CHOPPED
- 1 TABLESPOON COARSELY CHOPPED FRESH BASIL
- 2 TABLESPOONS COARSELY CHOPPED FRESH CHIVES
- 2 TEASPOONS COARSELY CHOPPED FRESH OREGANO
- ¾ CUP (60G) GRATED PARMESAN
- 2 EGGS, BEATEN LIGHTLY
- 1 CUP (250ML) MILK

1 Preheat oven to 200°C/400°F. Grease 18 holes of two 12-hole (⅓-cup/80ml) muffin pans.

2 Cook bacon in a small frying pan until crisp. Drain on absorbent paper towel.

3 Place flour in a large bowl; rub in butter. Add bacon, herbs and cheese, then combined eggs and milk; mix with a fork until just combined (mixture should be coarse and lumpy). Spoon mixture into pan holes.

4 Bake muffins about 20 minutes. Serve warm or cooled.

tip Muffins can be kept in an airtight container for 2 days or frozen for up to 2 months.

TEST
KITCHEN
Classic

Cut-and-keep BUTTER CAKE

- 125G (4 OUNCES) BUTTER, SOFTENED
- 1 TEASPOON VANILLA EXTRACT
- 1¼ CUPS (275G) CASTER SUGAR (SUPERFINE SUGAR)
- 3 EGGS
- 1 CUP (150G) PLAIN FLOUR (ALL-PURPOSE FLOUR)
- ½ CUP (75G) SELF-RAISING FLOUR
- ¼ TEASPOON BICARBONATE OF SODA (BAKING SODA)
- ½ CUP (125ML) MILK

1 Preheat oven to 180°C/350°F. Grease a deep 20cm (8-inch) round cake pan; line base with baking paper.

2 Beat ingredients in a medium bowl with an electric mixer on low speed until just combined. Increase speed to medium; beat for 3 minutes or until mixture is smooth and paler in colour. Spread mixture into pan.

3 Bake cake about 1¼ hours. Leave cake in pan for 5 minutes before turning, top-side up, onto a wire rack to cool. Serve dusted with sifted icing sugar (confectioners' sugar), if you like.

tip Store butter cake in an airtight container at room temperature for up to 2 days, or freeze for up to 2 months.

COTTEE'S REAL FRUIT JELLIES WITH THE *Locked in* FLAVOUR

Cottee's STRAWBERRY FRUIT JELLY TABLET

STRAWBERRY FRUIT JELLY TABLET "SEE THE FRUIT IN IT"

Strawberry Fruit Mould is fun to make and luscious to eat! Make up 1 packet of Cottee's Strawberry Jelly, as directed. Pour some of jelly (to a depth of about 1") in a wetted mould. When cool, but not set, arrange slices of peaches (or fruit in season) in this jelly and allow to set.

Here in each individually sealed cellophane cube is the real flavour of plump red strawberries . . . LOCKED IN until you are ready to release it! You'll actually see the fragments of strawberries as you savour the tantalising, fresh-fruit aroma. Once you've tried any of these Cottee's real fruit jellies, you'll never, never be content with any other STRAWBERRY, FRUIT SALAD, ORANGE, RASPBERRY, PINEAPPLE and a special favourite, LIME COOLA — they are all delicious.

Snow Tops are exciting and so easy. Make up a packet of Cottee's Lime Coola Jelly. Divide in two. Pour half into serving dishes to set and let the remainder stand until cold and beginning to "jell." Stir in one well-mashed ripe banana. Whip till thick and frothy and pile onto plain jelly. Chill before you serve—then watch the smiles.

Jelly Gems are real favourites. Make up two packets of Cottee's Jellies (different flavours). When set, chop into small particles and arrange in serving dishes. Top with cream or custard.

Strawberry Ice Cream. Combine in a small saucepan ½ a Cottee's Strawberry Jelly, 2 tablespoons sugar, ¾ measuring cup hot or cold water. Stir over a moderate heat till dissolved. Stir in ⅓ measuring cup Cottee's Strawberry Topping and a rounded teaspoon thinly grated lemon rind. Chill 1½ measuring cups Carnation Milk till ice crystals form. Whip till thick and fluffy with rotary beater or electric mixer. Beat in the cooled jelly mixture. Freeze quickly till firm.

Cottee's REAL FRUIT JELLIES

BY THE MAKERS OF THE WORLD-FAMOUS PASSIONA

71/FP.70

Coffee caramel CAKES

- 125G (4 OUNCES) BUTTER, SOFTENED
- ⅔ CUP (150G) FIRMLY PACKED BROWN SUGAR
- 2 TABLESPOONS INSTANT COFFEE GRANULES
- 1 TABLESPOON BOILING WATER
- 2 EGGS
- 2 CUPS (300G) SELF-RAISING FLOUR
- ½ CUP (125ML) MILK
- 18 (130G) JERSEY CARAMELS, HALVED

COFFEE CREAM

- 1 TABLESPOON INSTANT COFFEE GRANULES
- 1 TABLESPOON HOT WATER
- 1 CUP (250ML) THICKENED (HEAVY) CREAM

1 Preheat oven to 180°C/350°F. Grease a 12-hole (⅓-cup/80ml) muffin pan.

2 Beat butter and sugar in a small bowl with an electric mixer until light and fluffy. Add combined coffee and the water, then beat in eggs, one at a time. Transfer mixture to a large bowl.

3 Stir in sifted flour and milk, in two batches. Spoon mixture into pan. Press 3 caramel halves into centre of each cake, making sure they are covered with batter.

4 Bake cakes about 20 minutes. Leave cakes in pan for 5 minutes before turning, top-side up, onto a wire rack to cool.

5 Make coffee cream. Fit piping bag with a 2cm (¾ inch) fluted tube. Pipe coffee cream in swirls onto cooled cakes.

COFFEE CREAM Combine coffee and the water in a small bowl; cool. Whip coffee mixture and cream in a small bowl with an electric mixer until soft peaks form.

tips Cakes are best made on the day of serving. Uniced cakes are suitable to freeze for up to a month.

Coffee cream can simply be spread onto the cakes if you don't have a piping bag and tube.

Jersey caramels are delicious square bite-sized confections consisting of two layers of sweetened condensed milk caramel sandwiching a layer of white fondant. They is available from most supermarkets.

Mini banana BLUEBERRY CAKES

- 125G (4 OUNCES) BUTTER, CHOPPED
- ½ CUP (125ML) MILK
- 2 EGGS
- 1 CUP (220G) CASTER SUGAR (SUPERFINE SUGAR)
- ½ CUP MASHED BANANA

- 1½ CUPS (225G) SELF-RAISING FLOUR
- 1 CUP (150G) FROZEN BLUEBERRIES
- 1 TABLESPOON ICING SUGAR (CONFECTIONERS' SUGAR)

1 Preheat oven to 180°C/350°F. Grease two 12-hole (⅓-cup/80ml) muffin pans.

2 Place butter and milk in a small saucepan; stir over low heat until butter melts. Cool to room temperature.

3 Beat eggs in a small bowl with an electric mixer until thick and creamy. Gradually add sugar, beating until dissolved after each addition; stir in banana. Fold in flour and cooled butter mixture, in two batches. Spoon mixture into pan holes.

4 Bake cakes 10 minutes. Remove pan from oven; press frozen blueberries into tops of cakes. Bake cakes for a further 10 minutes. Leave cakes in pan for 5 minutes before turning, top-side up, onto wire racks to cool. Just before serving, dust with sifted icing sugar.

tips You will need 1 large over-ripe banana (230g) for the amount of mashed banana required in this recipe. Don't thaw frozen berries before using as they will bleed colour into the cake batter. Cakes can be stored in an airtight container for up to 3 days. Cakes are suitable to freeze for up to 1 month.

Irish SODA BREAD

- 2½ CUPS (375G) WHITE PLAIN (ALL-PURPOSE) FLOUR
- 2⅔ CUPS (420G) WHOLEMEAL PLAIN (ALL-PURPOSE) FLOUR
- 1 TEASPOON SALT
- 1 TEASPOON BICARBONATE OF SODA (BAKING SODA)
- 2¾ CUPS (680ML) BUTTERMILK, APPROXIMATELY

1 Preheat oven to 180°C/350°F. Grease an oven tray.

2 Sift flours, salt and soda into a large bowl; add any wholemeal husks from the sieve to the bowl. Stir in enough of the buttermilk to make a firm dough. Knead dough on a floured surface until just smooth.

3 Shape dough into a 20cm (8-inch) round; place on tray. Using a sharp knife, cut a cross into top of dough, about 1cm (½ inch) deep.

4 Bake bread about 50 minutes. Transfer, top-side up, onto a wire rack to cool.

serving suggestions Serve with butter and jam.

EDITOR'S
Favourite

BASIC SCONES

- 2½ CUPS (375G) SELF-RAISING FLOUR
- 1 TABLESPOON CASTER SUGAR (SUPERFINE SUGAR)
- ¼ TEASPOON SALT
- 30G (1 OUNCE) BUTTER, SOFTENED
- ¾ CUP (180ML) MILK
- ½ CUP (125ML) WATER, APPROXIMATELY
- YOUR FAVOURITE JAM OR CURD AND WHIPPED CREAM, TO SERVE

1 Preheat oven to 220°C/425°F. Grease a deep 19cm (8-inch) square cake pan.

2 Sift flour, sugar and salt into a large bowl; rub in butter with your fingertips. Make a well in centre of flour mixture; add milk and almost all of the water. Use a knife to cut the liquid through the flour mixture to form a soft, sticky dough. Add remaining water if needed. Knead dough on a floured surface until smooth.

3 Press dough out evenly into a 2cm (¾-inch) thickness. Using a 6cm (2½-inch) cutter, cut as many rounds as you can from the dough. Place the scones, just touching, in pan.

4 Gently knead scraps of dough together. Cut out more rounds; place in pan. Brush scones with a little extra milk.

5 Bake scones for 20 minutes or until browned and they sound hollow when tapped firmly on the top with your fingers.

tips Scones can be stored in an airtight container for up to 2 days. Add a further homemade touch by serving the scones with the berry jam, on page 245, or one of the curd butters on page 267.

VARIATION

DATE SCONES When making the basic scone mixture, stir ¾ cup (120g) finely chopped seeded dried dates into the flour mixture after the butter has been rubbed in. Replace milk and the water with 1¼ cups (310ml) buttermilk.

BANANA CAKE
with passionfruit icing

You need about two large over-ripe bananas (460g) to get the amount of mashed banana needed here.

- 125G (4 OUNCES) BUTTER, SOFTENED
- ¾ CUP (165G) FIRMLY PACKED BROWN SUGAR
- 2 EGGS
- 1½ CUPS (225G) SELF-RAISING FLOUR
- ½ TEASPOON BICARBONATE OF SODA (BAKING SODA)
- 1 TEASPOON MIXED SPICE
- 1 CUP MASHED BANANA
- ½ CUP (120G) SOUR CREAM
- ¼ CUP (60ML) MILK

PASSIONFRUIT ICING

- 1½ CUPS (240G) ICING SUGAR (CONFECTIONERS' SUGAR)
- 1 TEASPOON SOFTENED BUTTER
- 2 TABLESPOONS PASSIONFRUIT PULP, APPROXIMATELY

1 Preheat oven to 180°C/350°F. Grease a 15cm x 25cm (6-inch x 10-inch) loaf pan; line base with baking paper.

2 Beat butter and sugar in a small bowl with an electric mixer until light and fluffy. Beat in eggs, one at a time. Transfer mixture to a large bowl; stir in sifted dry ingredients, then banana, sour cream and milk. Spread mixture into pan.

3 Bake cake about 50 minutes. Leave cake in pan for 5 minutes before turning, top-side up, onto a wire rack to cool.

4 Make passionfruit icing. Spread cooled cake with icing.

PASSIONFRUIT ICING Sift icing sugar into a medium heatproof bowl; stir in butter and enough pulp to make a firm paste. Stir over a medium saucepan of simmering water until icing is of a spreading consistency, taking care not to overheat; use icing immediately.

tips It's important the bananas are over-ripe; if they are under-ripe, the cake will be too heavy.
The cake will keep for up to 3 days in an airtight container. Uniced cake can be frozen for up to 3 months.

Colour galore CUPCAKES

- 125G (4 OUNCES) BUTTER, CHOPPED
- 75G (2½ OUNCES) WHITE CHOCOLATE, CHOPPED COARSELY
- 1 CUP (220G) CASTER SUGAR (SUPERFINE SUGAR)
- ½ CUP (125ML) MILK
- ½ CUP (75G) PLAIN FLOUR (ALL-PURPOSE FLOUR)
- ½ CUP (75G) SELF-RAISING FLOUR
- 1 EGG

FLUFFY MOCK CREAM

- 2 TABLESPOONS MILK
- ⅓ CUP (80ML) WATER
- 1 CUP (220G) CASTER SUGAR (SUPERFINE SUGAR)
- 1 TEASPOON POWDERED GELATINE
- 2 TABLESPOONS WATER, EXTRA
- 250G (8 OUNCES) BUTTER, SOFTENED
- ½ TEASPOON VANILLA EXTRACT

DECORATIONS

- SMALL PURPLE, ORANGE, YELLOW AND PINK LOLLIES
- PURPLE, ORANGE, YELLOW AND PINK THIN BIRTHDAY CANDLES

1 Preheat oven to 160°C/325°F. Line a 12-hole (⅓-cup/80ml) muffin pan with paper cases.

2 Stir butter, chocolate, sugar and milk in a small saucepan over low heat until smooth. Transfer mixture to a medium bowl; cool 15 minutes.

3 Whisk sifted flours into chocolate mixture, then whisk in egg. Drop ¼-cups of mixture into paper cases.

4 Bake cakes about 30 minutes. Leave cakes in pan for 5 minutes before turning, top-side up, onto a wire rack to cool.

5 Make fluffy mock cream; spoon into a large piping bag fitted with a large fluted tube. Pipe a large star on top of cooled cakes.

6 Top mock cream with mounds of similar-coloured lollies and candles.

FLUFFY MOCK CREAM

Combine milk, the water and sugar in a small saucepan; stir over low heat, without boiling, until sugar is dissolved. Sprinkle gelatine over extra water in a cup, stand for 5 minutes to absorb the water then add to pan; stir syrup until gelatine is dissolved. Cool mixture to room temperature. Beat butter and extract in a small bowl with an electric mixer until as white as possible. While motor is operating, gradually pour in the cold syrup; beat until light and fluffy. The mixture will thicken on standing.

tip We used jubes, small jelly beans, mentos and bo-peeps, but you can use any lollies you like.

FRUIT & NUT CAKE

- ½ CUP (115G) COARSELY CHOPPED GLACÉ PINEAPPLE
- ½ CUP (125G) COARSELY CHOPPED GLACÉ APRICOTS
- 1½ CUPS (250G) SEEDED DRIED DATES
- ½ CUP (110G) RED GLACÉ CHERRIES
- ½ CUP (110G) GREEN GLACÉ CHERRIES
- 1 CUP (170G) BRAZIL NUTS
- ½ CUP (75G) MACADAMIA NUTS
- 2 EGGS
- ½ CUP (110G) FIRMLY PACKED BROWN SUGAR
- 1 TABLESPOON DARK RUM
- 100G (3 OUNCES) BUTTER, MELTED
- ⅓ CUP (50G) PLAIN FLOUR (ALL-PURPOSE FLOUR)
- ¼ CUP (35G) SELF-RAISING FLOUR

FRUIT AND NUT TOPPING

- ⅓ CUP (75G) COARSELY CHOPPED GLACÉ PINEAPPLE
- ¼ CUP (55G) RED GLACÉ CHERRIES, HALVED
- ¼ CUP (55G) GREEN GLACÉ CHERRIES, HALVED
- ¼ CUP (40G) BRAZIL NUTS
- ¼ CUP (35G) MACADAMIA NUTS

TOFFEE TOPPING

- ½ CUP (110G) CASTER SUGAR (SUPERFINE SUGAR)
- ¼ CUP (60ML) WATER

1 Preheat oven to 150°C/300°F. Grease a 20cm (8-inch) ring pan; line with baking paper, extending paper 5cm (2-inches) above the side.

2 Combine fruit and nuts in a large bowl.

3 Beat eggs and sugar in a small bowl with an electric mixer until thick. Add rum, butter and sifted flours; beat until just combined. Stir egg mixture into fruit and nut mixture. Press mixture firmly into pan.

4 Make fruit and nut topping. Gently press topping evenly over cake top.

5 Bake cake, covered, for 1 hour. Uncover; bake a further 45 minutes. Leave cake in pan for 10 minutes.

6 Meanwhile, make toffee topping. Turn cake, top-side up, onto a wire rack set over an oven tray; drizzle with toffee topping.

FRUIT AND NUT TOPPING Combine ingredients in a medium bowl.

TOFFEE TOPPING Combine ingredients in a small saucepan, stir over heat, without boiling, until sugar dissolves; bring to the boil. Reduce heat; simmer, uncovered, without stirring, about 10 minutes or until mixture is a golden colour. Remove from heat; stand until bubbles subside before using.

WHEATMEAL ROLLS

- 1¼ CUPS (185G) WHITE SELF-RAISING FLOUR
- 1¼ CUPS (200G) WHOLEMEAL SELF-RAISING FLOUR
- 2 TEASPOONS WHITE SUGAR (GRANULATED SUGAR)
- 1 TEASPOON SALT
- 60G (2 OUNCES) BUTTER, CHOPPED
- ¼ CUP (45G) COARSE-GROUND WHEATMEAL
- ¾ CUP (180ML) MILK, APPROXIMATELY
- 1 EGG YOLK
- 1 TABLESPOON MILK, EXTRA

ROLL TOPPINGS

- ½ TEASPOON WHOLEMEAL PLAIN (ALL-PURPOSE) FLOUR
- ½ TEASPOON FINE SEA SALT
- ½ TEASPOON DRIED MIXED HERBS
- ½ TEASPOON POPPY SEEDS
- ½ TEASPOON SESAME SEEDS
- ½ TEASPOON CARAWAY SEEDS

1 Preheat oven to 200°C/400°F. Lightly grease two oven trays.

2 Sift flours, sugar and salt into a large bowl; rub in butter with your fingertips. Stir in wheatmeal and enough milk to make a soft dough. Knead dough on a floured surface until smooth.

3 Divide dough into 12 portions. Knead each portion until smooth. Place one roll in the centre of each tray, and position five rolls, almost touching, around the centre roll.

4 Brush rolls with combined egg yolk and extra milk. Sprinkle one roll on each tray with ¼ teaspoon of one of the roll toppings, not repeating a topping on the same tray; each batch of rolls should have all the different toppings.

5 Bake rolls for 20 minutes or until browned and rolls sound hollow when tapped on the base.

tip Wheatmeal is the whole grain (it can be wheat or rye, etc), crushed and ground to a specific size. It is available in most health-food stores.

PARIS BREST

- ½ CUP (125ML) WATER
- 60G (2 OUNCES) BUTTER, CHOPPED FINELY
- 1 TABLESPOON CASTER SUGAR (SUPERFINE SUGAR)
- ½ CUP (75G) BAKER'S FLOUR
- 3 EGGS
- 2 TABLESPOONS FLAKED ALMONDS
- 1 TABLESPOON ICING SUGAR (CONFECTIONERS' SUGAR)

PRALINE CREAM

- ⅓ CUP (75G) CASTER SUGAR (SUPERFINE SUGAR)
- 2 TABLESPOONS WATER
- ⅓ CUP (25G) FLAKED ALMONDS, TOASTED
- 2 CUPS (500ML) THICKENED (HEAVY) CREAM

1 Preheat oven to 220°C/425°F. Grease oven trays.

2 To make choux pastry, combine the water, butter and caster sugar in a medium saucepan; bring to the boil. Add flour; beat with a wooden spoon over medium heat until mixture comes away from the base of the pan. Transfer pastry to a medium bowl; stand for 1 minute, then beat in two of the eggs, one at a time. Whisk remaining egg with a fork; beat enough of the egg into the pastry until it becomes smooth and glossy but still holds its shape.

3 Spoon pastry into a piping bag fitted with a 1.5cm (¾-inch) fluted tube; pipe 5.5cm (2¼-inch) rings, about 5cm (2 inches) apart, on trays. Sprinkle with nuts.

4 Bake for 10 minutes. Reduce oven temperature to 180°C/350°F; bake for a further 15 minutes. Using a serrated knife, split rings in half, remove any soft centres; return rings to trays, bake for a further 5 minutes or until puffs are dry. Cool on trays.

5 Meanwhile, make praline cream. Spread cream into cooled pastry bases; top with pastry tops. Dust with sifted icing sugar.

PRALINE CREAM Line an oven tray with baking paper. Stir sugar and the water in a small saucepan over high heat, without boiling, until sugar dissolves. Bring to the boil. Boil, uncovered, without stirring, until golden brown. Allow bubbles to subside, then add nuts; do not stir. Pour mixture onto tray; leave praline to set at room temperature. Beat cream in a small bowl with an electric mixer until soft peaks form. Break praline into pieces, then process until fine; fold into whipped cream.

tip To toast nuts, place nuts, in a single layer, in a small dry frying pan; cook, over low heat, stirring often, until nuts are fragrant and just changed in colour. Remove nuts immediately from pan.

Banana date MUFFINS

You need about two large over-ripe bananas (460g) to get the amount of mashed banana needed here.

- 2 CUPS (300G) SELF-RAISING FLOUR
- 1 TEASPOON MIXED SPICE
- ½ CUP (110G) FIRMLY PACKED BROWN SUGAR
- 1 CUP MASHED BANANA
- 1 CUP (160G) COARSELY CHOPPED SEEDED DATES
- 3 EGGS, BEATEN LIGHTLY
- ⅓ CUP (80ML) VEGETABLE OIL
- ⅓ CUP (80ML) BUTTERMILK

1 Preheat oven to 200°C/400°F. Grease a 12-hole (⅓-cup/80ml) muffin pan.

2 Stir ingredients in a large bowl until just combined; do not over-mix. Spoon mixture into pan holes.

3 Bake muffins about 20 minutes. Leave muffins in pan for 5 minutes before turning, top-side up, onto a wire rack to cool. Serve muffins warm or cooled.

tip These muffins can be stored in an airtight container for up to 2 days.

EDITOR'S
Favourite

PECAN SOUR CREAM CAKE

- 250G (8 OUNCES) BUTTER, SOFTENED
- 1 TEASPOON VANILLA EXTRACT
- ¾ CUP (165G) CASTER SUGAR (SUPERFINE SUGAR)
- 2 EGGS
- 300G (9½ OUNCES) SOUR CREAM
- 1½ CUPS (225G) PLAIN FLOUR (ALL-PURPOSE FLOUR)
- ½ CUP (75G) SELF-RAISING FLOUR

- 1 TEASPOON BICARBONATE OF SODA (BAKING SODA)
- ½ CUP (60G) FINELY CHOPPED PECANS
- 2 TABLESPOONS BROWN SUGAR
- ½ TEASPOON GROUND CINNAMON

1 Preheat oven to 180°C/350°F. Grease a deep 23cm (9-inch) round cake pan; line base with baking paper.

2 Beat butter, extract and sugar in a small bowl with an electric mixer until light and fluffy. Beat in eggs, one at a time. Transfer mixture to a large bowl; stir in sour cream, then sifted flours and soda.

3 Combine nuts, brown sugar and cinnamon in a small bowl.

4 Spread half the cake mixture over base of pan; sprinkle evenly with half the pecan mixture. Spread remaining cake mixture on top; sprinkle with remaining pecan mixture, pressing gently into the cake mixture.

5 Bake cake about 1 hour. Leave cake in pan for 5 minutes before turning, top-side up, onto a wire rack to cool.

Raspberry COCONUT SLICE

- 90G (3 OUNCES) BUTTER, SOFTENED
- ½ CUP (110G) CASTER SUGAR (SUPERFINE SUGAR)
- 1 EGG
- ⅓ CUP (50G) SELF-RAISING FLOUR
- ⅔ CUP (100G) PLAIN FLOUR (ALL-PURPOSE FLOUR)
- ½ CUP (160G) RASPBERRY JAM

COCONUT TOPPING

- 2 EGGS
- ⅓ CUP (75G) CASTER SUGAR (SUPERFINE SUGAR)
- 2 CUPS (160G) DESICCATED COCONUT

1 Preheat oven to 180°C/350°F. Grease a 20cm x 30cm (8-inch x 12-inch) rectangular pan; line base and long sides with baking paper, extending the paper 5cm (2 inches) above the sides.

2 Beat butter, sugar and egg in a small bowl with an electric mixer until light and fluffy. Stir in sifted flours, in two batches. Spread mixture over base of pan; spread jam evenly over mixture.

3 Make coconut topping; spread evenly over jam.

4 Bake slice for about 35 minutes. Cool in pan. Cut cooled slice into rectangles to serve.

COCONUT TOPPING Whisk eggs lightly with a fork in a medium bowl; stir in sugar and coconut.

VARIATION
APRICOT AND ALMOND

Replace raspberry jam with apricot jam. In the topping, replace 1 cup of the desiccated coconut with ground almonds.

Caramel apple PULL-APART

- 2 CUPS (300G) SELF-RAISING FLOUR
- 30G (1 OUNCE) BUTTER, CHOPPED
- 1 CUP (250ML) MILK, APPROXIMATELY
- ⅓ CUP (65G) FIRMLY PACKED BROWN SUGAR
- 400G (12½ OUNCES) CANNED PIE APPLES
- PINCH GROUND NUTMEG
- ½ TEASPOON GROUND CINNAMON
- 2 TABLESPOONS COARSELY CHOPPED ROASTED PECANS

CARAMEL TOPPING

- ¼ CUP (60ML) POURING CREAM
- 20G (¾ OUNCE) BUTTER
- ½ CUP (110G) FIRMLY PACKED BROWN SUGAR

1 Preheat oven to 200°C/400°F. Grease a deep 22cm (9-inch) round cake pan.

2 Sift flour into a medium bowl; rub in butter with fingertips. Make a well in centre of flour mixture; add enough milk to mix to a soft, sticky dough. Knead dough on a floured surface until smooth.

3 Roll dough on floured baking paper into a 21cm x 40cm (8-inch x 16-inch) rectangle. Sprinkle dough with sugar, spread with combined apple and spices leaving a 3cm (1-inch) border around long edge. Using paper as a guide, roll dough up from long side like a swiss roll. Use a floured serrated knife to cut roll into 12 slices. Place 11 slices upright around edge of pan; place remaining slice in the centre.

4 Bake pull-apart about 25 minutes or until golden brown in colour. Stand in pan for 5 minutes before turning, top-side up, onto a wire rack.

5 Meanwhile, make caramel topping.

6 Brush hot pull-apart evenly with hot caramel; sprinkle with nuts.

CARAMEL TOPPING Place ingredients in a small saucepan; stir constantly over heat, without boiling, until sugar is dissolved. Simmer, uncovered, without stirring, about 3 minutes or until mixture is thickened slightly.

ROCK CAKES

- 2 CUPS (300G) SELF-RAISING FLOUR
- ¼ TEASPOON GROUND CINNAMON
- ⅓ CUP (75G) CASTER SUGAR (SUPERFINE SUGAR)
- 90G (3 OUNCES) BUTTER, CHOPPED

- 1 CUP (160G) SULTANAS
- 1 EGG
- ½ CUP (125ML) MILK
- 1 TABLESPOON CASTER SUGAR (SUPERFINE SUGAR), EXTRA

1 Preheat oven to 200°C/400°F. Grease oven trays.

2 Sift flour, cinnamon and sugar into a medium bowl; rub in butter with your fingertips. Stir in sultanas, egg and milk. Do not over mix.

3 Drop rounded tablespoons of mixture onto trays about 5cm (2 inches) apart; sprinkle with extra sugar.

4 Bake cakes about 15 minutes. Cool on trays.

tip Rock cakes are not scones, but they are related. Don't overcook the rock cakes as they firm up as they cool. When they look brown and firm-ish, give one a gentle push and, if it slides on the oven tray, they're all done.

EDITOR'S
Favourite

Cinnamon DOUGHNUTS

You need an 8cm (3-inch) round cutter and a 2.5cm (1-inch) round cutter to make these doughnuts.

- 3 TEASPOONS (10G) DRY YEAST
- ¼ CUP (60ML) LUKEWARM WATER
- 80G (2½ OUNCES) BUTTER
- 1 CUP (250ML) MILK
- ¼ CUP (55G) CASTER SUGAR (SUPERFINE SUGAR)
- ½ TEASPOON SALT
- 2 EGG YOLKS
- 3 CUPS (450G) PLAIN FLOUR (ALL-PURPOSE FLOUR)
- CANOLA OIL, FOR DEEP-FRYING
- 1 CUP (220G) CASTER SUGAR (SUPERFINE SUGAR), EXTRA
- 2 TEASPOONS GROUND CINNAMON

1 Combine yeast and the water in a small bowl, stir until yeast dissolves.
2 Place butter and milk in a small saucepan over high heat; stir until butter is melted. Cool until lukewarm.
3 Place yeast mixture, butter mixture, sugar, salt, egg yolks and sifted flour in a large bowl; beat with a wooden spoon until mixture forms a soft, sticky dough. Cover bowl; stand in a warm place for about 1 hour or until dough has doubled in size.
4 Turn dough onto a lightly floured surface; knead gently until smooth. Roll dough out until 1cm (½-inch) thick. Flour both round cutters; cut rounds from dough, removing the centres with the smaller cutter. Repeat with remaining dough, re-rolling when necessary. Place rounds on baking-paper-lined oven trays. Stand for 15 minutes.
5 Heat oil in a large saucepan until it reaches 150°C/300°F on a sugar thermometer (or until the base of a wooden spoon bubbles when placed in the oil). Deep-fry doughnuts three at a time for 2 minutes each side or until golden brown. Drain on paper towel; toss doughnuts immediately in combined extra sugar and cinnamon. Serve warm.

GLAZE VARIATIONS

To create the doughnut toppings as pictured on pages 412-413, use the glazes below with your favourite sprinkles, crushed nuts and shredded coconut.

PLAIN GLAZE Stir 2 cups (320g) sifted pure icing (confectioners') sugar and ¼ cup (60ml) lukewarm milk in a bowl until combined. Dip the top half of the cooled doughnuts in icing; place on a wire rack to set.

COLOURED GLAZE Use food colourings to tint the plain glaze mixture (above) your favourite colour (or colours).

CHOCOLATE GLAZE Sift ¼ cup (25g) cocoa powder with the pure icing sugar when making the plain glaze mixture. Add a little more lukewarm milk if necessary.

tips Never walk away from hot oil. If doughnuts are over browning, reduce the heat of the oil. The doughnuts are best eaten at the time of making. Reheat cold doughnuts in 10-second bursts in the microwave oven until just warm.

Doughnut TOPPINGS

OLD-TIME

FAVOURITES

Classic APPLE PIE

- 10 MEDIUM APPLES (1.5KG)
- ½ CUP (125ML) WATER
- ¼ CUP (55G) CASTER SUGAR (SUPERFINE SUGAR)
- 1 TEASPOON FINELY GRATED LEMON RIND
- ¼ TEASPOON GROUND CINNAMON
- 1 EGG WHITE
- 1 TABLESPOON CASTER SUGAR (SUPERFINE SUGAR), EXTRA

PASTRY

- 1 CUP (150G) PLAIN FLOUR (ALL-PURPOSE FLOUR)
- ½ CUP (75G) SELF-RAISING FLOUR
- ¼ CUP (35G) CORNFLOUR (CORNSTARCH)
- ¼ CUP (30G) CUSTARD POWDER
- 1 TABLESPOON CASTER SUGAR (SUPERFINE SUGAR)
- 100G (3 OUNCES) COLD BUTTER, CHOPPED COARSELY
- 1 EGG YOLK
- ¼ CUP (60ML) ICED WATER

1 Make pastry.

2 Peel, core and slice apples thickly. Place apples and the water in a large saucepan; bring to the boil. Reduce heat; simmer, covered, for 10 minutes or until apples soften. Drain; stir in sugar, rind and cinnamon. Cool.

3 Preheat oven to 220°C/425°F. Grease a deep 25cm (10-inch) pie dish.

4 Divide pastry in half. Roll one half between sheets of baking paper until large enough to line dish. Lift pastry into dish; press into base and side. Spoon apple mixture into pastry case; brush edge with egg white.

5 Roll remaining pastry until large enough to cover filling; lift onto filling. Press pastry edges together; trim off excess pastry. Brush pastry with egg white; sprinkle with extra sugar.

6 Bake pie for 20 minutes. Reduce oven temperature to 180°C/350°F; bake for a further 25 minutes or until golden brown.

PASTRY Process dry ingredients with butter until crumbly. Add egg yolk and the water; process until just combined. Knead on a floured surface until smooth. Wrap in plastic wrap; refrigerate for 30 minutes.

tips The apple filling must be well drained and cooled to room temperature before adding to the pastry case. Also, brushing the pastry case with a little egg white before adding the filling will help stop the apples making the pastry soggy.

PRIZE
WINNING

Orange poppy seed
SYRUP CAKE

- ⅓ CUP (50G) POPPY SEEDS
- ¼ CUP (60ML) MILK
- 185G (6 OUNCES) BUTTER, SOFTENED
- 1 TABLESPOON FINELY GRATED ORANGE RIND
- 1 CUP (220G) CASTER SUGAR (SUPERFINE SUGAR)
- 3 EGGS
- 1½ CUPS (225G) SELF-RAISING FLOUR
- ½ CUP (75G) PLAIN FLOUR (ALL-PURPOSE FLOUR)
- ½ CUP (60G) GROUND ALMONDS
- ½ CUP (125ML) ORANGE JUICE

ORANGE SYRUP

- 1 CUP (220G) CASTER SUGAR (SUPERFINE SUGAR)
- ⅔ CUP (160ML) ORANGE JUICE
- ⅓ CUP (80ML) WATER

1 Combine seeds and milk in a small bowl; stand for 20 minutes.
2 Preheat oven to 180°C/350°F. Grease a deep 22cm (9-inch) round cake pan; line base and side with baking paper.
3 Beat butter, rind and sugar in a small bowl with an electric mixer until light and fluffy; beat in eggs, one at a time. Transfer mixture to a large bowl; using a wooden spoon, stir in sifted flours, ground almonds, juice and poppy-seed mixture. Spread mixture into pan; bake about 1 hour.
4 Meanwhile, make orange syrup.
5 Leave cake in pan for 5 minutes before turning, top-side up, onto a wire rack set over a tray. Pour hot syrup over hot cake; serve warm.

ORANGE SYRUP Using a wooden spoon, stir ingredients in a small saucepan over heat, without boiling, until sugar dissolves. Bring to the boil; reduce heat, simmer, uncovered, without stirring, for 2 minutes.

tips Lemon or mandarin flavours also blend well with the taste of poppy seeds; substitute, in equal amounts, for the orange rind and juice given in the recipe.

Store the cake, coated with syrup, in an airtight container for up to 2 days. The cake, without syrup, can be stored in an airtight container for up to 2 days, and can also be frozen for up to 3 months.

Classic TRIFLE

- 85G (3 OUNCES) RASPBERRY JELLY CRYSTALS
- 250G (8-OUNCE) SPONGE CAKE, CUT INTO 2.5CM (1-INCH) PIECES
- ¼ CUP (60ML) SWEET SHERRY
- ¼ CUP (30G) CUSTARD POWDER
- ¼ CUP (55G) CASTER SUGAR (SUPERFINE SUGAR)
- ½ TEASPOON VANILLA EXTRACT
- 1½ CUPS (375ML) MILK
- 825G (1¾ POUNDS) CANNED SLICED PEACHES, DRAINED
- 600ML THICKENED (HEAVY) CREAM

1 Make jelly according to directions on packet; pour into a shallow container. Refrigerate jelly for 20 minutes or until almost set.

2 Arrange cake in a 3-litre (12-cup) bowl; sprinkle over sherry.

3 Blend custard powder, sugar and extract with a little of the milk in a small saucepan; stir in remaining milk. Stir over heat until mixture boils and thickens. Cover surface of custard with plastic wrap; cool.

4 Pour jelly over cake; refrigerate for 15 minutes. Top with peaches. Stir ⅓ cup of the cream into custard; pour over peaches.

5 Whip remaining cream; spread half over custard. Spoon remaining whipped cream into a piping bag fitted with a large fluted tube; pipe over top of trifle. Refrigerate for 3 hours or overnight. Serve trifle topped with maraschino cherries, if you like.

TEST ...KITCHEN... *Classic*

SPICED APRICOT & PLUM PIE

- 2 X 825G (1¾ POUNDS) CANNED DARK PLUMS IN LIGHT SYRUP
- 2 CUPS (300G) DRIED APRICOTS
- 1 CINNAMON STICK
- 3 CLOVES
- ½ TEASPOON MIXED SPICE
- ½ TEASPOON GROUND GINGER
- 2 SHEETS PUFF PASTRY
- 1 EGG, BEATEN LIGHTLY
- 1 TABLESPOON ICING SUGAR (CONFECTIONERS' SUGAR)

SPICED YOGHURT CREAM

- ½ CUP (140G) YOGHURT
- ½ CUP (120G) SOUR CREAM
- 1 TABLESPOON GROUND CINNAMON
- ¼ TEASPOON GROUND GINGER

1 Preheat oven to 200°C/400°F. Grease a deep 1.25 litre (5-cup) rectangular baking dish or a 26cm (10½-inch) pie dish.

2 Drain plums; reserve 1 cup of the syrup. Halve plums, discard stones; place plums in dish.

3 Place reserved syrup, apricots, cinnamon, cloves, mixed spice and ginger in a medium saucepan; simmer, uncovered, until liquid is reduced to ½ cup. Remove and discard cinnamon stick and cloves. Cool syrup to room temperature. Pour over plums.

4 Cut pastry into 2.5cm (1-inch) strips. Brush edges of the dish with a little of the egg; press pastry strips around edges of the dish. Twist the remaining strips, place over filling in a lattice pattern; trim ends, brush top with remaining egg.

5 Bake pie for 40 minutes or until pastry is browned lightly.

6 Make spiced yoghurt cream.

7 Dust pie with icing sugar; serve with spiced yoghurt cream.

SPICED YOGHURT CREAM

Combine ingredients in a small bowl.

tip See pages 344-345 for more ideas on decorating the pie top.

Raspberry CREAM SPONGE

- 4 EGGS
- ¾ CUP (165G) CASTER SUGAR (SUPERFINE SUGAR)
- ⅔ CUP (100G) WHEATEN CORNFLOUR (CORNSTARCH)
- ¼ CUP (30G) CUSTARD POWDER
- 1 TEASPOON CREAM OF TARTAR
- ½ TEASPOON BICARBONATE OF SODA (BAKING SODA)
- 1½ CUPS (375ML) THICKENED (HEAVY) CREAM
- ¾ CUP (240G) RASPBERRY JAM

RASPBERRY GLACÉ ICING

- 45G (1½ OUNCES) FRESH RASPBERRIES
- 2 CUPS (320G) ICING SUGAR (CONFECTIONERS' SUGAR)
- 15G (½ OUNCE) BUTTER, SOFTENED
- 2 TEASPOONS HOT WATER, APPROXIMATELY

1 Preheat oven to 180°C/350°F. Grease a deep 22cm (9-inch) square cake pan.

2 Beat eggs and sugar in a small bowl with an electric mixer for 10 minutes or until thick and creamy and sugar has dissolved; transfer to a large bowl. Sift dry ingredients twice, then sift a third time over egg mixture; fold dry ingredients into egg mixture. Spread mixture into pan.

3 Bake sponge about 25 minutes. Turn sponge immediately onto a baking-paper-covered wire rack, then turn top-side up to cool.

4 Beat cream in a small bowl with an electric mixer until firm peaks form.

5 Make raspberry glacé icing.

6 Split cooled sponge in half. Sandwich with jam and whipped cream. Spread top of sponge with icing; top with extra fresh raspberries, if you like.

RASPBERRY GLACÉ ICING Push raspberries through a fine sieve into a small heatproof bowl; discard solids. Sift icing sugar into same bowl; stir in butter and enough of the water to make a thick paste. Place bowl over a small saucepan of simmering water; stir until icing is spreadable.

tip Use a serrated or electric knife to split the sponge.

MIXED BERRY & RICOTTA TART

- 1⅓ CUPS (200G) PLAIN FLOUR (ALL-PURPOSE FLOUR)
- 185G (6 OUNCES) COLD BUTTER, CHOPPED COARSELY
- ¼ CUP (60ML) ICED WATER, APPROXIMATELY
- 500G (1 POUND) SOFT RICOTTA
- ⅓ CUP (80ML) POURING CREAM
- ⅓ CUP (75G) CASTER SUGAR (SUPERFINE SUGAR)
- 3 EGGS
- 1 TABLESPOON FINELY GRATED LEMON RIND
- 200G (6½ OUNCES) STRAWBERRIES, HALVED
- 125G (4 OUNCES) BLUEBERRIES
- 125G (4 OUNCES) RASPBERRIES
- 2 TEASPOONS ICING SUGAR (CONFECTIONERS' SUGAR)

1 Sift flour into a large bowl; rub in butter until crumbly. Mix in enough of the water to make ingredients just come together. Knead dough gently on a floured surface until smooth. Flatten pastry slightly, wrap in plastic wrap; refrigerate for 30 minutes.

2 Grease a 22cm (9-inch) round loose-based fluted flan pan. Roll out pastry between sheets of baking paper until large enough to line pan. Ease pastry into pan, press into base and side; trim edge. Prick base all over with a fork; refrigerate for 30 minutes.

3 Preheat oven to 200°C/400°F.

4 Place pan on an oven tray. Line pastry with baking paper; fill with dried beans or rice. Bake for 15 minutes. Remove paper and beans; bake for a further 10 minutes or until pastry is browned lightly and crisp. Cool.

5 Reduce oven temperature to 180°C/350°F.

6 Meanwhile, beat ricotta, cream, caster sugar, eggs and rind in a small bowl with an electric mixer until smooth. Pour mixture into tart shell.

7 Bake tart for 35 minutes or until filling is just set. Refrigerate until cold. Just before serving, top tart with berries and dust with sifted icing sugar.

tips To make the pastry using a food processor: Process flour and butter until crumbly; with motor operating, add the water and process until ingredients just come together. You could also use ready-made shortcrust pastry.

This tart is best made on the day of serving.

PREP + COOK TIME 1½ HOURS (+ REFRIGERATION & COOLING) **SERVES** 6

Custard TART

- 1¼ CUPS (185G) PLAIN FLOUR (ALL-PURPOSE FLOUR)
- ¼ CUP (35G) SELF-RAISING FLOUR
- ¼ CUP (55G) CASTER SUGAR (SUPERFINE SUGAR)
- 90G (3 OUNCES) BUTTER, CHOPPED
- 1 EGG, BEATEN LIGHTLY
- 2 TEASPOONS WATER, APPROXIMATELY
- ¼ TEASPOON GROUND NUTMEG
- 300ML THICKENED (HEAVY) CREAM
- 80G (2½ OUNCES) STRAWBERRIES, SLICED

CUSTARD

- 3 EGGS
- 1 TEASPOON VANILLA EXTRACT
- 2 TABLESPOONS CASTER SUGAR (SUPERFINE SUGAR)
- 2 CUPS (500ML) MILK

1 Sift flours and sugar into a large bowl; rub in butter. Add egg and enough water to make ingredients just come together. Knead dough on a floured surface until smooth. Wrap dough in plastic wrap; refrigerate for 30 minutes.

2 Preheat oven to 220°C/425°F.

3 Roll dough on a floured surface until large enough to line a greased 20cm (8-inch) pie dish. Lift pastry into pie dish, ease into side; trim edge. Pinch around edge of pastry.

4 Place pie dish on an oven tray. Line pastry with baking paper, fill with dried beans or rice. Bake for 10 minutes. Remove paper and beans; bake a further 10 minutes or until pastry is browned lightly. Cool.

5 Reduce oven temperature to 180°C/350°F.

6 Make custard.

7 Pour custard into pastry case; bake for 15 minutes. Sprinkle custard with nutmeg; bake for a further 15 minutes or until custard is just set (custard will firm as it cools). Cool.

8 Beat cream in a small bowl with an electric mixer until firm peaks form. Spoon cream into a piping bag fitted with a fluted tube. Pipe cream on tart; top with strawberries.

CUSTARD Whisk eggs, extract and sugar in a small bowl until combined. Heat milk in a small saucepan over low heat until hot. Whisk hot milk into egg mixture.

EDITOR'S
Favourite

TEST
KITCHEN
Classic

Biscotten TORTE

- 24 MILK COFFEE BISCUITS
- ½ CUP (125ML) MILK
- 1½ TABLESPOONS RUM
- 300ML THICKENED (HEAVY) CREAM

ALMOND FILLING

- 2 EGGS, SEPARATED
- 125G (4 OUNCES) BUTTER, CHOPPED COARSELY, SOFTENED
- ½ CUP (110G) CASTER SUGAR (SUPERFINE SUGAR)
- FEW DROPS ALMOND ESSENCE
- 1 CUP (120G) GROUND ALMONDS
- ½ CUP (125ML) MILK

1 Make almond filling.

2 Arrange six biscuits lengthways, in two rows of three each, on a large sheet of aluminium foil; brush biscuits generously with combined milk and rum. Spread biscuits with one-third of the almond filling. Repeat layering with remaining biscuits, milk and rum mixture, and almond filling, ending with a layer of biscuits. Wrap torte in foil; refrigerate for 8 hours or overnight.

3 Beat cream in a small bowl with an electric mixer until soft peaks form. Cover torte with cream, running a fork lightly through the cream for a swirled effect. Top with fresh strawberries, if you like.

ALMOND FILLING Beat egg whites in a small bowl with an electric mixer until soft peaks form. Beat butter, sugar, essence and egg yolks in a medium bowl with an electric mixer until just combined; do not overmix. Stir in ground almonds; gradually beat in milk. Gently fold egg white into almond mixture.

CRÊPES SUZETTE

- ¾ CUP (110G) PLAIN FLOUR (ALL-PURPOSE FLOUR)
- 3 EGGS
- 2 TABLESPOONS VEGETABLE OIL
- ¾ CUP (180ML) MILK

ORANGE SAUCE

- 125G (4 OUNCES) UNSALTED BUTTER
- ½ CUP (110G) CASTER SUGAR (SUPERFINE SUGAR)
- 1½ CUPS (375ML) ORANGE JUICE
- 2 TABLESPOONS LEMON JUICE
- ⅓ CUP (80ML) ORANGE-FLAVOURED LIQUEUR

1 Sift flour into a medium bowl, make a well in the centre; add eggs and oil then gradually whisk in milk until smooth. Pour batter into a large jug, cover; stand for 1 hour.

2 Heat a greased heavy-based crêpe pan or small frying pan; pour ¼ cup of batter into pan, tilting pan to coat base. Cook, over low heat, until browned lightly, loosening edge of crêpe with a spatula. Turn crêpe; brown the other side. Remove crêpe from pan; cover to keep warm. Repeat with remaining batter to make a total of eight crêpes, greasing the pan each time.

3 Make orange sauce.

4 Fold crêpes in half then in half again, place in sauce; warm over low heat.

5 Remove crêpes to serving plates; pour hot sauce over crêpes. Serve with orange slices, if you like.

ORANGE SAUCE Melt butter in a large frying pan, add sugar; cook, stirring, until mixture begins to brown. Add strained juices; bring to the boil. Reduce heat; simmer, uncovered, for about 3 minutes or until sauce turns a golden colour. Remove from heat; add liqueur, ignite (see tips).

tips Be very careful when igniting the sauce – use extra long matches, available from supermarkets or camping stores, and make sure overhead exhaust fans are turned off. Igniting the sauce burns off the alcohol, leaving a more intense flavour. If you prefer, the sauce can be served as is, without first igniting it.

TEST

··· KITCHEN ···

Classic

Marshmallow PAVLOVA

- 4 EGG WHITES
- 1 CUP (220G) CASTER SUGAR (SUPERFINE SUGAR)
- ½ TEASPOON VANILLA EXTRACT
- ¾ TEASPOON WHITE VINEGAR
- 300ML THICKENED (HEAVY) CREAM, WHIPPED
- 250G (8 OUNCES) STRAWBERRIES, HALVED
- 125G (4 OUNCES) RASPBERRIES
- 125G (4 OUNCES) BLUEBERRIES
- ¼ CUP (60ML) PASSIONFRUIT PULP

1 Preheat oven to 130°C/260°F. Line an oven tray with foil; grease foil, dust with a little cornflour (cornstarch) shake away excess cornflour. Mark an 18cm (7¼-inch) circle on foil.

2 Beat egg whites in a small bowl with an electric mixer until soft peaks form; gradually add sugar, beating until sugar dissolves between additions. Add extract and vinegar; beat until combined.

3 Spread meringue into circle on foil, building up at the side to 8cm (3¼ inches) in height. Smooth side and top of pavlova gently. Using a spatula blade, mark decorative grooves around side of pavlova; smooth top again.

4 Bake pavlova for 1½ hours. Turn oven off; cool pavlova in oven with door slightly ajar.

5 Cut around top edge of pavlova (the crisp meringue top will fall on top of the marshmallow centre). Top pavlova with cream, berries and passionfruit.

Pineapple UPSIDE-DOWN CAKE

- 60G (2 OUNCES) BUTTER
- ½ CUP (110G) FIRMLY PACKED BROWN SUGAR
- 450G (14½ OUNCES) CANNED PINEAPPLE SLICES IN SYRUP
- 13 RED GLACÉ CHERRIES
- 125G (4 OUNCES) BUTTER, EXTRA
- ½ CUP (110G) FIRMLY PACKED BROWN SUGAR, EXTRA
- 2 EGGS
- 2 CUPS (300G) SELF-RAISING FLOUR
- ¼ CUP (60ML) MILK

1 Preheat oven to 180°C/350°F. Grease a deep 20cm (8-inch) round cake pan; line base and sides with baking paper.

2 Beat butter and sugar in a small bowl with an electric mixer until just combined. Spread mixture over base of pan.

3 Drain pineapple slices, reserving ¼ cup of the syrup. Arrange pineapple and cherries on butter mixture.

4 Beat extra butter and extra sugar in a small bowl with an electric mixer until light and fluffy. Beat in eggs, one at a time, until just combined. Fold in sifted flour and combined reserved syrup and milk, in batches, until smooth. Spread mixture carefully over pineapple.

5 Bake cake for 45 minutes. Leave cake in pan for 5 minutes before turning out onto a serving plate.

TEST KITCHEN
... KITCHEN ...
Classic

CAKE STAND

MATERIALS

- 2 STEMMED CUT-GLASS SWEET DISHES
- PRETTY DINNER PLATE
- CRAFT GLUE FOR GLASS AND CERAMICS
- PACKET OF RECTANGULAR PAPER DOILIES
- SCISSORS
- DOUBLE-SIDED TAPE

1 Turn one glass dish upside down; run glass glue around the base then place second glass dish, right-side up, on top. Wait until glue has dried and hardened, according to the glue instructions.

2 Run glue around rim of top dish; centre the plate on top of the glass. Wait for glue to harden.

3 Measure around plate. Cut lacy edge off long sides of doilies; tape together with double-sided tape, overlapping ends to make a neat join, until doily wraps around plate.

4 Place double-sided tape at 2cm (¾-inch) intervals on wrong side of doily. Stick doily to the underside of the plate edge.

tip The doily needs to be replaced after each use.

STEP 1
Get together your materials: 2 stemmed cut-glass sweet dishes; a dinner plate, ceramic or glass glue and doilies.

STEP 2
Turn one dish upside down; run the glue around the base then place the second glass dish, right-side up, on top.

STEP 3
Run glue around rim of top dish; centre plate on top. Cut lacy edge off long sides of doily; join ends with double-sided tape.

STEP 4
Place double-sided tape at 2cm intervals on the wrong side of the doily. Attach the doily around the edge of the plate.

Pink VELVET CAKE

- 125G (4 OUNCES) BUTTER, SOFTENED
- 1 TEASPOON VANILLA EXTRACT
- 1½ CUPS (330G) CASTER SUGAR (SUPERFINE SUGAR)
- 2 EGGS
- 1½ CUPS (225G) PLAIN FLOUR (ALL-PURPOSE FLOUR)
- 2 TABLESPOONS CORNFLOUR (CORNSTARCH)
- 2 TABLESPOONS COCOA POWDER
- 1 CUP (250ML) BUTTERMILK
- 1 TABLESPOON ROSE PINK FOOD COLOURING
- 1 TEASPOON WHITE VINEGAR
- 1 TEASPOON BICARBONATE OF SODA (BAKING SODA)
- 1 CUP (50G) FLAKED COCONUT

MASCARPONE FROSTING

- 250G (8 OUNCES) CREAM CHEESE, SOFTENED
- 250G (8 OUNCES) MASCARPONE CHEESE
- 1 CUP (160G) ICING SUGAR (CONFECTIONERS' SUGAR)
- 1 TEASPOON VANILLA EXTRACT
- 300ML THICKENED (HEAVY) CREAM

1 Preheat oven to 180°C/350°F. Grease two deep 22cm (9-inch) round cake pans; line bases and sides with baking paper.

2 Beat butter, extract, sugar and eggs in a small bowl with an electric mixer until light and fluffy. Transfer mixture to a large bowl; stir in sifted flours and cocoa and combined buttermilk and colouring, in two batches.

3 Combine vinegar and soda in a cup; allow to fizz then fold into cake mixture. Divide mixture between pans.

4 Bake cakes about 25 minutes. Leave cakes in pans for 10 minutes before turning, top-side up, onto wire racks to cool. Wrap cakes in plastic; freeze for 40 minutes.

5 Make mascarpone frosting.

6 Split cold cakes in half. Place one layer on a serving plate, cut-side up; spread with ⅔ cup of frosting. Repeat layering, finishing with remaining frosting, spreading all over top and side of the cake; press coconut onto the side of the cake.

MASCARPONE FROSTING

Beat cream cheese, mascarpone, sugar and extract in a small bowl with an electric mixer until smooth. Beat in cream.

tip To make your own buttermilk equivalent, combine 1 tablespoon fresh lemon juice with enough reduced-fat milk to make 1 cup. Stand mixture for a few minutes until thickened, then stir.

Black forest SOUFFLÉS

- ⅔ CUP (150G) CASTER SUGAR (SUPERFINE SUGAR)
- 400G (12½ OUNCES) CHERRIES, SEEDED, HALVED
- 2 TABLESPOONS KIRSCH
- 1 TABLESPOON LEMON JUICE
- 50G (1½ OUNCES) BUTTER
- 1 TABLESPOON COCOA POWDER
- ½ CUP (125ML) BUTTERMILK
- 125G (4 OUNCES) DARK (SEMI-SWEET) CHOCOLATE, CHOPPED
- 2 EGG YOLKS
- 4 EGG WHITES

1 Preheat oven to 220°C/425°F. Grease six ¾-cup (180ml) soufflé dishes. Sprinkle inside of dishes with 1 tablespoon of the sugar; shake away excess sugar. Place dishes on an oven tray.

2 Stir cherries, kirsch, juice and ⅓ cup of the sugar in a small saucepan over heat, without boiling, until sugar dissolves. Simmer, uncovered, without stirring, about 10 minutes or until mixture is syrupy. Cool.

3 Meanwhile, melt butter in a small saucepan; stir in cocoa until smooth. Stir in buttermilk, heat without boiling. Remove from heat; stir in chocolate and 1½ tablespoons of the remaining sugar until smooth. Transfer mixture to a large bowl; stir in egg yolks.

4 Beat egg whites in a small bowl with an electric mixer until soft peaks form; gradually add remaining sugar, beating until sugar dissolves between additions. Fold egg white mixture into chocolate mixture, in two batches.

5 Divide cherry mixture among dishes; top with chocolate mixture.

6 Bake soufflés about 12 minutes or until puffed. Serve immediately.

Caramelised apple CLAFOUTIS

- 6 MEDIUM APPLES (900G)
- 50G (1½ OUNCES) UNSALTED BUTTER
- ½ CUP (110G) FIRMLY PACKED BROWN SUGAR
- ⅓ CUP (75G) CASTER SUGAR (SUPERFINE SUGAR)
- ⅓ CUP (50G) PLAIN FLOUR (ALL-PURPOSE FLOUR)
- ⅓ CUP (50G) SELF-RAISING FLOUR

- 4 EGGS
- 80G (2½ OUNCES) UNSALTED BUTTER, EXTRA, MELTED
- ⅔ CUP (160ML) MILK
- ⅔ CUP (160ML) POURING CREAM
- 1 TEASPOON VANILLA EXTRACT
- 1 TEASPOON ICING SUGAR (CONFECTIONERS' SUGAR)

1 Preheat oven to 200°C/400°F. Grease a shallow 2.5-litre (10-cup) ovenproof dish.

2 Peel, core and halve apples; cut each half into four wedges.

3 Melt butter in a large frying pan over medium heat; cook apples, stirring, for 5 minutes or until browned lightly. Add brown sugar; cook for 5 minutes or until mixture thickens. Transfer to dish; cool for 5 minutes.

4 Combine caster sugar and sifted flours in a medium bowl. Lightly whisk eggs, extra butter, milk, cream and extract in a small bowl. Gradually whisk egg mixture into flour mixture until smooth. Pour mixture over apples.

5 Bake clafoutis for 40 minutes. Serve hot, dusted with sifted icing sugar.

tip Clafoutis is originally from the Limousin region of central France where, in the local dialect, it translates as 'brimming over'. It is one of the easiest desserts to make: a sweet batter is poured into a baking dish 'brimming' with cherries, prunes or the fresh fruit of your choice, such as apple, and baked. Traditionally, cherries native to the region were used.

serving suggestion Cream or custard.

Black forest LAYER CAKE

- 250G (8 OUNCES) BUTTER, CHOPPED
- 1 TABLESPOON INSTANT COFFEE GRANULES
- 1½ CUPS (375ML) HOT WATER
- 200G (6½ OUNCES) DARK (SEMI-SWEET) CHOCOLATE, CHOPPED
- 2 CUPS (440G) CASTER SUGAR (SUPERFINE SUGAR)
- 1½ CUPS (225G) SELF-RAISING FLOUR
- 1 CUP (150G) PLAIN FLOUR (ALL-PURPOSE FLOUR)
- ¼ CUP (25G) COCOA POWDER
- 2 EGGS
- 2 TEASPOONS VANILLA EXTRACT
- 600ML THICKENED (HEAVY) CREAM
- ¼ CUP (60ML) CHERRY-FLAVOURED LIQUEUR
- 850G (1¾ POUNDS) CANNED PITTED BLACK CHERRIES, DRAINED, HALVED
- SHAVED DARK (SEMI-SWEET) CHOCOLATE AND MARASCHINO CHERRIES, TO DECORATE

1 Preheat oven to 150°C/300°F. Grease a deep 23cm (9-inch) round cake pan; line base and side with baking paper.

2 Melt butter in a medium saucepan over low heat, add combined coffee and hot water, then chocolate and sugar; stir, over low heat, without boiling, until smooth. Transfer to a large bowl of an electric mixer; cool until warm.

3 Beat mixture on low speed with an electric mixer; gradually beat in sifted dry ingredients, in three batches. Beat in eggs, one at a time, then extract. Pour mixture into pan.

4 Bake cake about 1¾ hours. Leave cake in pan for 5 minutes before turning, top-side up, onto a wire rack to cool.

5 Beat cream in a small bowl with an electric mixer until firm peaks form.

6 Level top of cake. Split cake into three even layers. Place one cake layer on a serving plate, brush with 1 tablespoon of the liqueur; top with one-third of the cream and half the black cherries. Repeat layering, finishing with a cake layer. Brush top of cake with remaining liqueur; top with remaining cream. Decorate with chocolate shavings and the maraschino cherries. Just before serving, dust with a little sifted cocoa, if you like.

Passionfruit & lemon
SYRUP CAKE

- ⅔ CUP (160ML) PASSIONFRUIT PULP
- 250G (8 OUNCES) BUTTER, SOFTENED
- 1 TABLESPOON FINELY GRATED LEMON RIND
- 1 CUP (220G) CASTER SUGAR (SUPERFINE SUGAR)
- 3 EGGS
- 1 CUP (250ML) BUTTERMILK
- 2 CUPS (300G) SELF-RAISING FLOUR

LEMON SYRUP

- ⅓ CUP (80ML) LEMON JUICE
- ¼ CUP (60ML) WATER
- ¾ CUP (165G) CASTER SUGAR (SUPERFINE SUGAR)
- RESERVED PASSIONFRUIT SEEDS FROM STEP 2

1 Preheat oven to 180°C/350°F. Grease a deep 22cm (9-inch) round cake pan well; line base and sides with baking paper.

2 Strain passionfruit over a medium jug; reserve both juice and seeds.

3 Beat butter, rind and sugar in a small bowl with an electric mixer until light and fluffy. Beat in eggs, one at a time; transfer to a large bowl. Fold in combined passionfruit juice and buttermilk, and the sifted flour in two batches. Spread mixture into pan.

4 Bake cake about 1 hour. Leave cake in pan for 5 minutes before turning, top-side up, onto a wire rack set over a tray.

5 Meanwhile, make lemon syrup. Pour hot syrup over hot cake; serve cake warm.

LEMON SYRUP Combine juice, the water, sugar and half the reserved passionfruit seeds (discard the remaining seeds or freeze for a future use) in a small saucepan; stir over heat, without boiling, until sugar dissolves. Simmer, uncovered, without stirring, for 5 minutes.

Chocolate SPONGE ROLL

- 4 EGGS, SEPARATED
- ½ CUP (110G) CASTER SUGAR (SUPERFINE SUGAR)
- 2 TABLESPOONS HOT WATER
- 60G (2 OUNCES) DARK (SEMI-SWEET) CHOCOLATE, GRATED COARSELY
- ½ CUP (75G) SELF-RAISING FLOUR
- 2 TABLESPOONS CASTER SUGAR (SUPERFINE SUGAR), EXTRA
- 150G (4½ OUNCES) DARK (SEMI-SWEET) CHOCOLATE, EXTRA
- 250G (8 OUNCES) FRESH RASPBERRIES

RASPBERRY VANILLA CREAM

- 1½ CUPS (375ML) THICKENED (HEAVY) CREAM
- 1 TABLESPOON ICING SUGAR (CONFECTIONERS' SUGAR)
- 2 TEASPOONS VANILLA EXTRACT
- 1 CUP FRESH OR FROZEN RASPBERRIES, PUREED

1 Preheat oven to 180°C/350°F. Grease a 23cm x 32cm (9-inch x 13-inch) swiss roll pan; line base and long sides with baking paper, extending the paper 5cm (2 inches) above the sides.

2 Beat egg yolks and sugar in a small bowl with an electric mixer for 5 minutes or until thick and creamy. Transfer mixture to a large bowl; fold in the hot water and grated chocolate, then fold in sifted flour.

3 Beat egg whites in a small bowl with an electric mixer until soft peaks form; fold into chocolate mixture. Spread mixture into pan. Bake sponge about 12 minutes.

4 Meanwhile, place a piece of baking paper cut the same size as the pan on bench; sprinkle with extra sugar.

5 Turn hot sponge onto the sugared paper; peel away lining paper. Using paper as a guide, loosely roll sponge from long side. Stand for 2 minutes; unroll. Cool; trim all sides of sponge.

6 Make raspberry vanilla cream.

7 Melt extra chocolate (see tips). Spread cooled sponge with cream. Using paper as a guide, roll sponge up from long side. Drizzle roll with melted chocolate; sprinkle with raspberries. Stand until chocolate sets. Dust with a little icing sugar, if you like.

RASPBERRY VANILLA CREAM

Beat cream, sifted icing sugar and extract in a small bowl with an electric mixer until soft peaks form. Fold in raspberry puree.

tips For information on melting chocolate, see glossary entry under 'Chocolate, Melting', page 483.

Filled sponge roll is best eaten on the day it is made; store in an airtight container, in the fridge, until ready to serve.

Vanilla CITRUS TART

- 2 SHEETS SHORTCRUST PASTRY
- ⅔ CUP (160ML) WATER
- 50G (1½ OUNCES) BUTTER, CHOPPED FINELY
- 1 TABLESPOON CASTER SUGAR (SUPERFINE SUGAR)
- ⅔ CUP (100G) BAKER'S FLOUR
- 2 EGGS
- 100G (3 OUNCES) CANDIED ORANGE SLICES, CHOPPED FINELY
- ⅓ CUP (80G) REDCURRANT JELLY
- 15 SLICES CANDIED ORANGE (200G), EXTRA

PASTRY CREAM

- 1⅓ CUPS (330ML) MILK
- 1 VANILLA BEAN, SPLIT IN HALF LENGTHWAYS
- 3 EGG YOLKS
- ⅓ CUP (75G) CASTER SUGAR (SUPERFINE SUGAR)
- 2 TABLESPOONS CORNFLOUR (CORNSTARCH)
- 20G (¾ OUNCE) BUTTER

1 Place oven tray in oven; preheat oven to 220°C/425°F.

2 Join pastry sheets, overlapping about 5mm (¼ inch); brush between overlap with a little tap water, press firmly to seal. Line a lightly greased 34cm x 11cm (13½-inch x 4½-inch) rectangular loose-based fluted tart pan with pastry. Trim excess pastry, leaving about 5mm (¼ inch) above edges to account for shrinkage; prick base all over with a fork. Place pan on preheated oven tray. Line pastry with baking paper; fill with dried beans or rice. Bake pastry case for 10 minutes. Remove paper and beans; bake for a further 5 minutes. Remove pastry from oven. Reduce oven temperature to 200°C/400°F.

3 Meanwhile, make pastry cream.

4 To make choux pastry, combine the water, butter and sugar in a medium saucepan; bring to the boil. Add flour; beat with a wooden spoon over medium heat until mixture comes away from the base of the pan. Transfer pastry to a medium bowl; stand for 1 minute. Beat in eggs, one at a time, until pastry becomes smooth and glossy.

5 Cover base of tart shell with chopped candied orange.

6 Beat pastry cream and choux pastry in a medium bowl with an electric mixer until combined. Spoon mixture into tart shell; smooth surface.

7 Bake tart for 45 minutes or until puffed and browned lightly (cover with aluminium foil if it starts to over-brown). Stand tart in pan for 15 minutes before transferring to a wire rack.

8 Gently heat jelly in microwave oven until warm; pour over warm tart. Place orange slices on tart. Serve warm.

PASTRY CREAM Place milk in a medium saucepan; scrape vanilla seeds into milk, add bean. Bring milk mixture to the boil. Meanwhile, whisk egg yolks, sugar and cornflour in a medium heatproof bowl. Gradually whisk hot milk mixture into egg mixture. Strain mixture back into pan, discard bean; whisk over medium heat until mixture boils and thickens. Remove from heat; whisk in butter until smooth. Cover surface with plastic wrap.

Traditional APPLE STRUDEL

This recipe uses a traditional strudel pastry; while it is not too hard to make, it can be time consuming and a little fiddly, however, the result is delicious.

- 1.2KG (2½ POUNDS) APPLES
- ½ CUP (110G) CASTER SUGAR (SUPERFINE SUGAR)
- 1 TEASPOON VANILLA EXTRACT
- 30G (1 OUNCE) BUTTER
- 1 CUP (70G) STALE BREADCRUMBS
- ½ CUP (100G) LIGHTLY PACKED BROWN SUGAR
- ¾ CUP (120G) SULTANAS
- 1 TEASPOON FINELY GRATED LEMON RIND
- 1 TEASPOON GROUND CINNAMON
- ¼ TEASPOON GROUND NUTMEG
- FLOUR, EXTRA, FOR ROLLING PASTRY
- 185G (6 OUNCES) BUTTER, EXTRA, MELTED
- 1 TABLESPOON ICING SUGAR (CONFECTIONERS' SUGAR)

PASTRY
- 1½ CUPS (225G) PLAIN FLOUR (ALL-PURPOSE FLOUR)
- 1 EGG
- 1 TABLESPOON OLIVE OIL
- ⅓ CUP (80ML) WARM WATER, APPROXIMATELY

1 Peel, core and slice apples thinly. Combine apple slices with caster sugar and extract in a medium bowl. Cover; stand for 1 hour.

2 Meanwhile, make pastry.

3 Melt butter in a small frying pan over low heat; stir in breadcrumbs until golden brown. Cool. Combine breadcrumb mixture and brown sugar in a small bowl.

4 Drain excess liquid from apples; return apples to bowl. Add sultanas, rind, cinnamon and nutmeg; stir gently until combined.

5 Preheat oven to 200°C/400°F. Grease a large oven tray.

6 Cover a large table with a clean cloth; rub flour over cloth. Roll out dough as far as it goes. Flour your hands, slip them under the dough; gently and carefully, start lifting and stretching the dough from the centre using the back of your hands, rather than your fingers. Continue stretching the dough until it is paper-thin and approximately 87cm (36 inches) square.

7 Brush pastry with two thirds of the extra melted butter. Sprinkle breadcrumb mixture over half the pastry. Spoon the apple mixture along one end of the pastry, leaving a 5cm (2-inch) border. Fold in the sides of the pastry, covering both ends of the apple filling. Gather the cloth in your hands and carefully roll up the strudel, pulling the cloth toward you as you roll. Place strudel on the tray, gently curving into a horseshoe shape. Brush with the remaining melted butter.

8 Bake strudel for 40 minutes or until golden. Cool. Dust with icing sugar before serving.

PASTRY Sift flour into a medium bowl, make a well in the centre; add egg and oil. Gradually add the water, mixing to a soft dough with your hands. Knead on a floured surface into a ball. Pick up the dough, then throw it down on the floured surface about 100 times. Knead dough for 5 minutes. (The more the dough is banged and kneaded, the lighter it will be.) Form dough into a ball; place in a lightly oiled bowl. Cover; stand in a warm place for 45 minutes.

Mocha WALNUT CAKE

- 1 CUP (220G) CASTER SUGAR (SUPERFINE SUGAR)
- 125G (4 OUNCES) DARK (SEMI-SWEET) CHOCOLATE, CHOPPED COARSELY
- 1 TEASPOON INSTANT COFFEE GRANULES
- 2 TABLESPOONS WATER
- 125G (4 OUNCES) UNSALTED BUTTER, SOFTENED
- 6 EGGS, SEPARATED
- 2 CUPS (250G) FINELY CHOPPED WALNUTS
- 2 TABLESPOONS PLAIN FLOUR (ALL-PURPOSE FLOUR)

- ½ CUP (60G) COARSELY CHOPPED WALNUTS, EXTRA
- ½ CUP (125ML) THICKENED (HEAVY) CREAM, WHIPPED

MOCHA FROSTING

- 60G (2 OUNCES) DARK (SEMI-SWEET) CHOCOLATE, CHOPPED COARSELY
- 90G (3 OUNCES) UNSALTED BUTTER, SOFTENED
- 1¼ CUPS (200G) ICING SUGAR (CONFECTIONERS' SUGAR)
- 1 TEASPOON INSTANT COFFEE GRANULES
- 2 TEASPOONS HOT WATER

1 Preheat oven to 180°C/350°F. Grease two deep 20cm (8-inch) round cake pans; line bases with baking paper.

2 Combine sugar, chocolate, coffee and the water in a small saucepan; stir over low heat, without boiling, until mixture is smooth. Cool.

3 Meanwhile, beat butter in a small bowl with an electric mixer until pale and creamy; beat in egg yolks. Transfer to a large bowl; stir in chocolate mixture, walnuts and sifted flour.

4 Beat egg whites in a medium bowl with an electric mixer until soft peaks form. Fold into cake mixture in two batches; pour into pans.

5 Bake cakes about 35 minutes. Leave cakes in pans for 5 minutes before turning, top-side up, onto wire racks to cool.

6 Make mocha frosting. Join cold cakes with one-third of the frosting. Spread remaining frosting over top and side of cake. Press coarsely chopped walnuts around side of cake. Fit piping bag with a 1.5cm (¾-inch) fluted tube; pipe cream around top of cake.

MOCHA FROSTING Melt chocolate in a medium heatproof bowl over a medium saucepan of simmering water (don't let water touch the base of the bowl); cool. Beat butter in a small bowl with an electric mixer until pale and creamy; gradually beat in sifted icing sugar, chocolate and combined coffee and water.

Pressure cooker steamed PLUM PUDDING

- 2 CUPS (300G) CHOPPED MIXED DRIED FRUIT
- ½ CUP (75G) FINELY CHOPPED SEEDED DRIED DATES
- ½ CUP (85G) FINELY CHOPPED RAISINS
- ½ CUP (125ML) WATER
- ¾ CUP (165G) FIRMLY PACKED BROWN SUGAR
- 75G (2½ OUNCES) BUTTER, CHOPPED COARSELY
- ½ TEASPOON BICARBONATE OF SODA (BAKING SODA)
- 2 EGGS, BEATEN LIGHTLY
- ¾ CUP (110G) PLAIN FLOUR (ALL-PURPOSE FLOUR)
- ½ CUP (75G) SELF-RAISING FLOUR
- 1 TEASPOON MIXED SPICE
- ½ TEASPOON GROUND CINNAMON
- 2 TABLESPOONS DARK RUM

1 Wash combined fruit under cold water; drain. Combine fruit, the water, sugar and butter in a medium saucepan. Stir over high heat until butter melts and sugar dissolves; bring mixture to the boil. Reduce heat; simmer, uncovered, for 5 minutes. Transfer mixture to a large heatproof bowl, stir in soda; cool.

2 Stir eggs, sifted dry ingredients and rum into cooled fruit mixture.

3 Grease a 1.25-litre (5-cup) pudding steamer; spoon mixture into steamer. Top with pleated baking paper and foil; secure with kitchen string or steamer lid.

4 Place steamer basket in an 8-litre (32-cup) pressure cooker; add 2 cups (500ml) water. Place the pudding steamer on a tea towel; use tea towel to lower steamer into basket in cooker. Fold tea towel overhang over top of steamer; secure lid of cooker. Bring cooker to high pressure. Reduce heat to stabilise pressure; cook for 1¼ hours.

5 Release pressure using the quick release method (see glossary entry under 'Pressure Cookers', page 486); remove lid. Remove steamer from cooker; stand pudding for 10 minutes before turning out to serve.

tip If you have an electric pressure cooker you won't need to reduce the heat to stabilise pressure, your cooker will automatically stabilise itself. Before using your appliance, you should always check the manufacturer's instructions.

serving suggestion Custard, brandy butter, cream or ice-cream.

'BIG SISTER'

...fruit cake

...into a ...nderful

Christmas cake

You can't improve on the rich, fruity goodness of 'Big Sister'! Every bite has the flavour of juicy, red cherries, sun-ripe raisins and currants, tender citrus peels and fine old brandy and rum.

But you, yourself, can turn it into the finest Christmas cake ever iced, with the wonderful, up-to-date yet simple icing that has been made specially for 'Big Sister' by one of the foremost cooking authorities in this country.

GET YOUR 'BIG SISTER' FRUIT CAKE
FROM YOUR GROCER TODAY . . .
AND DON'T FORGET
'BIG SISTER' PLUM PUDDING

Exclusive 'BIG SISTER'

Christmas Icing

by *Janet Blan*

3 lbs. pure icing sugar
3 ozs. liquid glucose
2 egg whites
½ teaspoon lemon juice
½ teaspoon vanilla
red and green food colouring

Reserve half of one egg white. Drop balance (unbeaten) into middle of sifted icing sugar in bowl. Add melted glucose, lemon juice and vanilla. Work sugar in from the sides until a smooth, stiff paste is formed. Lift on to board dusted with sifted icing sugar. Knead like pastry until icing has absorbed sufficient sugar to hold its shape. Cut off a small portion for decoration. Roll balance to a 12" square, barely ¼" thick with rolling pin coated with icing sugar. Brush cake with remaining egg white, lift icing on to cake. Mould and smooth over top and sides of cake with hands coated with icing sugar. Trim excess icing from bottom edges with sharp knife. Add dabs of green colouring to threequarters of portion saved for decoration, knead until evenly coloured. Roll to ¼" thickness. Cut out Christmas trees as illustrated, using paper pattern and small sharp-pointed knife. Moisten trees underneath with egg white, press lightly on to cake. Colour balance of icing red and cut tubs for trees. Apply to cake in same way.

BUTTER ICING FOR PIPING

3 tablespoons soft butter icing made by creaming 1 level tablespoon butter with 1 cup sifted icing sugar and 1 or 2 teaspoons orange juice or sherry. Colour half the butter icing red, balance green. Use to pipe "Merry Christmas", edge decoration and lattice on sides.

Allow cake to stand for 24 hours before cutting.

Merry Christmas

Big Sister
RICH FRUIT CAKE

STICKY DATE PUDDING
with butterscotch sauce

- 1¼ CUPS (200G) SEEDED DRIED DATES
- 1¼ CUPS (310ML) BOILING WATER
- 1 TEASPOON BICARBONATE OF SODA (BAKING SODA)
- 50G (1½ OUNCES) BUTTER, CHOPPED
- ½ CUP (110G) FIRMLY PACKED BROWN SUGAR
- 2 EGGS, BEATEN LIGHTLY
- 1 CUP (150G) SELF-RAISING FLOUR

BUTTERSCOTCH SAUCE

- ¾ CUP (150G) FIRMLY PACKED BROWN SUGAR
- 300ML POURING CREAM
- 80G (2½ OUNCES) BUTTER

1 Preheat oven to 180°C/350°F. Grease a deep 20cm (8-inch) round cake pan; line base and side with baking paper.

2 Combine dates and the water in a medium heatproof bowl. Stir in soda; stand for 5 minutes.

3 Blend or process date mixture with butter and sugar until smooth. Add eggs and flour; blend or process until just combined. Pour mixture into pan.

4 Bake cake about 1 hour. Leave cake in pan for 10 minutes before turning, top-side up, onto a serving plate.

5 Make butterscotch sauce. Serve cake warm with sauce.

BUTTERSCOTCH SAUCE Stir ingredients in a medium saucepan over low heat until smooth.

EDITOR'S Favourite

Plum COBBLER

- 825G (1¾ POUNDS) CANNED PLUMS IN SYRUP
- ¾ CUP (110G) SELF-RAISING FLOUR
- ¼ CUP (55G) CASTER SUGAR (SUPERFINE SUGAR)
- 1 TEASPOON GROUND CINNAMON
- 60G (2 OUNCES) BUTTER, CHOPPED COARSELY
- 1 EGG YOLK
- ¼ CUP (60ML) BUTTERMILK, APPROXIMATELY
- 2 TABLESPOONS COARSELY CHOPPED ROASTED HAZELNUTS
- 2 TABLESPOONS ICING SUGAR (CONFECTIONERS' SUGAR)

1 Preheat oven to 180°C/350°F.

2 Drain plums over a medium saucepan. Halve plums; discard stones. Add plums to pan; bring to the boil. Reduce heat; simmer, uncovered, for 5 minutes or until plums soften. Strain plums; reserve ½ cup liquid.

3 Place plums and reserved liquid into a 1-litre (4-cup) ovenproof dish; place dish on an oven tray.

4 Sift flour, caster sugar and cinnamon into a medium bowl; rub in butter. Stir in egg yolk and enough of the buttermilk to make a soft, sticky dough. Drop heaped teaspoons of the mixture over hot plums; sprinkle with nuts.

5 Bake cobbler for 30 minutes or until browned lightly. Serve warm, dusted with sifted icing sugar.

tip Swap plums for canned peaches or apricots.

serving suggestion Thick (double) cream or ice-cream.

Chocolate
SELF-SAUCING PUDDING

- 60G (2 OUNCES) BUTTER
- ½ CUP (125ML) MILK
- ½ TEASPOON VANILLA EXTRACT
- ¾ CUP (165G) CASTER SUGAR (SUPERFINE SUGAR)
- 1 CUP (150G) SELF-RAISING FLOUR
- 1 TABLESPOON COCOA POWDER
- ¾ CUP (165G) FIRMLY PACKED BROWN SUGAR
- 1 TABLESPOON COCOA POWDER, EXTRA
- 2 CUPS (500ML) BOILING WATER

1 Preheat oven to 180°C/350°F. Grease a 1.5-litre (6-cup) ovenproof dish well.

2 Melt butter with milk in a medium saucepan. Remove from heat; stir in extract and caster sugar then sifted flour and cocoa. Spread mixture into dish.

3 Sift brown sugar and extra cocoa over mixture; gently pour boiling water over mixture.

4 Bake pudding for 40 minutes or until the centre is firm. Stand for 5 minutes before serving; dust with extra sifted cocoa, if you like.

tip When pouring the boiling water over the pudding, run the water over the back of a large spoon to distribute the water evenly and to stop large holes forming in the pudding.

serving suggestion Cream or ice-cream.

Ice-cream SANDWICHES

Make the patty cakes on page 334 do double duty as these delightful little treats.

NEAPOLITAN

Split uniced patty cakes in half crossways, sandwich with a round of neapolitan ice-cream. Pipe whipped cream on cake; drizzle with chocolate sauce. Decorate with pink, white and chocolate sprinkles and a maraschino cherry.

HOKEY POKEY

Split uniced patty cakes in half crossways, sandwich with a round of hokey pokey ice-cream. Pipe whipped cream on cakes; drizzle with caramel sauce. Decorate with chopped honeycomb and a maraschino cherry.

MINTY CHOC-CHIP

Split uniced patty cakes in half crossways, sandwich with
a round of choc-mint ice-cream. Pipe whipped cream
on cakes; drizzle with chocolate sauce. Decorate with
chopped peppermint crisp bars and a maraschino cherry.

CARAMEL CHOC SWIRL

Split uniced patty cakes in half crossways, sandwich with a
round of caramel chocolate swirl ice-cream. Pipe whipped
cream on cakes; drizzle with caramel sauce. Decorate with
chopped jersey caramels and a maraschino cherry.

COFFEE LIQUEUR ROLL

- 5 EGGS
- ¾ CUP (165G) CASTER SUGAR (SUPERFINE SUGAR)
- 1 CUP (150G) SELF-RAISING FLOUR
- 90G (3 OUNCES) BUTTER, MELTED
- 1 TABLESPOON INSTANT COFFEE GRANULES
- 1 TABLESPOON HOT WATER
- 1 TABLESPOON COCOA POWDER
- 1 TABLESPOON CASTER SUGAR (SUPERFINE SUGAR), EXTRA

COFFEE LIQUEUR CREAM

- 2 TEASPOONS INSTANT COFFEE GRANULES
- 1 TABLESPOON HOT WATER
- 1 TABLESPOON COFFEE-FLAVOURED LIQUEUR
- 300ML THICKENED (HEAVY) CREAM

1 Preheat oven to 200°C/400°F. Grease a 25cm x 30cm (10-inch x 12-inch) swiss roll pan; line with baking paper, extending the paper 5cm (2-inches) above long sides.

2 Beat eggs in a medium bowl with an electric mixer for 5 minutes or until thick and creamy. Gradually beat in sugar, about a tablespoon at a time; beat until dissolved between additions. Fold in sifted flour, then the combined butter, coffee and water. Spread mixture into pan.

3 Bake sponge about 15 minutes. Turn immediately onto baking paper sprinkled with combined sifted cocoa and extra sugar. Trim edges from sponge. Using baking paper as a guide, roll up sponge from short side; stand for 2 minutes. Unroll sponge; cool.

4 Make liqueur cream. Spread cooled sponge with liqueur cream. Using paper as a guide, roll sponge up from short side.

COFFEE LIQUEUR CREAM

Dissolve coffee with the hot water in a cup; cool. Beat coffee mixture, liqueur and cream in a small bowl with an electric mixer until soft peaks form.

Raspberry almond CRUMBLE TART

- 1½ CUPS (225G) FROZEN RASPBERRIES
- 1 TEASPOON ICING SUGAR (CONFECTIONERS' SUGAR)

ALMOND PASTRY

- 150G (4½ OUNCES) BUTTER, SOFTENED
- 1 TEASPOON VANILLA EXTRACT
- ⅔ CUP (150G) CASTER SUGAR (SUPERFINE SUGAR)
- 1 EGG
- ½ CUP (60G) GROUND ALMONDS
- 1½ CUPS (225G) PLAIN FLOUR (ALL-PURPOSE FLOUR)

1 Make almond pastry.

2 Roll two-thirds of the pastry between sheets of baking paper until large enough to line an 11cm x 35cm (4½-inch x 14-inch) rectangular loose-based flan pan. Ease pastry into pan, press into base and sides; trim edges. Prick pastry base with a fork; refrigerate for 30 minutes. Crumble remaining pastry; reserve.

3 Preheat oven to 200°C/400°F.

4 Place flan pan on an oven tray; bake for 10 minutes or until browned lightly. Sprinkle raspberries over base; top with reserved crumbled pastry. Bake for a further 20 minutes or until browned. Cool in pan. Dust with icing sugar before serving.

ALMOND PASTRY Beat butter in a small bowl with an electric mixer until smooth. Add extract, sugar and egg; beat until combined. Stir in ground almonds and half the flour. Work in remaining flour using your hands. Knead pastry on a floured surface until smooth. Wrap pastry in plastic wrap; refrigerate for 30 minutes.

tip This recipe is best made on the day of serving as the raspberries will soften the pastry.

serving suggestion Thick (double) cream, custard or ice-cream.

QUINCE & RHUBARB PIE

- 2 CUPS (500ML) WATER
- 2 CUPS (440G) CASTER SUGAR (SUPERFINE SUGAR)
- 4 MEDIUM QUINCES (1.2KG), PEELED, QUARTERED
- 2 STRIPS LEMON RIND
- 500G (1 POUND) RHUBARB, CHOPPED COARSELY
- ¼ CUP (60ML) LEMON JUICE, APPROXIMATELY
- 1 CUP (150G) PLAIN FLOUR (ALL-PURPOSE FLOUR)
- ⅓ CUP (55G) ICING SUGAR (CONFECTIONERS' SUGAR)
- 100G (3 OUNCES) COLD BUTTER, CHOPPED COARSELY
- 1 EGG, SEPARATED
- 1 TABLESPOON ICED WATER, APPROXIMATELY
- 1 TABLESPOON RAW SUGAR

1 Stir the water and caster sugar in a medium saucepan, over heat, without boiling, until sugar dissolves. Add quince and rind; bring to the boil. Reduce heat; simmer, covered, about 2 hours, or until quince is tender and a rosy colour. Add rhubarb to pan; cook for 5 minutes or until softened. Add juice to taste (to reduce sweetness). Cool quince and rhubarb in the syrup.

2 Meanwhile, process flour, icing sugar and butter until crumbly. Add egg yolk and iced water, process until ingredients just come together. Knead gently on a floured surface until smooth. Cover; refrigerate for 30 minutes.

3 Preheat oven to 180°C/350°F. Grease a 22cm (9-inch) pie dish.

4 Drain fruit mixture, reserving ⅓ cup of syrup. Spoon fruit mixture and reserved syrup into dish.

5 Roll out pastry until large enough to cover pie. Cut a few 1cm (½-inch) rounds from pastry, reserve. Place pastry over filling, trim edge with a knife. Place rounds on pastry, brush a little lightly beaten egg white over the pastry; sprinkle with raw sugar. Place pie on an oven tray.

6 Bake pie for 30 minutes or until well browned. (Cover the edges of the pastry with foil after 20 minutes to prevent over-browning). Stand for 10 minutes before serving with double (thick) cream, if you like.

CYGNE CHANTILLY

(choux swans)

Once filled, the choux will soften, so assemble 1-2 hours before serving.

- ⅔ CUP (160ML) WATER
- 50G (1½ OUNCES) BUTTER, CHOPPED FINELY
- 1 TABLESPOON CASTER SUGAR (SUPERFINE SUGAR)
- ⅔ CUP (100G) BAKER'S FLOUR
- 3 EGGS
- PURE ICING SUGAR (CONFECTIONERS' SUGAR), FOR DUSTING

CHANTILLY CREAM

- 1½ CUPS (375ML) THICKENED (HEAVY) CREAM
- 1 TEASPOON VANILLA EXTRACT
- 2 TABLESPOONS PURE ICING SUGAR (CONFECTIONERS' SUGAR)

1 Preheat oven to 220°C/425°F. Grease oven trays.

2 To make choux pastry, combine the water, butter and sugar in a medium saucepan; bring to the boil. Add flour; beat with a wooden spoon over medium heat until the mixture comes away from the base of the pan. Transfer pastry to a medium bowl; stand for 1 minute. Beat in two of the eggs, one at a time, until pastry becomes smooth and glossy but still holds its shape.

3 Spoon three-quarters of the pastry into a piping bag fitted with a 1cm (½-inch) plain tube. Pipe eight 4cm x 6cm (1½-inch x 2½-inch) swan bodies, about 5cm (2 inches) apart, on trays (see tips). Spoon remaining pastry into a piping bag fitted with a 5mm (¼-inch) plain tube; pipe eight swan necks, 6.5cm (2¾ inches) in length on second tray (see tips). Brush bodies with lightly beaten remaining egg.

4 Bake swan necks for 5 minutes; remove from oven. Cool on trays.

5 Bake swan bodies for 10 minutes. Reduce oven to 160°C/325°F; bake a further 20 minutes. Turn off oven; cool puffs in oven with door ajar.

6 Make chantilly cream.

7 Using a serrated knife, cut the top third off the swan bodies; cut this piece in half to make wings.

8 Spoon three-quarters of the cream into a piping bag fitted with a 1.5cm (¾-inch) fluted tube; pipe cream into bodies. Arrange wings and neck on bodies.

9 Spoon remaining cream into another piping bag fitted with a 5mm (¼-inch) fluted tube. Pipe cream between wings; dust with sifted icing sugar.

CHANTILLY CREAM Beat ingredients in a small bowl with an electric mixer until firm peaks form. Refrigerate until required.

tips To pipe the swan's body, place the tube close to the tray and press down to finish the choux with a small point. To pipe the neck, start at the base of the neck and finish at the head. As you finish the head, press down on the tube to make a point for the beak. When piping the neck, pipe over it again to thicken (too thin and they will burn). Double the number of necks, as it can take a few attempts to get the hang of it.

GLOSSARY

ALMOND flat, pointy-ended nut with a pitted brown shell enclosing a creamy white kernel covered by a brown skin.

blanched brown skins removed.

flaked paper-thin almond slices.

ground also known as almond meal; nuts are pounded to a coarse flour-like texture.

slivered small almond pieces cut lengthways.

vienna toffee-coated almonds.

BAKING PAPER also known as parchment paper or baking parchment – is a silicone-coated paper that is primarily used for lining baking pans and oven trays so cakes and biscuits won't stick, making removal easy.

BAKING POWDER a raising agent consisting mainly of two parts cream of tartar to one part bicarbonate of soda (baking soda).

BAY LEAVES aromatic leaves from the bay tree available fresh or dried; adds a peppery flavour.

BEANS

broad (fava) also called windsor and horse beans; available dried, fresh, canned and frozen. Fresh should be peeled twice (discarding both the outer long green pod and the beige-green tough inner shell); the frozen beans have had their pods removed but the beige shell still needs removal.

green also called french or string beans (although the tough string they once had has been bred out of them); long thin fresh bean eaten in its entirety once cooked.

haricot a white bean with a delicate flavour; traditionally used to make the classic 'baked bean' dish.

white a generic term we use for canned or dried cannellini, haricot, navy or great northern beans.

BEETROOT also known as 'beets'; a firm, round root vegetable.

BICARBONATE OF SODA also known as baking or carb soda; a mild alkali used as a leavening (raising agent) in baking.

BREADCRUMBS

panko (japanese) are available in two kinds: larger pieces and fine crumbs; they are lighter in texture than Western-style breadcrumbs. Available from Asian food stores and most supermarkets.

stale crumbs made by grating, blending or processing one- or two- day-old bread.

BROCCOLINI a cross between broccoli and chinese kale; long asparagus-like stems with a long loose floret, both completely edible. Resembles broccoli but is milder and sweeter in taste. Also known as 'broccolette' and 'tender stem'.

BUTTER we use salted butter unless stated otherwise; 125g is equal to 1 stick (4 ounces).

unsalted butter also known as 'sweet' butter, has no added salt.

BUTTERMILK originally the term given to the slightly sour liquid left after butter was churned from cream, today it is made from no-fat or low-fat milk to which specific bacterial cultures have been added. Despite its name, it is low in fat.

CAPERS the grey-green buds of a warm climate shrub, sold either dried and salted or pickled in a vinegar brine; tiny young ones, called baby capers, are available in brine or dried in salt.

CAPSICUM also called pepper or bell pepper; comes in different shapes, sizes and colours. Discard seeds and membranes before use.

CHEESE

cream cheese commonly called Philadelphia or Philly; a soft cow's-milk cheese, its fat content ranges from 14% to 33%.

fetta Greek in origin; a crumbly textured goat- or sheep-milk cheese with a sharp, salty taste. Ripened and stored in salted whey.

goat's made from goat's milk, has an earthy, strong taste. Available in soft, crumbly and firm textures, and in various shapes and sizes; is sometimes rolled in ash or herbs.

mascarpone an Italian fresh cultured-cream product made in much the same way as yoghurt. Is whiteish to creamy yellow in colour, with a soft, creamy buttery-rich, luscious texture.

parmesan also called parmigiano; is a hard, grainy cow's-milk cheese originating in Italy. Reggiano is the best variety.

ricotta a soft, sweet, moist, white cow's-milk cheese with a low fat content and a slightly grainy texture. The name roughly translates as 'cooked again' and refers to ricotta's manufacture from whey, which is a by-product of other cheese making.

CHICKEN

breast fillet breast halved, skinned and boned.

tenderloin thin strip of meat lying just under the breast; good for stir-frying.

thigh skin and bone intact.

thigh cutlet thigh with skin and centre bone intact; sometimes found skinned with bone intact.

CHICKPEAS also known as garbanzo beans, hummus or channa; an irregularly round, sandy-coloured legume. Has a firm texture even after cooking, a floury mouth-feel and robust nutty flavour; available canned or dried.

CHILLI use rubber gloves when handling fresh chillies as they can burn your skin. We use unseeded chillies because the seeds contain the heat; use fewer chillies rather than seeding the lot.

chipotle chillies in adobo sauce these are sold in small cans from delicatessens and specialist food stores; they have a medium-hot smoky taste.

green any unripened chilli; also some particular varieties that are ripe when green, such as jalapeño, habanero, poblano or serrano.

long red available both fresh and dried; a generic term used for any moderately hot, long, thin chilli (about 6cm to 8cm long).

thai also known as 'scuds'. Fresh small, very hot and bright red to dark green in colour; can be substituted with fresh serrano or habanero chillies.

CHOCOLATE

dark also called semi-sweet or luxury chocolate; made of a high percentage of cocoa liquor and cocoa butter, and little added sugar. Unless stated otherwise, we use dark eating chocolate as it's ideal for use in desserts and cakes.

milk the most popular eating chocolate, mild and very sweet; similar in make-up to dark chocolate, with the difference being the addition of milk solids.

white contains no cocoa solids but derives its sweet flavour from cocoa butter. Is very sensitive to heat so watch carefully if melting.

CHOCOLATE, MELTING place roughly chopped chocolate into a heatproof bowl over a pan of barely simmering water – the water mustn't touch the base of the bowl. Stir the chocolate until smooth, remove from the pan as soon as it's melted to stop it from overheating.

CINNAMON available in sticks (quills) and ground into powder; one of the world's most common spices.

CLOVES dried flower buds of a tropical tree; available whole or ground. Has a strong scent and taste so use sparingly.

COCOA POWDER also called unsweetened cocoa; fermented, roasted and shelled cocoa beans (cacao seeds) that are ground into powder then cleared of most of the fat content.

COCONUT

desiccated dried, unsweetened, finely shredded coconut flesh.

flaked dried flaked coconut flesh.

shredded unsweetened thin strips of dried coconut flesh.

CORNFLOUR also known as cornstarch. Available made from corn (maize – gluten free) or wheat (contains gluten). Can either be used in baking, or as a thickening agent in cooking.

CREAM

pouring also called fresh, single or pure cream. It has no additives, unlike thickened cream. Minimum fat content 35%.

thick (double) a dolloping cream with a minimum fat content of 45%.

thickened (heavy) a whipping cream containing a thickener. Minimum fat content 35%.

CREAM OF TARTAR the acid ingredient in baking powder; added to confectionery mixtures to help prevent sugar from crystallising. Improves volume when beating egg whites, so add a little when making meringues, and helps to keep frostings creamy.

CRÈME FRÂICHE a mature, naturally fermented cream with a velvety texture and slightly tangy, nutty flavour; has a minimum fat content of 35%. A French variation of sour cream, it boils without curdling and can be used in sweet and savoury dishes.

CUCUMBER, LEBANESE a short, slender and thin-skinned cucumber. Probably the most popular variety because of its tender, edible skin, tiny, yielding seeds, and sweet, fresh and flavoursome taste.

CUMIN also called zeera or comino; resembling caraway in size, cumin is the dried seed of a plant related to the parsley family. It has a spicy, almost curry-like flavour. Available dried as seeds or ground.

EGGPLANT also called aubergine. Ranging in size from tiny to very large and in colour from pale green to deep purple. Can also be purchased char-grilled, packed in oil, in jars.

EGGS we use large chicken eggs weighing an average of 60g unless stated otherwise. If a recipe calls for raw or barely cooked eggs, exercise caution if there is a salmonella problem in your area; the risk is greater for those who are pregnant, elderly or very young, and those with impaired immune systems.

FENNEL also called finocchio or anise; a crunchy green vegetable slightly resembling celery that's eaten raw in salads; fried as an accompaniment; or used as an ingredient in soups and sauces. Also the name given to the dried seeds of the plant which have a stronger licorice flavour.

FLOUR

plain (all-purpose) a general all-purpose flour made from wheat.

rice very fine, almost powdery, gluten-free flour made from rice.

self-raising plain flour sifted with baking powder in the proportion of 1 cup flour to 2 teaspoons baking powder. Also known as self-rising.

wholemeal milled from whole wheat grains (bran, germ and endosperm).

GELATINE we use powdered (dried) gelatine; is also available in sheet form called leaf gelatine. Three teaspoons of dried gelatine (8g or one sachet) is about the same as four leaves. The two types are interchangeable, but leaf gelatine gives a clearer mixture than dried.

GINGER

crystallised fresh ginger, cubed and preserved in syrup then coated in sugar.

fresh also called green or root ginger; the thick gnarled root of a tropical plant. Can be kept, peeled, and covered with dry sherry, in a jar and refrigerated, or frozen in an airtight container.

glacé fresh ginger root preserved in sugar syrup; crystallised ginger can be used if rinsed with warm water and dried before using.

ground also called powdered ginger; used as a flavouring in baking but cannot be substituted for fresh ginger.

GLACÉ CHERRIES boiled in a heavy sugar syrup and then dried.

GLUCOSE SYRUP also known as liquid glucose; is made from wheat starch. Available at most supermarkets.

GOLDEN SYRUP a by-product of refined sugar cane; pure maple syrup or honey can be substituted. Treacle is similar, however, it is more viscous and has a stronger flavour and aroma – golden syrup has been refined further and contains fewer impurities, so is lighter in colour and more fluid.

HAM HOCK the lower portion of the leg of a pig, made up of meat, fat and bone. Most are cured, smoked or both, but fresh hocks can sometimes also be found. Are often used to flavour dishes that require lengthy, slow cooking.

HORSERADISH a white, pungently spicy, root vegetable, purchased in bottles at the supermarket in two forms: horseradish cream and prepared horseradish. While these can't be substituted one for the other in cooking, they can both be used as table condiments.

cream commercially prepared creamy paste consisting of grated horseradish, vinegar, oil and sugar.

prepared preserved grated horseradish.

JELLING to test if your jam has reached setting consistency or has 'jelled', take the pan off the heat, then drop a heaped teaspoon of the jam on a cold plate (chilled in the fridge or freezer). Run your finger through the jam, it should leave a distinct trail through the middle of the jam. If the jam runs back into the trail, it needs to be cooked a little longer.

KAFFIR LIME LEAVES also called bai magrood; looks like two glossy dark green leaves joined end to end, forming a rounded hourglass shape. Used fresh or dried like bay leaves or curry leaves. Dried leaves are less potent, so double if using them instead of fresh; a strip of fresh lime peel may be substituted for each kaffir lime leaf.

KITCHEN STRING made of a natural product, so it neither affects the flavour of the food it's tied around nor melts when heated.

KUMARA the Polynesian name of an orange-fleshed sweet potato that is often confused with yam. Is good baked, boiled, mashed or fried similarly to other potatoes. Is also known as orange sweet potato.

LAMINGTON PAN 20cm x 30cm (8-inch x 12-inch) slab cake pan, 3cm (1¼-inch) deep.

MAPLE SYRUP, PURE distilled from the sap of sugar maple trees.

maple-flavoured syrup is made from sugar cane and is also known as golden or pancake syrup. It is not a substitute for pure maple syrup.

MARZIPAN basically almond paste to which more sugar has been added. (Almond paste is simply ground almonds, sugar and water cooked together until smooth.) Marzipan is more pliable, easier to roll and is used for moulding and decorating.

MILK we use full-cream milk unless otherwise stated.

sweetened condensed a canned milk product consisting of milk with more than half the water content removed and sugar added to the remaining milk.

MIXED DRIED FRUIT sultanas, raisins, currants, peel and cherries.

MIXED PEEL candied citrus peel.

MIXED SPICE a classic spice mixture generally containing cumin, caraway, allspice, coriander, nutmeg and ginger, although cinnamon and other spices can be added.

MUSHROOMS

button small, cultivated white mushrooms with a mild flavour. When a recipe in this book calls for an unspecified mushroom, use button.

flat large, flat mushrooms with a rich earthy flavour, ideal for filling and barbecuing. Are sometimes misnamed field mushrooms, which are wild mushrooms.

shiitake, fresh also known as chinese black, forest or golden oak mushrooms. Although cultivated, they have the earthiness and taste of wild mushrooms. They are large and meaty.

swiss brown also known as roman or cremini. Light to dark brown mushrooms with a full-bodied flavour; suited for use in casseroles or being stuffed and baked.

MUSTARD

dijon also called french. Pale brown, creamy, distinctively flavoured, fairly mild french mustard.

powder can be either hot or mild; finely ground white (yellow) mustard seeds mixed into a paste with water.

wholegrain also known as seeded mustard. A french-style coarse-grain mustard made from crushed mustard seeds and dijon mustard.

NECTAR is a form of fruit juice that tends to be very sweet and rich. It is made by pressing the fruit, and often includes some of the pulp, making it very thick.

NUTMEG a strong, pungent spice; found ground or as a whole nut that is grated with a fine grater.

OIL

cooking spray we use a cholesterol-free cooking spray made from canola oil.

olive made from ripened olives. Extra virgin and virgin are the first and second press, respectively, of the olives and are considered the best; the 'extra light' or 'light' name on other types refers to taste not fat levels.

peanut pressed from ground peanuts; the most commonly used oil in Asian cooking because of its high smoke point (capacity to handle high heat without burning).

sesame made from roasted, crushed, white sesame seeds; a flavouring rather than a cooking medium.

vegetable sourced from plants.

ONION

brown and white these two are interchangeable. Their pungent flesh adds flavour to a vast range of dishes.

green (scallions) also called, incorrectly, shallot; an immature onion picked before the bulb has formed, having a long, bright-green edible stalk.

red also known as spanish, red spanish or bermuda onion; a large, sweet tasting, purple-red onion.

shallots also called french shallots, golden shallots or eschalots. Small and elongated, with a brown-skin, they grow in tight clusters similar to garlic.

spring a small onion with a sweet white bulb and long, narrow, crisp green-leafed tops.

PANCETTA an Italian unsmoked bacon; pork belly is cured in salt and spices then rolled into a sausage shape and dried for several weeks.

PAPRIKA ground dried sweet red capsicum; there are many grades and types available, including hot, sweet, mild and smoked.

PARSLEY flat-leaf parsley is also known as continental or italian parsley; it has a stronger peppery, fresh-flavoured taste than the curly variety, which is more often found as a garnish.

PASTRY, READY-ROLLED packaged sheets of frozen pastry, available from supermarkets.

fillo unique in that no fat is added to the dough. The dough is very elastic in texture and is stretched, rather than rolled, into the desired thickness. If required in a recipe, we use commercially-made fillo.

puff a crisp, light pastry; layers of dough and margarine are folded and rolled many times making many layers. When baked, it becomes a high, crisp, flaky pastry.

butter puff uses butter for the shortening, whereas puff pastry uses a commercially-made blend of vegetable and animal fats.

shortcrust is a tender, crunchy, melt-in-the-mouth buttery pastry.

PINE NUTS also called pignoli; not a nut but a small, cream-coloured kernel from pine cones.

POLENTA also known as cornmeal; a flour-like cereal made of ground corn (maize). Also the name of the dish made from it.

POTATOES

all-rounders such as sebago, desiree and coliban, are good for mashing and roasting.

baby new also known as chats; not a separate variety but an early harvest with very thin skin; good steamed or in salads.

kipfler small, finger-shaped potato with a nutty flavour; great baked and in salads.

PRESSURE COOKERS always read the appliance instruction manual before you start cooking.

quick release method each time the lid is removed from the cooker, the pressure must first be released quickly. Use tongs (steam can burn your fingers) to turn the pressure valve on top of the cooker to open the valve and release the steam. We use this method when adding ingredients and when checking the food toward the end of cooking time.

PROSCIUTTO unsmoked Italian ham; salted and air-cured.

QUINCE yellow-skinned fruit with a hard texture and astringent, tart taste; eaten cooked or as a preserve. Long, slow cooking turns the flesh a deep rose pink.

RADICCHIO Italian in origin; a member of the chicory family. The dark burgundy leaves and strong, bitter flavour can be cooked or eaten raw in salads.

RAISINS dried sweet grapes.

RHUBARB has thick, celery-like stalks that can reach up to 60cm (2 feet) long; the stalks are the only edible portion of the plant.

RICE

arborio small, round-grain rice suited to absorb a large amount of liquid; is especially suitable for risottos, giving the dish its classic creaminess.

ROASTING/TOASTING nuts and dried coconut can be roasted in the oven to restore their fresh flavour and release their aromatic oils. Spread them evenly onto an oven tray then roast in a moderate oven for about 5 minutes.

desiccated coconut, pine nuts and sesame seeds toast more evenly if stirred over low heat in a heavy-based frying pan; their natural oils will help turn them golden brown. Once golden, remove them from the oven tray/frying pan immediately to stop them from burning.

ROCKET also known as arugula, rugula and rucola; a peppery green leaf eaten raw in salads or used in cooking. *Baby rocket* leaves are smaller and less peppery.

ROSEWATER extract made from crushed rose petals.

SAUSAGE

chipolata coarse-textured, highly spiced beef sausage. Also called 'little fingers'.

chorizo of Spanish origin; made of coarsely ground pork and highly seasoned with garlic and chilli. They are deeply smoked, very spicy and dry-cured. Also available raw.

SEAFOOD

prawns also known as shrimp. Can be bought uncooked (green) or cooked, with or without shells.

white fish fillets means non-oily fish; includes bream, flathead, whiting, snapper, dhufish, redfish and ling.

SICHUAN PEPPER the peppercorns are reddish-brown in colour, with a strong, pungent aroma and a sharp, tingling and mildly spicy taste. Dry-roast to bring out their full flavour, then grind with a mortar and pestle.

SILVER BEET also known as swiss chard and, incorrectly, spinach; has fleshy stalks and large leaves.

SILVERSIDE also known as topside roast; used for making corned beef, usually sold vacuum-sealed in brine.

SOY SAUCE also known as sieu; made from fermented soya beans. Several variations are available in supermarkets and Asian grocery stores; we use japanese soy sauce unless indicated otherwise.

japanese an all-purpose low-sodium soy sauce with more wheat content than its Chinese counterparts. It is fermented in barrels and aged, and is possibly the best table soy and the one to choose if you only want one variety.

SPINACH (english spinach) also incorrectly called silver beet. Its thick, soft oval leaves and green stems are both edible.

SPLIT PEAS a variety of yellow or green pea grown specifically for drying. When dried, the peas usually split along a natural seam. Whole and split dried peas are available packaged in supermarkets and in bulk in health-food stores. Found in the classic pea and ham soup.

SPONGE FINGER BISCUITS also known as savoiardi, savoy biscuits or lady's fingers; they are long, oval-shaped italian-style crisp fingers made from sponge cake mixture. Used as a base for tiramisu.

SRIRACHA (see-rah-jah) also known as 'rooster sauce' because of the picture on the bottle; is a hot sauce named after the city in Thailand where it was produced, Si Racha. It is made with chilli, sugar, garlic, vinegar and salt. The sauce is hot and tangy with a hint of sweetness and adds a spicy kick.

STAR ANISE a dried star-shaped pod whose seeds have an astringent aniseed flavour.

STERILISING JARS it's important the jars be as clean as possible; make sure your hands, the preparation area, tea towels and cloths etc, are clean, too. The aim is to finish sterilising the jars and lids at the same time the preserve is ready to be bottled; the hot preserve should be bottled into hot, dry clean jars. Jars that aren't sterilised properly can cause deterioration of the preserves during storage. You must always start with cleaned washed jars and lids, before following one of these methods:

(1) Put the jars and lids through the hottest cycle of a dishwasher without using any detergent.

(2) Lie the jars down in a boiler with the lids, cover them with cold water then cover the boiler with a lid. Bring the water to the boil over a high heat and boil the jars for 20 minutes.

(3) Stand the jars upright, without touching each other, on a wooden board on the lowest shelf in the oven. Turn the oven to the lowest possible temperature, close the oven door and leave the jars to heat through for 30 minutes.

After following methods (1), (2) or (3), next remove the jars from the oven or dishwasher with a towel, or from the boiling water with tongs and rubber-gloved hands; the water will evaporate from hot wet jars quite quickly. Stand the jars upright and not touching each other on a wooden board, or a bench covered with a towel to protect and insulate the bench. Fill the jars as directed in the recipe; secure the lids tightly, holding jars firmly with a towel or an oven mitt. Leave the preserves at room temperature to cool before labelling and storing.

SUGAR

brown a soft, finely granulated sugar retaining molasses for its characteristic colour and flavour.

caster (superfine) finely granulated table sugar.

dark brown a moist sugar with a rich distinctive full flavour coming from natural molasses syrup.

demerara has a golden colour and subtle molasses flavour. The fine syrup coating on the crystal, together with its coarseness, gives a good colour to crusts when baked.

icing (confectioners') also known as powdered sugar; pulverised granulated sugar crushed together with a small amount of cornflour.

pure icing (confectioners') also called powdered sugar; similar to icing sugar, but without cornflour.

raw natural brown granulated sugar.

white a coarse, granulated table sugar, also known as crystal sugar.

SUMAC a purple-red, astringent spice ground from berries growing on wild Mediterranean shrubs; adds a tart, lemony flavour. Can be found in Middle Eastern food stores.

TARRAGON the most common tarragon available is french tarragon; it has a subtle aniseed flavour.

THYME is a member of the mint family; its tiny grey-green leaves have a pungent minty, light-lemon aroma. Store fresh thyme in the fridge, wrapped in a damp paper towel and placed in a sealed bag for a few days only.

lemon thyme a herb with a lemony scent, which is due to the high level of citral (an oil also found in lemon, orange, verbena and lemon grass) in its leaves. The citrus scent is enhanced by crushing the leaves in your hands before using the herb.

TOMATOES

bottled pasta sauce a blend of tomatoes, herbs and spices.

paste triple-concentrated puree.

roma are also known as egg or plum. These smallish, oval-shaped tomatoes are much used in Italian cooking or salads.

semi-dried partially dried tomato pieces in olive oil; softer and juicier than sun-dried, these are not a preserve so do not keep as long as sun-dried tomatoes.

sun-dried tomato pieces that have been dried with salt; this dehydrates the tomato and concentrates the flavour. We use sun-dried tomatoes packaged in oil.

truss small vine-ripened tomatoes with the vine still attached.

TREACLE thick, dark syrup not unlike molasses; a by-product of sugar refining.

VANILLA

bean dried long, thin pod from a tropical golden orchid grown in Central and South America and Tahiti; the minuscule black seeds inside the bean are used to impart a luscious vanilla flavour in baking and desserts. A bean can be used three or four times before discarding. Place a whole bean in a jar of sugar to make vanilla sugar.

extract made by extracting the flavour from the vanilla bean pod; pods are soaked, usually in alcohol, to capture the authentic flavour.

paste made from vanilla pods and contains real seeds. It is highly concentrated; 1 teaspoon of vanilla paste replaces a whole vanilla pod. Found in most supermarkets in the baking section.

VINEGAR

balsamic originally from Modena, Italy, there are now many balsamic vinegars on the market. Quality can be determined up to a point by price; use the most expensive sparingly. Aged balsamic is thicker.

cider made from fermented apples.

malt made from fermented malt and beech shavings.

sherry made from a blend of wines and left in wood vats to mature and develop a rich mellow flavour.

white made from the spirit of cane sugar.

white wine made from a blend of white wines.

WATERCRESS is a slightly peppery, dark-green leafy vegetable commercially cultivated but also found growing in the wild. Highly perishable, so must be used as soon as possible after purchase. Also known as winter rocket.

WOMBOK also called napa, chinese or peking cabbage; elongated in shape with pale green, crinkly leaves, this is the most common cabbage in South-East Asia.

WORCESTERSHIRE SAUCE thin, dark-brown spicy sauce developed by the British when in India; used as a seasoning for meat, gravies and cocktails.

YEAST raising agent used in dough making. Granular (7g sachets) and fresh compressed (20g blocks) yeast can almost always be substituted one for the other when yeast is called for. These days, dried yeast is more readily available than fresh.

YOGHURT we use plain full-cream yoghurt in our recipes.

greek-style plain yoghurt strained in a muslin cloth to remove the whey and give it a creamy consistency.

ZUCCHINI also called courgette; small, pale- or dark-green or yellow vegetable of the squash family. Harvested when young, its edible flowers can be stuffed and deep-fried.

Conversion CHART

MEASURES

One Australian metric measuring cup holds approximately 250ml; one Australian metric tablespoon holds 20ml; one Australian metric teaspoon holds 5ml.

The difference between one country's measuring cups and another's is within a two- or three-teaspoon variance, and will not affect your cooking results. North America, New Zealand and the United Kingdom use a 15ml tablespoon. All cup and spoon measurements are level. The most accurate way of measuring dry ingredients is to weigh them. When measuring liquids, use a clear glass or plastic jug with the metric markings.

We use large eggs with an average weight of 60g.

DRY MEASURES

metric	imperial
15g	½oz
30g	1oz
60g	2oz
90g	3oz
125g	4oz (¼lb)
155g	5oz
185g	6oz
220g	7oz
250g	8oz (½lb)
280g	9oz
315g	10oz
345g	11oz
375g	12oz (¾lb)
410g	13oz
440g	14oz
470g	15oz
500g	16oz (1lb)
750g	24oz (1½lb)
1kg	32oz (2lb)

LIQUID MEASURES

metric	imperial
30ml	1 fluid oz
60ml	2 fluid oz
100ml	3 fluid oz
125ml	4 fluid oz
150ml	5 fluid oz
190ml	6 fluid oz
250ml	8 fluid oz
300ml	10 fluid oz
500ml	16 fluid oz
600ml	20 fluid oz
1000ml (1 litre)	1¾ pints

LENGTH MEASURES

metric	imperial
3mm	⅛in
6mm	¼in
1cm	½in
2cm	¾in
2.5cm	1in
5cm	2in
6cm	2½in
8cm	3in
10cm	4in
13cm	5in
15cm	6in
18cm	7in
20cm	8in
22cm	9in
25cm	10in
28cm	11in
30cm	12in (1ft)

OVEN TEMPERATURES

The oven temperatures in this book are for conventional ovens; if you have a fan-forced oven, decrease the temperature by 10-20 degrees.

	°C (Celsius)	°F (Fahrenheit)
Very slow	120	250
Slow	150	300
Moderately slow	160	325
Moderate	180	350
Moderately hot	200	400
Hot	220	425
Very hot	240	475

The imperial measurements used in these recipes are approximate only. Measurements for cake pans are approximate only. Using same-shaped cake pans of a similar size should not affect the outcome of your baking. We measure the inside top of the cake pan to determine sizes.

INDEX

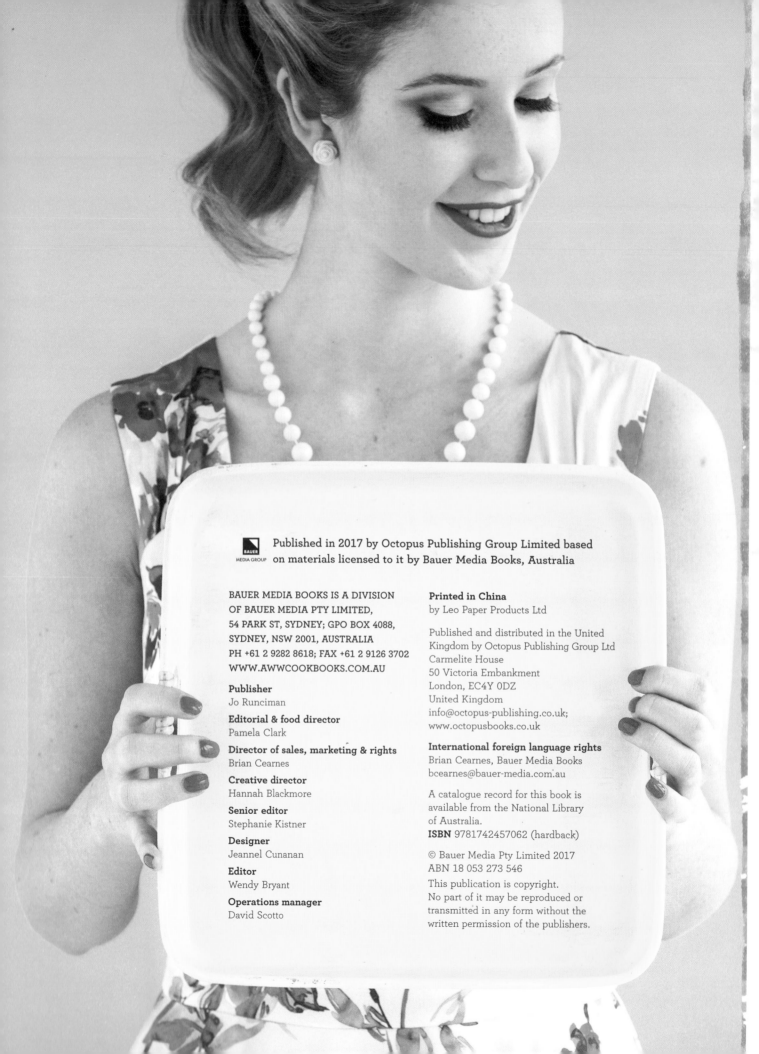

Published in 2017 by Octopus Publishing Group Limited based on materials licensed to it by Bauer Media Books, Australia

BAUER MEDIA BOOKS IS A DIVISION OF BAUER MEDIA PTY LIMITED, 54 PARK ST, SYDNEY; GPO BOX 4088, SYDNEY, NSW 2001, AUSTRALIA PH +61 2 9282 8618; FAX +61 2 9126 3702 WWW.AWWCOOKBOOKS.COM.AU

Publisher
Jo Runciman

Editorial & food director
Pamela Clark

Director of sales, marketing & rights
Brian Cearnes

Creative director
Hannah Blackmore

Senior editor
Stephanie Kistner

Designer
Jeannel Cunanan

Editor
Wendy Bryant

Operations manager
David Scotto

Printed in China
by Leo Paper Products Ltd

Published and distributed in the United Kingdom by Octopus Publishing Group Ltd Carmelite House 50 Victoria Embankment London, EC4Y 0DZ United Kingdom info@octopus-publishing.co.uk; www.octopusbooks.co.uk

International foreign language rights
Brian Cearnes, Bauer Media Books bcearnes@bauer-media.com.au

A catalogue record for this book is available from the National Library of Australia.
ISBN 9781742457062 (hardback)